battles
that changed
history

battles
that changed
history

DK

DK | Penguin Random House

Senior Editors	Hugo Wilkinson, Andrew Szudek
Senior Art Editor	Anthony Limerick
Editors	Jemima Dunne, Joanna Micklem
US Editors	Lori Hand, Jill Hamilton
Managing Editor	Gareth Jones
Senior Managing Art Editor	Lee Griffiths
Picture Researchers	Sarah Hopper, Sarah Smithies
Jacket Designer	Surabhi Wadhwa-Gandhi
Jacket Design	
Development Manager	Sophia MTT
Jacket Editor	Claire Gell
Pre-production Producers	Gillian Reid, David Almond
Producer	Mandy Inness
Publisher	Liz Wheeler
Art Director	Karen Self
Publishing Director	Jonathan Metcalf

DK INDIA

Senior Editor	Arani Sinha
Assistant Editors	Priyadarshini Gogoi, Devangana Ojha
Project Art Editor	Vikas Chauhan
Art Editors	Jomin Johny, Anukriti Arora
Assistant Art Editor	Amrai Dua
Managing Editor	Soma B. Chowdhury
Senior Managing Art Editor	Arunesh Talapatra
Picture Researcher	Aditya Katyal
Picture Research Manager	Taiyaba Khatoon
Senior DTP Designers	Shanker Prasad, Jagtar Singh
DTP Designer	Ashok Kumar
Production Manager	Pankaj Sharma
Pre-production Manager	Balwant Singh
Senior Jackets DTP Designer	Harish Aggarwal
Jacket Designer	Juhi Sheth
Senior Jackets Coordinator	Priyanka Sharma-Saddi
Managing Jackets Editor	Saloni Singh

First published in Great Britain in 2023 by
Dorling Kindersley Limited
DK, One Embassy Gardens, 8 Viaduct Gardens,
London, SW11 7BW

The authorised representative in the EEA is
Dorling Kindersley Verlag GmbH. Arnulfstr. 124,
80636 Munich, Germany

Copyright © 2023 Dorling Kindersley Limited
A Penguin Random House Company
Content previously published in 2018
10 9 8 7 6 5 4 3 2 1
002-337597-May/2023

A CIP catalogue record for this book is
available from the British Library.
ISBN 978-0-2416-4148-4

Printed and bound in UAE

For the curious
www.dk.com

MIX
Paper | Supporting
responsible forestry
FSC™ C018179

This book was made with Forest Stewardship
Council™ certified paper — one small step
in DK's commitment to a sustainable future.
For more information go to
www.dk.com/our-green-pledge

Contents

BEFORE 1000 CE

1000—1500

Contributors

Philip Parker
Philip Parker is a historian specializing
in the classical and medieval world. He is
the author of the *Eyewitness Companion
Guide to World History*, *The Empire Stops
Here: A Journey Around the Frontiers
of the Roman Empire*, *The Northmen's
Fury: A History of the Viking World*, and
general editor of *The Great Trade
Routes: A History of Cargoes and
Commerce Over Land and Sea*. He was
a contributor to DK's *The History Book*
and *History Year by Year*. He previously
worked as a diplomat and a publisher
of historical atlases.

R.G. Grant
R.G. Grant has written extensively on
history, military history, current affairs,
and biography. His publications include
Flight: 100 Years of Aviation, *A Visual
History of Britain*, and *World War I: The
Definitive Visual Guide*. He was consultant
editor on DK's *The History Book*.

Andrew Humphreys
Andrew Humphreys is an author and travel
writer who has written or co-written more
than 35 books for DK, Lonely Planet,
National Geographic, and *Time Out*. His
journalism often involves travel with a
historical slant and has appeared in the
Financial Times, the *Telegraph*, and *Condé
Nast Traveller*. He is the author of two
books on the golden age of travel in Egypt.

Foreword by Sir Tony Robinson
Award-winning writer, presenter, and
actor Sir Tony Robinson is Britain's
foremost face of popular history. His
television credits include *Time Team*
(Channel 4), *Blackadder* (BBC1), *The
Worst Jobs In History* (Channel 4),
Walking Through History (Channel 4),
Me and My Mum (ABC), *Tony Robinson's
Coast to Coast* (Channel 5), *Britain's*

1500–1700

Ancient Tracks (Channel 4), and more. As a children's television writer, he has won two RTS awards, a BAFTA, and the International Prix Jeunesse, and his work includes Central TV's *Fat Tulip's Garden, Odysseus – the Greatest Hero of Them All*, and *Blood and Honey*. He has also made a range of television documentaries, written 30 children's books, winning the Blue Peter Factual Book Award twice, and several books for adults, including his autobiography *No Cunning Plan*. He is an ambassador for the Alzheimer's Society, and received a knighthood in 2013.

1700–1900

1900–PRESENT

Foreword

How many battles did change the course of history? It's a good question. When we read about some troop deployment on an ancient battlefield, it's easy to think of it as a mere historical curiosity rather than as a confrontation still relevant to us today.

The reality is, though, that the outcome of historic battles has shaped countries, empires, civilizations, and the lives of each and every one of us. In Europe, nations were born from the crucible of warring powers, while in the mountains and deserts of the East, ancient rivalries created borders and moulded cultures in ways that are still central to the lives of their inhabitants today. Across the great landmass of central Europe, the expansion of Genghis Khan's Mongol empire changed the face of a huge swathe of the world. In South America the use of Spanish as a *lingua franca* can be traced to Cortés's conquest of the Aztec city of Tenochtitlán, while the US owes much of its political and cultural heritage to the War of Independence and the American Civil War. Closer to the present, the behind-the-scenes dealings of the Cold War have had an enormous influence both on contemporary geopolitics and on modern combat.

But it's not only the great defining moments of history that are revealed in these battles. Each military engagement is a snapshot of the political and cultural background in which it took place; the anger, frustrations, and terror of the local inhabitants; the clothes and weapons of the fighting forces, the fateful decisions taken by civilian and military leaders – all are reflected in, and are illuminated by, the clash of arms. And while this book isn't intended as a comprehensive compendium of the world's wars or as a manual on the art of warfare, it does aim to offer a glimpse of the broader world in which each battle took place, as well as the ways in which history was made at a particular moment in time.

Finally, as tempting as it is to look back at historical events simply as fascinating echoes of years gone by, it's always worth remembering the sacrifices of the fallen. Military history is forged not only by bravery but by loss of life, and we would do well to remember this when we look back at the struggles of the past.

SIR TONY ROBINSON

Introduction

Conflicts have been an ever-present part of human history around the globe since the emergence of the first civilizations in Egypt and Mesopotamia. Warfare has played a key role in shaping our history, with defeat in battle often precipitating the decline of cultures, of empires, or more recently, of nation-states – and victory leading to the acquisition of land, people, and resources. *Battles That Changed History* takes a chronological look at a selection of the world's most infamous and influential wars. Its content spans more than 3,000 years, from the Battle of Kadesh of 1274 BCE between the Egyptians and Hittites (see p.42), to the second multi-national coalition invasion of Saddam Hussein's Iraq launched in 2003 (see p.247), and examines battles on every continent, with the exception of Antarctica.

Tactics and techology

Throughout the centuries, emperors, military commanders, generals, and admirals have faced the same objectives and challenges: to outmanoeuvre their enemy, to gather maximum resources to apply to the other side's weak point, to avoid becoming entrapped, and to capitalize on the effects of victory, as well as to mitigate the consequences of defeat. While modes of transport and weaponry have changed and adapted over the centuries – the spears and chariots employed by the Egyptians and Hittites at the Battle of Kadesh may seem very different to the hi-tech tanks and cruise missiles deployed by the US during the 1991 Desert Storm offensive (see pp.244–45) – but each has had the power to change history. Critically, too, no battle sits in isolation. They are always the consequence of other developments: for example, the ambition of emperors, politicians, or peoples, of the failure of diplomacy, or of competition for scarce resources.

Types of battle

Battles That Changed History looks at many different types of campaign both on land and at sea. These include everything from straightforward field encounters between two sides, as seen at the 1187 Battle of Hattin between the crusaders and Saladin's Muslim army (see pp.56–57), to complex manoeuvres such as the Battle of Kursk during World War II, which featured one the world's largest tank battles (see pp.224–45). Marine engagements range from the Spanish Armada Campaign of 1588 (see pp.100–103),

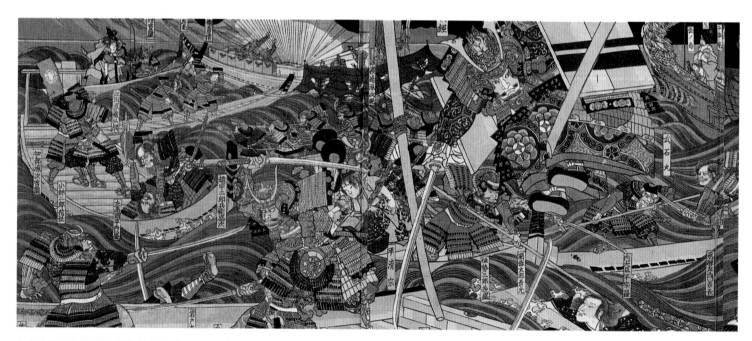

▲ **SEA BATTLE IN FEUDAL JAPAN** The Battle of Dan-no-ura (see pp.54–55) took place in the 12th century between warring Japanese clans. Their ships' crews boarded each other and engaged in fierce hand-to-hand combat.

to the 1905 Battle of Tsushima (see pp.184–87), which saw a Japanese fleet humiliate the might of Tsarist Russia's navy. This book also examines the sieges that formed part of longer campaigns for example, at the French city of Orléans 1429 during the Hundred Years' War (see pp.76–77), the Fall of Constantinople to the Ottoman Turks in 1453 that marked the end of the Byzantine empire (see pp.78–81), and the Siege of Vienna in 1683 that signalled the beginning of the end for the Ottomans (see pp.118–21).

Landmarks in history

Every entry in the book marks a key moment in military history, and attempts to outline its context, actions, and consequences. Some battles led to the fall of an empire – for example, Hannibal's defeat at Zama ended his military conquests (see p.42) – or the creation of one: Babur's victory over the Delhi sultan at Panipat in 1526 (see pp.90–91) resulted in the emergence of the Mughal empire. Others are included as they mark the end of a long campaign – for example, World War II's Battle for Berlin in 1945 – or the beginning of one, such as the German rush for Paris at the start of the World War I, which was halted at the Battle of the Marne in 1914 (see p.190–91). Some potentially less well-known battles mark the first significant use of a piece of military technology – for example, the Battle of Pavia in 1525 saw the earliest outcome of a battle determined by hand-held firearms (see pp.88–89). Others highlight brilliant

◀ **ZULU WEAPONS AT THE BATTLE OF ISANDLWANA** Most Zulu warriors (see pp.176–77) were armed with an *iklwa,* the Zulu refinement of the *assegai* thrusting spear, and a shield made of cowhide. The Zulus were trained in the use and coordination of this weapons system. They saw firearms as the weapons of cowards.

tactical innovations, such as Hannibal's victory at Cannae in 216 BCE, won by enveloping the Roman Army's wings (see pp.26–27) – a manoeuvre that has been repeated in various forms by dozens of generals since.

Each battle is illustrated with contemporary or other artworks, paintings, photographs, and artefacts, while both modern and historical maps show how the action of certain battles unfolded. The book explains examples of key weaponry – from the trebuchets and the earliest cannon, to the first engagement of aircraft and tanks in warfare – as well as profiling military and political leaders throughout history, from Alexander the Great and Julius Caesar to Napoleon Bonaparte, Genghis Khan, Símon Bolívar, and George Washington.

With coverage of the backgrounds, events, and aftermaths of some of the most significant battles in world history, this book aims to help anyone understand the profound political, social, and economic consequences of these military conflicts, and in so doing how kingdoms and empires have been won and lost on the battlefield.

> War is a matter not so much of arms as of money, for it is money alone that makes arms serviceable.

THUCYDIDES, ATHENIAN HISTORIAN, SPEAKS ON WAR IN HIS BOOK *HISTORY OF THE PELOPONNESIAN WAR*, C.400 BCE

BEFORE 1000 CE

CHAPTER 1

▶ **GRECO-PERSIAN DUEL** A Persian soldier (left) and a Greek hoplite (right) are depicted fighting to the death on this *kylix* (wine cup) dating from the 5th century BCE. The hoplite's shield bears the emblem of Pegasus, the divine winged stallion of Greek mythology.

Marathon

490 BCE ■ CENTRAL GREECE ■ PERSIAN EMPIRE VS. ATHENS AND PLATAEA

GRECO-PERSIAN WARS

In 499 BCE, the Greek cities of Ionia, on Asia Minor's west coast, revolted against Persia. Only Athens and Eretria in central Greece answered their appeal for aid, and the Ionian revolt was put down after five years. But Darius I, king of Persia, did not forget the affront, and in 490 BCE he despatched an enormous fleet to exact revenge. Eretria fell after a week-long siege, and then the Persian armada descended on Marathon, a short march away from Athens. The Athenians had been forewarned so they sent messengers – runners such as Pheidippides – hundreds of miles to the other Greek cities to plead for reinforcements. The Spartans agreed to help, but observance of their festival of Carneia delayed them for 10 days.

Without immediate allies, the Athenian generals Callimachus and Miltiades led 10,000 hoplites on the 40-km (26-mile) march from Athens, reaching Marathon just in time to prevent the Persians making their attack. After several days – during which the Persians re-embarked their cavalry onto ships to be sent on a direct attack on Athens, and the Athenian army was reinforced by a contingent from the Greek city of Plataea – the two armies clashed. The hoplite phalanx's success in almost enveloping their opponents might have been fruitless had not the battle-weary Athenians marched straight back to their city and prevented a Persian landing. With the final arrival of the Spartans, the Persian commanders Datis and Artaphernes withdrew their fleet, granting Greece a 10-year respite before the next Persian invasion.

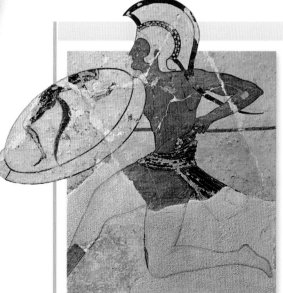

THE HOPLITE **PHALANX**

Around 700 BCE, the aristocratic military culture of Greece's Homeric age was replaced by the disciplined tactics of the phalanx – a compact formation up to eight ranks deep composed of land-owning citizens. Armed with long thrusting spears, short swords, and thick bronze breastplates, each soldier bore a large round shield, or hoplon, which gave them their name. In close formation, the shields protected the unguarded side of the man to the left and the spears projecting from the phalanx made it almost impenetrable. In hoplite warfare, most casualties occurred when one side's ranks broke and fled.

◀ **This image** from the 6th-century-BCE shows a hoplite soldier on the battlefield.

In detail

On arriving at Marathon, the Greeks camped beside a grove of trees, blocking the Persians' route to Athens. However, they did not advance further, afraid to face the more mobile Persians on the open plain and hoping for the arrival of reinforcements from Sparta. When part of the Persian fleet, including most of its cavalry, left for Athens, the Greek general Miltiades persuaded a divided council of Greek generals to unite and attack.

Thinning the centre of his line, the Greek commander Callimachus reinforced his wings and closed rapidly, giving the Persian archers little time to unleash their deadly volleys. Although the Greek centre buckled, this drew their opponents forwards, and when the Persian wings were in turn pushed back by the force of the reinforced phalanx facing them, the hoplites swung inwards, threatening to envelope Darius's troops. The Persians broke and fled towards their ships; thousands died as the pursuing hoplites cut them down while they floundered in the marshes. The Greeks captured seven Persian ships, but the rest made their escape. For the loss of just 192 hoplites, the Athenians and Plataeans had won an important victory. However, Athens still lay exposed to the escaping fleet and the Persian cavalry that was still heading towards the city. In the event, the city was successfully defended.

▼ **MARATHON, 490 BCE** The Greeks felled trees to create obstacles to defend their flanks as they advanced from their camp. Denied manoeuvrability by these and the marshes, the Persians risked being pinned against the shore when the Greek wings broke the Persian flanks. The resulting retreat was chaotic, and in it, according to some accounts, the Persian general Datis was killed.

▶ **KING DARIUS** Darius I of Persia (r.522–486 BCE) annexed Thrace in 512 BCE, but his attempt to exact revenge for the Ionian revolt by conquering Greece foundered at Marathon. A revolt in Egypt delayed a second expedition, and his death gave the Greeks six years of further respite.

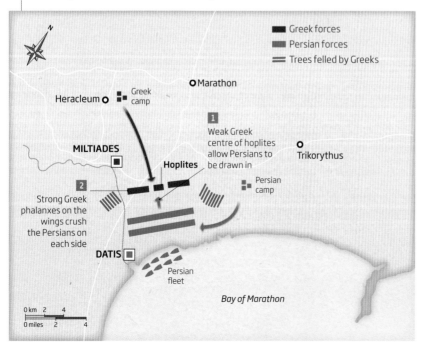

- ■ Greek forces
- ■ Persian forces
- ≡ Trees felled by Greeks

Heracleum ○   Greek camp   ○ Marathon

MILTIADES ■

Hoplites

1 Weak Greek centre of hoplites allow Persians to be drawn in

○ Trikorythus

Persian camp ■■

2 Strong Greek phalanxes on the wings crush the Persians on each side

DATIS ■

Persian fleet

Bay of Marathon

0 km 2   4
0 miles 2   4

◄ **IMMORTALS** The Immortals were a unit of 10,000 men that formed the bodyguard of the Persian king. They were tasked with protecting the king and breaking down stubborn opposition on the battlefield. Other elite formations, similarly equipped with long spears and bows, made up the Persian centre at Marathon, while less experienced troops formed the flanks.

▼ **ON THE BATTLEFIELD** The Greek phalanx crashes into the Persian line at Marathon in this frieze from a sarcophagus found in Italy. After nearly a week in which the two armies had stood off against each other, the attack caught the Persians by surprise, and by the time Datis had realized the trap Miltiades had set him, it was too late for him to react.

▶ **TACTICAL ADVANTAGE**
In an attempt to block the advance of the Persian invaders, Leonidas placed his forces at the Middle Gates of Thermopylae in central Greece. The 15-m (45-ft) gap was flanked on one side by water and on the other by a sheer slope which, together with a wall that had been built decades earlier, made passage by an attacking force almost impossible.

Mountain path taken by Persian outflanking force

Middle Gates of Thermopylae

Spartan defensive position and wall at Middle Gates

Site of Spartan last stand

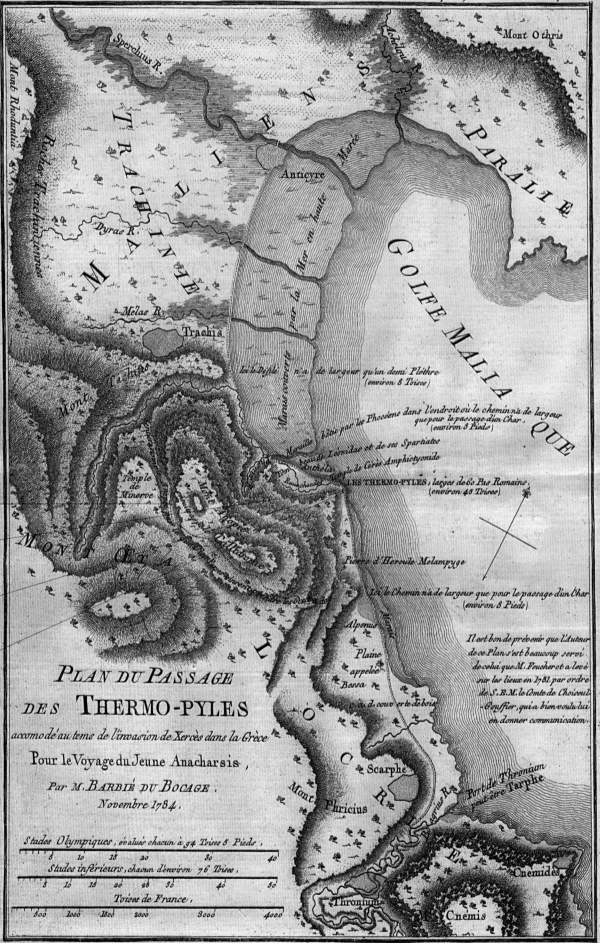

Thermopylae

480 BCE ▪ CENTRAL GREECE ▪ GREECE VS. PERSIA

GRECO-PERSIAN WARS

In 480 BCE, Xerxes I restarted the Persian invasion of Greece that had ended at Marathon 10 years earlier (see pp.12–15), bridging the Hellespont (Dardenelles) with pontoons to transport his huge army. Unable to oppose such a force, the northern Greek cities quickly capitulated and the Persians swept through Thessaly in central Greece. An anti-Persian resistance coalesced around Athens and Sparta, however, and resolved to halt the invaders. The Spartan army under Leonidas marched to Thermopylae in Boeotia, where a narrow pass could be held by a small number of hoplites. Simultaneously, the Athenian fleet blocked the Persian navy at the Straits of Artemisium to the north-east.

Xerxes approached on 18 August with around 70,000 men, 10 times that of the Spartan-led defenders. He unleashed a volley of arrows, followed by a headlong charge and an assault by his elite forces, the Immortals, all of which the Greeks withstood. With Persian losses mounting on the second day,

KING **LEONIDAS** (C.548–480 BCE)

The third son of King Anaxandridas of Sparta, Leonidas received the rigorous martial training typical of high-born Spartan males, and his military experience included service in a campaign against Argos in 494 BCE. He became king in 490 BCE and was selected to lead the anti-Persian alliance in 480 BCE. Ignoring a prophecy from the Delphic oracle that predicted his death, his heroic stand at Thermopylae, stubbornly resisting and then refusing to retreat with the rest of the army, made Leonidas's name a byword for bravery among future Greek generations.

▶ **Depicting the hero of the battle**, this statue of Leonidas was found at the city of Sparta in Greece.

Xerxes's campaign was only saved by the discovery of a mountain path that enabled him to attack from the rear. Outflanked, Leonidas sent most of the army away, and fought to the death with a smaller force. The Greek fleet retired, and Xerxes marched on Athens and into the Peloponnese.

In detail

▶ **LEONIDAS'S LAST STAND**
A local man betrayed the Greek forces by revealing a track over the mountain that allowed the Persians to circumvent Leonidas's defences. Xerxes used the path to send 10,000 men to attack from the rear. Facing the Persian forces with 300 Spartan warriors, accompanied by 700 Thespians and a force of Thebans, Leonidas made a heroic last stand while the remaining Greek forces retreated. This painting from 1963 depicts the final moments of the battle.

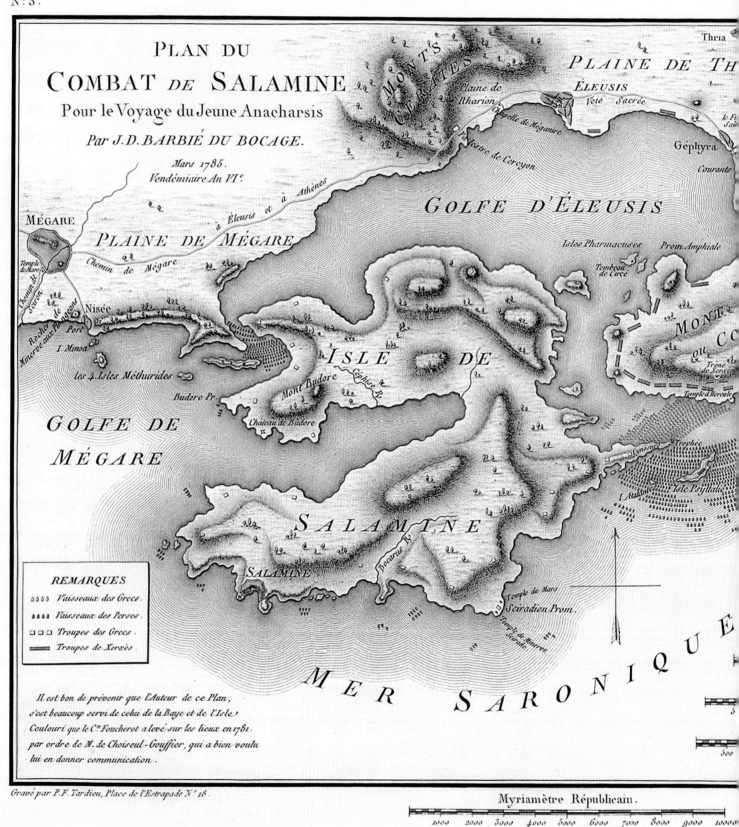

N.º 5.

PLAN DU
COMBAT DE SALAMINE
Pour le Voyage du Jeune Anacharsis

Par J. D. BARBIÉ DU BOCAGE.

Mars 1785.
Vendémiaire An VI.ᵉ

MÉGARE

PLAINE DE MÉGARE

GOLFE DE
MÉGARE

GOLFE D'ÉLEUSIS

ISLE DE

SALAMINE

SALAMINE

MER SARONIQUE

REMARQUES

∿∿∿∿ Vaisseaux des Grecs.
▲▲▲▲ Vaisseaux des Perses.
□□□ Troupes des Grecs.
▬▬▬ Troupes de Xerxès.

Il est bon de prévenir que l'Auteur de ce Plan,
s'est beaucoup servi de celui de la Baye et de l'Isle
Coulouri que le C.ᵉⁿ Foucherot a levé sur les lieux en 1781.
par ordre de M. de Choiseul-Gouffier, qui a bien voulu
lui en donner communication.

Gravé par P. F. Tardieu, Place de l'Estrapade N.º 18.

Myriamètre Républicain.

1000   2000   3000   4000   5000   6000   7000   8000   9000   10000

▲ **BATTLE MAP OF SALAMIS** This map from 1825 shows the Persian and Greek fleets clustered at the narrow entrance to the Gulf of Eleusis, east of the island of Salamis. The Greek line (north) consisted of the Athenians on its left and the Spartans and Aeginetans on its right. The Persians tried to block the Greek rear by sending an Egyptian detachment to sail northwest around Salamis, but in the event it was the Persian fleet that had to retreat, and was ambushed by the Aeginetans as it did so.

The map on the left shows the region around Athens.

L. Aubert scripsit.

Salamis

480 BCE ▪ WESTERN GREECE ▪ SPARTA AND ATHENS VS. PERSIA

GRECO-PERSIAN WARS

The Persian king Xerxes captured northern Greece and burned the city of Athens in September 480 BCE. He then intended to transport his army by sea to move against the Spartans. In the Gulf of Eleusis, the Greek navy, led by the Athenian admiral Themistocles and the Spartan Eurybiades, blocked the narrow straits opposite the island of Salamis, so denying Xerxes use of the harbours of Athens. The Persian flotilla that approached on the night of 28 September – drawn in by rumours artfully spread by Themistocles that the Greeks might escape – consisted of around 800 triremes (see below), more than double the Greeks' numbers.

Themistocles had chosen his location well. Once the Persians sailed into the narrow straits, their numerical advantage was nullified. Persian triremes ploughed into each other and ships became entangled in the wreckage. Seeing the disorder, Themistocles pounced, and the Greeks smashed into the Persian line, their rams splintering the enemy triremes or shearing their oars. Many vessels were captured by Greek marines or sunk. A horrified Xerxes, who had been watching from a promontory high above the straits, ordered a retreat. Having lost 200 ships, his navy was shattered and he withdrew much of his army to Asia Minor. This gave the Greek city-states invaluable breathing space to rebuild their forces and finally drive the Persians out of Greece.

TRIREMES

Triremes, which had three banks of oars on each side, first appeared in around 700 BCE, and formed the backbone of eastern Mediterranean fleets for the following four centuries. Fast and highly manoeuvrable, they were capable of sailing through an opposing line and turning about to attack from the rear. Many were also equipped with metal spikes designed for ramming enemy vessels. The discovery of a silver mine in around 483 BCE gave Athens funds to build 200 triremes; without these ships it would have struggled to face the large Persian trireme force.

▲ **An Athenian trireme**, complete with oarsmen, depicted in bas-relief, c.400 BCE.

Issus

333 BCE ▪ SOUTHERN TURKEY ▪ MACEDONIA VS. PERSIA

CONQUESTS OF ALEXANDER THE GREAT

Having put down a series of revolts in Greece after his accession to the Macedonian throne in 336 BCE, Alexander the Great began an attack on the Persian Empire. His crossing into Asia Minor in 334 BCE caught Persian ruler Darius III unprepared, and it was not until the following year, with the Macedonian army deep in the interior, that Darius mounted a counter-strike.

He wrong-footed Alexander by crossing the Taurus Mountains at the Amanic Gates (in modern Turkey) and appearing unexpectedly at the Macedonians' rear. Undaunted, Alexander ordered an arduous descent of the narrow Jonah Pass into a narrow plain by the Pinarus River. He deployed his forces with cavalry at the wings, hoping to use the force of his infantry phalanxes, armed with the 6-m (20-ft) Macedonian sarissa pike, to overwhelm the Greek mercenary hoplites who faced them. Instead, Alexander's elite Companion cavalry smashed through the Persian left, began to envelop the Greek mercenaries, and threatened the person of Darius directly. When Darius fled, most of the Persian army followed, and the Greek mercenaries had to conduct a fighting withdrawal.

Darius's humiliation was total: his mother, wife, and children had been captured. However, a force of 10,000 Greek mercenaries had escaped to form the core of a new Persian army. Darius, aware that one more defeat would cost him his empire, offered Alexander generous terms – including the cession of much of Asia Minor – but Alexander summarily dismissed them. After Issus, Alexander the invader had become Alexander the conqueror.

ALEXANDER THE GREAT (356–323 BCE)

The son of Philip II of Macedon (who defeated the Greek city-states at Chaeronea in 338 BCE), Alexander proved his military talent when he became the commander of his father's army. His mastery of enveloping tactics defeated Darius III three times – at Granicus, Issus, and Gaugamela (see pp.24–25) – and secured the entire Persian empire. His conquests were so great that his realm would have been almost impossible to govern had he not died of fever in 323 BCE.

▶ **Alexander** on his favourite horse, Bucephalus, after which he named a city in India.

▼ **FLEEING THE FIELD** This 2nd-century BCE Roman mosaic from Pompeii is thought to depict the battle of Issus. Overwhelmed by the oncoming Macedonian cavalry, Darius orders his charioteer to flee.

In detail

The Persian and Macedonian forces deployed along the Pinarus River, an unidentified stream some 15 km (9 miles) north of the Pass of Jonah (today, near the Turkey-Syria border). Alexander placed his phalanxes, including the elite *hypaspist* ("shield bearer") infantry, to the centre and left of his line, facing the Greek mercenaries across the stream. On either flank Alexander placed his cavalry (see right) opposite the Persian horse, while Darius kept his large infantry reserve to the rear. At first, Alexander's left flank was forced back by the heavy Persian cavalry under Nabarzanes, then he sent a contingent of Thessalians to support it, protected by his phalanx.

At the same time Alexander's elite cavalry dislodged a Persian force that had tried to outflank him on the right. They scattered the Persian horse, then wheeled inwards, threatening Darius's bodyguard and the rear of the Greek mercenary phalanx. Narrowly escaping capture, Darius fled the field. Meanwhile, the Greek mercenaries who had stubbornly resisted Macedonian attempts to cross the stream, attacked from both the front and the rear, began to buckle. The Thessalians scattered the Persian cavalry charge on the left, and a Persian retreat ensued. Despite pursuing Darius for 40 km (25 miles), Alexander failed to catch him; had he done so, the war might have come to an early end.

▲ **DARIUS III** The king is portrayed as an archer on this Persian coin. In reality, the Persian Great Kings were kept well back from the fighting, since any threat to them might ruin their armies' morale.

◄ **ISSUS, 333 BCE** At Issus, Alexander chose his ground well, with the sea protecting his left flank. The Persian heavy cavalry pushed at his left in the early stages of the battle, but his centre held against strong pressure from the Greek mercenaries in Darius's army. The Macedonian cavalry were able to break through to their right and envelop the Persians from the rear.

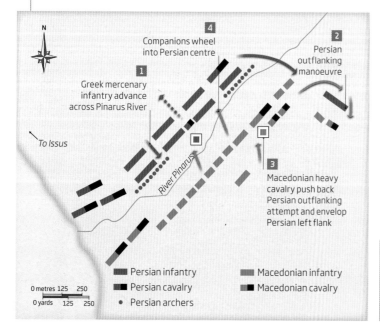

N

4 Companions wheel into Persian centre

2 Persian outflanking manoeuvre

1 Greek mercenary infantry advance across Pinarus River

To Issus

River Pinarus

3 Macedonian heavy cavalry push back Persian outflanking attempt and envelop Persian left flank

■ Persian infantry   ■ Macedonian infantry
■ Persian cavalry   ■ Macedonian cavalry
• Persian archers

0 metres 125   250
0 yards   125   250

> … the Persian left **collapsed** the very **moment** he was on them ❞
>
> **ARRIAN,** *THE ANABASIS OF ALEXANDER*

▲ **MACEDONIAN INFANTRY IN BATTLE** A Macedonian infantry phalanx (see p.24) lines up (top). The long sarissas and overlapping shields of the elite *pezhetairoi* ("foot companions") and the regular *hypaspists* presented a formidable obstacle to attackers, as the sarissas of the first five ranks projected beyond the front of the phalanx. Alexander was a master at combining infantry tactics with those of the cavalry (below). In general, the infantry, positioned in the centre, held the enemy line in place while the cavalry charged the often ill-disciplined Persian cavalry on the wings.

◄ **HOPLITES** The Macedonians retained the traditional phalanx used by Greek armies since the 7th century BCE. By Alexander's time the Greek hoplite spear had doubled in length to become the 6-m (20-ft) long sarissa of the Macedonian phalangite. With a sharp point at one end and a spiked butt for use as a secondary weapon if the shaft broke, the effect on opponents of hundreds of such weapons projecting from the phalanx was terrifying.

▲ **CAVALRY CHARGE** Alexander brought 1,800 of his elite Companion cavalry on the Persian campaign. Organized into 300-strong squadrons, they attacked in a wedge formation that could penetrate, pivot around, and envelop enemy lines. The infantry phalanx held off often vastly superior numbers, but it was generally the cavalry that delivered the killing blow.

Gaugamela

331 BCE ▪ MODERN-DAY IRAQI KURDISTAN ▪ MACEDON AND HELLENIC LEAGUE VS. ACHAEMENID EMPIRE

CONQUESTS OF ALEXANDER THE GREAT

After his victory against Darius III at Issus (see pp.20–23), Alexander the Great occupied Syria and Palestine, and then travelled to Egypt in 332 BCE. It was only in the summer of the following year that he returned, intent on pushing into the Persian Empire's eastern province. The Persians allowed Alexander to reach the Euphrates, in Mesopotamia, but put up just enough resistance to deny him the easier river route down to Babylon. Instead, the Macedonian army marched north towards Arbela (modern Irbil), where Darius lay in wait near a hill called Gaugamela. A series of bad omens shook Persian morale, and Darius sent a peace proposal to Alexander, which Alexander summarily rejected. After pausing just a few kilometres from the Persian line, Alexander attacked on 30 September.

Alexander approach obliquely, concentrating his cavalry on the right to draw out the enemy horse, and then sending a reinforced phalanx crashing through the weak point in the Persian centre that this exposed. This outwitted Darius, who fled as he saw his army crumbling. Alexander followed him eastwards, occupying the Persian ceremonial capital at Persepolis, which his troops burnt following a drunken argument. Finally, in July 330 BCE, Darius was murdered on the orders of one of his generals. Although resistance continued in the north-east, most of Darius's governors surrendered, leaving Alexander the master of the Persian Empire.

THE **MACEDONIAN PHALANX**

The Macedonian infantry adopted a Greek-style phalanx formation. Known as Foot Companions, its members were armed with 6-m (20-ft)-long pikes, or sarissas. In battle, the phalanx was drawn up eight or 16 ranks deep, and the sarissas of the first four ranks projected beyond it, making the formation very difficult to penetrate. Training enabled the phalanx to push forwards and break up less disciplined opponents, resist attacks by numerically superior enemies, and even to open up to allow chariots to pass harmlessly through.

▲ **During the fierce fighting** at Gaugamela, the phalanx's offensive power proved invaluable.

In detail

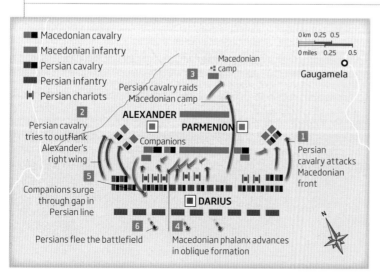

- ▪ Macedonian cavalry
- ▪ Macedonian infantry
- ▪ Persian cavalry
- ▪ Persian infantry
- |▪| Persian chariots

0 km 0.25 0.5
0 miles 0.25 0.5

Macedonian camp

Gaugamela

3 Persian cavalry raids Macedonian camp

2 Persian cavalry tries to outflank Alexander's right wing

ALEXANDER
■ PARMENION ■

Companions

1 Persian cavalry attacks Macedonian front

5 Companions surge through gap in Persian line

■ DARIUS

6 Persians flee the battlefield **4** Macedonian phalanx advances in oblique formation

N

◄ GAUGAMELA, 331 BCE
Alexander's oblique attack and concentration of troops on his right nullified the Persians' advantage in numbers. Charges by Persian heavy cavalry, chariots, and even elephants served only to disorder and over-extend the Persian line. The Persians wasted their one breakthrough by attacking Alexander's baggage train.

▲ **ASTRONOMICAL DIARY** This Babylonian tablet describes heavenly phenomena that spread fear among the Persian soldiers: first a blood-red moon, then fire falling from the sky. Persian priests interpreted these as omens of military disaster.

◄ **CAVALRY AT GAUGAMELA** Fierce cavalry engagements took place on both the right and left wings at Gaugamela. On the Macedonian right, Alexander and the Companion cavalry succeeded in drawing the Persian heavy cavalry away form the centre, opening up a gap in the line that the phalanx could exploit. On the Macedonian left, however, the light cavalry faired relatively poorly. This 16th-century Persian miniature depicts the melee between opposing horsemen.

Cannae

216 BCE ■ SOUTHERN ITALY ■ CARTHAGE VS. ROMAN REPUBLIC

SECOND PUNIC WAR

The invasion of Italy in 218 BCE by Carthage's young military leader Hannibal Barca met with early success, but two years later the Romans had regrouped, helped by a series of delaying campaigns fought by Fabius Maximus. Now impatient to drive the invader out, the Roman Senate ordered the recruitment of an army of 80,000 men, including eight infantry legions. This headed south to confront Hannibal, who had just seized a supply depot at Cannae, in southern Italy.

The legions found Hannibal on the banks of the Aufidius River, but with command alternating daily between the consuls Aemilius Paullus and Terentius Varro, the Romans' strategy was unclear. Hannibal knew that Varro was the more impetuous, and on 30 August he tempted him to battle with a deployment that had weak infantry units in its centre and cavalry on its wings. Varro ordered a charge, and the Roman legions closed in, pushing back Hannibal's centre. However, the undefeated African infantry on the wings then closed in against the Romans' flanks, and the Carthaginian cavalry, which had routed the Roman horsemen, returned and sealed off the Roman rear. Stuck in a trap, almost 70,000 Romans perished, including Paullus.

With the main field force destroyed, Rome itself was only saved by Hannibal's hesitancy in marching on the city – a delay that gave the Romans time to recover. The Carthaginian campaign in Italy subsequently lost momentum, ending in 202 BCE, when Hannibal was recalled to Africa to stave off a Roman invasion.

▶ **CANNAE, 216 BCE** Hannibal formed his centre in a crescent facing the Roman infantry. As the legionaries advanced, the Carthaginian line bowed back, and Varro's men were drawn in. Hannibal's African infantry then attacked their flanks and the Carthaginian cavalry on the left wing wheeled and completed the encirclement. It was the Roman Republic's worst ever military defeat.

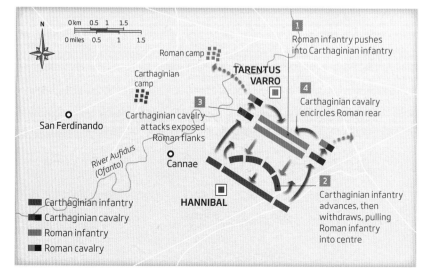

N

0 km   0.5   1   1.5
0 miles   0.5   1   1.5

Roman camp

Carthaginian camp

San Ferdinando

River Aufidus (Ofanto)

Cannae

TARENTUS VARRO

HANNIBAL

1 Roman infantry pushes into Carthaginian infantry

3 Carthaginian cavalry attacks exposed Roman flanks

4 Carthaginian cavalry encircles Roman rear

2 Carthaginian infantry advances, then withdraws, pulling Roman infantry into centre

▬ Carthaginian infantry
▬ Carthaginian cavalry
▬ Roman infantry
▬ Roman cavalry

There was **no longer** any Roman camp, any general, any single soldier in existence.

LIVIUS TITUS, ROMAN HISTORIAN, DESCRIBING HANNIBAL'S INVASION IN *THE HISTORY OF ROME, BOOK 22*

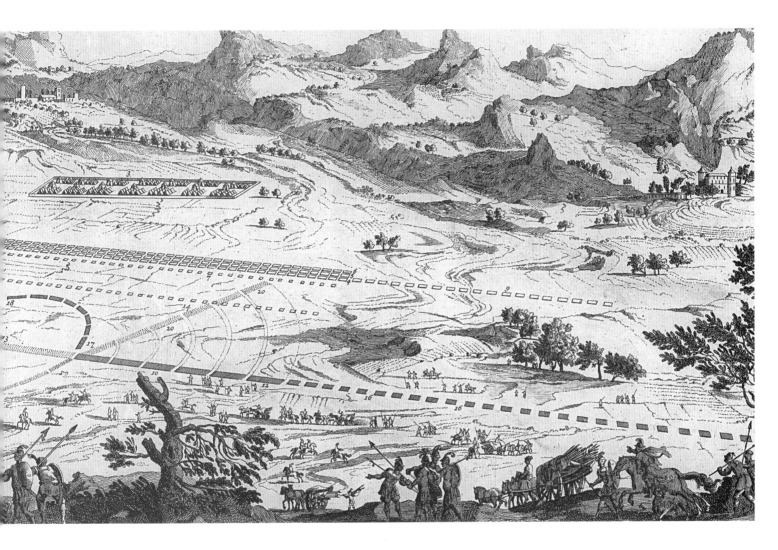

▲ **FIELD OF BATTLE**
Produced by K. de Putter in 1729, this engraving gives an idealized impression of the forces arrayed at the battle of Cannae. The Aufidius River lies to the left, with the greater Roman camp on its western side. In the foreground, Hannibal's army of Spanish, Gallic, and African infantry, plus Carthaginian and Numidian cavalry, assembles before its adversaries.

THE **PUNIC WARS** (264–146 CE)

Rome fought three wars with the North African city-state of Carthage between 264 and 146 BCE. In the second of these, sparked by Roman fears of Carthage's burgeoning empire in Spain and tensions over competing interests in Sicily, the brilliant Carthaginian general Hannibal Barca brought an army over the Alps – which the Romans had thought impassable. Despite his stunning victories in Italy, the war ended after Hannibal suffered his only battlefield defeat at the hands of Scipio Africanus at Zama in 202 BCE (see p.42). Stripped of its army and most of its lands, a much-weakened Carthage was finally captured and destroyed by Rome in 146 BCE.

▶ **Hannibal brought** 38 war elephants with him on his Italian campaigns, but almost all died during the crossing of the Alps.

QVANTA STRA
CE VIRVM SVBLI
MIS ALEXIA CESSIT
CÆSAREIS AQVI
LIS. PICTA TABEL
LA NOTAT

Alesia

52 BCE ■ CENTRAL FRANCE ■ ROMAN EMPIRE VS. GAUL

CAESAR'S GALLIC WAR

Julius Caesar's successful conquest of Gaul between 58 and 54 BCE provoked a backlash among the conquered peoples. Gaulish tribes, angry at the savagery with which an uprising by Ambiorix of the Eburones had been put down, rallied around Vercingetorix, the young chieftain of the Arverni. In the spring of 52 BCE, Caesar began a counter-offensive, using siege earthworks to smash the defences of Avaricum, the capital of Vercingetorix's allies, the Bituriges. However, at Gergovia, in February 52 BCE, Vercingetorix trapped Caesar by luring him into a siege against the Gauls, and the Roman army only extracted itself at the price of a thousand dead.

After the siege, it appeared that the Romans might retreat to southern Gaul, so Vercingetorix decided to repeat the ruse on a larger scale, selecting the easily defended high promontory of Alesia. However, the massive 250,000-strong

JULIUS CAESAR (100–44 BCE)

Politically ruthless, Caesar used the First Triumvirate (his alliance with Crassus and Pompey) as a springboard for a consulship in 59 BCE and then the governorship of Cisalpine Gaul. From there, he conquered Gaul in four campaigning seasons. With expeditions to Britain in 55 and 54 BCE behind him, he became Rome's premier general, turning on Pompey after the Gallic Wars and fighting a civil war that ended in his victory in 48 BCE. In 45 BCE, he declared himself "dictator for life", which led to his assassination by rivals the following year.

➤ **Julius Caesar** laid the foundations of the Roman Empire.

army sent to relieve Vercingetorix was delayed by heavy rains, giving Caesar time to reach Alesia and build a pair of walls – one to hem Vercingetorix in, the other to keep the relief force out. Disrupted, the Gaulish armies failed co-ordinate their attacks, and a final assault on 15 September was beaten off by Caesar's timely commitment of his final reserves. With the relief force suffering thousands of casualties and the besieged unable to break out, the Gauls held out for a further week in Alesia before Vercingetorix surrendered, his men starving and desperate. He was taken a captive to Rome, where he was murdered six years later. Leaderless, the Gaulish revolt collapsed.

◀ **ALESIA BESIEGED** This 16th-century painting shows the wall encircling Vercingetorix's Gauls at Alesia. Despite their entrenched defensive positions, the Gauls' final attack nearly overwhelmed the Roman legions, and it required Caesar's masterful deployment of his German mercenary cavalry at the critical moment to turn the tide of the battle. The German imperial eagle on the Romans' standard is an anachronism dating to the painter's day.

In context

➤ **THE CIRCUMVALLATION OF ALESIA** Although Alesia was easily defended, once encircled by the Roman wall – as in this Roman siege in 54 BCE – it became a trap. Attempts by the relieving force to use the surrounding mountains to screen an attack on a lightly held Roman camp failed to break the deadlock.

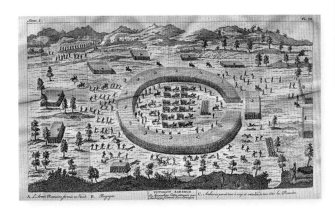

▲ **VERCINGETORIX SURRENDERS** At the height of the siege, Vercingetorix released Alesia's non-combatants, but the Romans refused to let them pass. Six days later, with supplies all but exhausted, Vercingetorix rode out to surrender to Caesar in person.

▲ **CONTEMPORARY WARSHIP** This 1st-century CE frieze may depict
a large Egyptian warship (the crocodile was a symbol of the Nile), even
though its figures bear arms characteristic of Roman soldiers. The
tower at the front of the vessel would have been used as a platform
for hurling missiles at enemy ships.

Actium

31 BCE ▪ WESTERN GREECE ▪ OCTAVIAN VS. MARK ANTONY AND EGYPT

REPUBLICAN CIVIL WAR

The assassination of Julius Caesar in 44 BCE unleashed a violent struggle between the Republican partisans of his killers, Brutus and Cassius, and the defenders of Caesar's legacy, notably Octavian (his adopted son), and Mark Antony. However, relations between Antony and Octavian deteriorated. Accusations that Antony had promised his mistress Cleopatra VII of Egypt the cession of several Roman provinces led to a final rupture with the Roman Senate, which declared war on the pair in 33 BCE.

Octavian gathered an army and sailed for Greece to bring Antony to heel. By September 31 BCE, he and his deputy Agrippa had seized key garrisons loyal to Antony and positioned themselves with a fleet of 230 ships north of the Gulf of Ambracia, where Antony's smaller fleet of 170 vessels was moored. Antony resolved to break out to save what he could and, on 2 September, sailed out to open water. His vessels engaged Octavian's squadrons, allowing Cleopatra to get away with their treasure. Antony then broke off with a small flotilla, leaving the rest of his navy to fight an increasingly desperate struggle. Surrounded by Octavian's marines, Antony's heavy ships were boarded, rammed, or set alight. His land-force rapidly surrendered, and by the summer of 30 BCE, when Octavian arrived in Egypt, Antony had virtually no forces left. Faced with certain defeat, he and Cleopatra committed suicide, leaving Octavian the unchallenged master of Rome.

THE REIGN OF **AUGUSTUS**

Octavian's victory at Actium enabled him to reshape the Roman world. In 27 BCE, he induced the Senate to grant him unprecedented powers: personal control over key provinces, successive consulships, and the title Augustus (meaning "venerable"). These changes marked the shift of Rome from a Republic to an Empire, and Augustus's reorganization of the army (he dismissed legions previously loyal to his competitors) rendered it answerable to him alone. During his reign, his troops pushed the Roman border beyond the Rhine in Germany and to the Danube in the Balkans. His political authority, augmented by the right to propose and veto legislation, enabled him to bequeath his position to his step-son Tiberius, the second emperor, in 14 CE.

➤ **Augustus Caesar**, founder of the Roman Empire.

In detail

On 1 September, Octavian approached the Gulf of Ambracia, but did not pass through its shallow entrance. Intent on escape, Antony had burnt his spare ships, leaving him with mostly heavy sixes and nines (ships with six and nine banks of oars respectively) to face Octavian's lighter but more numerous fleet. Antony left the bay westwards with his squadron on the right, Marcus Octavius in the centre, and Gaius Sosius on the left, while Cleopatra brought up the rear. Agrippa, Octavian's deputy, at first refused to engage, and a stalemate ensued until midday. Then Antony's left wing advanced, hoping to draw out Octavian's fleet, and gave Cleopatra room to escape.

Amid a hail of catapult bolts, and volleys of arrows and slingshots, the fleets moved to close quarters, Agrippa doubling his line to stop Antony's heavy ships breaking through. Agrippa extended his line to the left to outflank Octavian, pulling Antony's right wing northward, where it became detached from the rest, opening a gap through which Cleopatra's squadron sped into open water. Seeing this, Antony shifted to a smaller vessel (a five) and about three hours after the battle began, he fled with a few ships to join Cleopatra.

The rest of Antony's fleet fought on until nightfall, but they were eventually sunk, burnt, or captured. Although a few swift liburnians (small galleys) pursued Antony, he drove them off and escaped with 60–70 ships, eventually returning to Egypt.

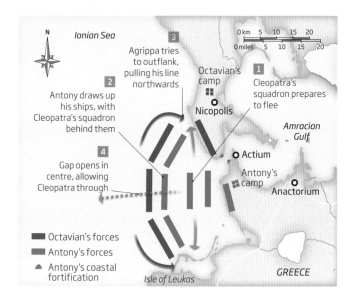

ACTIUM, 31 BCE Although Antony was safe in the Ambracian Gulf, his fleet was trapped there. As battle commenced, he put pressure on the wings of Octavian and Agrippa's fleet, which tried to outflank him and opened up a gap in the centre through which Cleopatra's squadron was able to escape, together with a small number of Antony's ships.

RAMMING AND BOARDING This late-15th-century painting by Italian artist Neroccio de' Landi shows the masses of troops aboard opposing fleets at Actium. Roman warships typically carried dozens of marines; the main tactic was to immobilize vessels by ramming or grappling, after which marines boarded and fought hand-to-hand to take control.

▼ **FLOATING BATTLEFIELD** The Romans' close-combat tactics in sea battles were adapted from their particular style of land warfare. This 1st-century CE depiction shows the melee caused by the combatants boarding each others' ships at Actium.

▲ **GODDESS OF WAR** This bronze prow-fitting depicting Athena, the Greek goddess of war, is thought to have belonged to a ship that was sunk at the battle of Actium. The Romans saw Athena as the Greek equivalent of Minerva, their own goddess of war, trade, and wisdom.

▲ **SOLDIER'S PAY** One of thousands minted by Mark Antony to pay his troops during the Actium campaign, this coin shows a Roman trireme with its characteristically curved prow. The legend beneath it refers to Antony as a *triumvir* – one of the three men (along with Octavian and Marcus Lepidus) who had shared power at Rome before the Civil War broke out.

> About **five thousand men** were slain in the action...
> and Caesar took **three hundred ships**
>
> **PLUTARCH**, *BATTLE OF ACTIUM*

▲ **END IN FLAMES** Cao Cao ordered his ships to be chained together to compensate for his inexperienced sailors' inability to manoeuvre them. As a result, they were easy targets for the rebel admiral Huang Gai's fireships, and flames rapidly took hold of Cao Cao's fleet.

Red Cliffs

208 CE ■ EASTERN CHINA ■ HAN LOYALISTS VS. REBEL ALLIANCE

LATE HAN CIVIL WAR

The authority of the Han emperors of China was shattered by a peasant uprising of 184 CE – then the generals who suppressed the uprising turned against each other, and China became a patchwork of warring states. The emperor, Xian, became a pawn in the hands of rival military strongmen, until Cao Cao, a former garrison commander, took control of the imperial household in 196 CE. Gradually, he secured the north of China, then he set out to conquer the south in 208 CE. First, he had to gain control of the Yangzi river, which was defended by warlords Liu Bei and Sun Quan.

Initially, things went Cao Cao's way. He seized Lui Bei's naval base – and the fleet that came with it – at Jiangling. Then he sailed east to seize Sun Quan's power base at Chaisang. Meanwhile, Sun's general Zhou Yu sailed 50,000 soldiers west to meet Cao Cao, whose forces numbered 220,000. The fleets met at Red Cliffs, and the fighting was inconclusive. Pretending to seek peace, rebel admiral Huang Gai sailed to Cao Cao, leading a fleet filled with dry reeds and inflammable wax. Cao Cao had bound his ships together for stability and was unable to manoeuvre when the blazing fleet of fireships came his way. Panic gripped the Han forces, and Cao Cao ordered a retreat. Thousands died as they fled overland, where the road turned into a swamp. Eventually, Cao Cao reversed his territorial losses, but the chance to unify China under a single ruler had been lost.

CAO CAO (c.150-220 CE)

A junior Han army officer, Cao Cao rose to prominence during the suppression of a peasant uprising known as the Yellow Turban Revolt. Although later disgraced, he rescued the Emperor Xian in 196 CE after the declaration of a rival emperor, securing him the allegiance of Han loyalists. Shortly after being declared imperial chancellor in 208 CE, he launched the abortive campaign to conquer the middle Yangzi. After Red Cliffs, he retained control of the north as de facto emperor, although it was only after his death in 220 CE that his son, Cao Pi, formally became the first ruler of the Wei dynasty.

▶ **Cao Cao contemplates** his approaching fate on the eve of the battle of Red Cliffs.

... our infantry were exhausted by toil and danger... they had neither strength left to fight, nor spirits to plan anything...

AMMIANUS MARCELLINUS DESCRIBING THE DECIMATION OF THE ROMANS IN *LATER ROMAN HISTORY*, c.380 CE

▲ **ROMAN INFANTRY IN ACTION** Although this mid-3rd-century CE synagogue fresco depicts a Biblical battle, it shows equipment similar to that of the late Roman infantry. The longer swords and chain mail armour are characteristic of the *comitatenses*, the mobile forces that later Roman emperors relied upon in the field as the backbone of their efforts to defend the empire against barbarian invasions.

Adrianople

378 CE ■ NORTHWESTERN TURKEY ■ ROMAN EMPIRE VS. GOTHIC TRIBES

ROMAN-GOTHIC WARS

In the mid-370s CE, the eastern Roman frontier on the Danube came under growing pressure from the Goths, a Germanic people who had been forced westward by the migration of the Huns. In 376 CE, one group of Goths, the Tervingi, was permitted to enter Roman territory. However, the cruel treatment meted out to them by the Roman commander Lupicinus, which included denying them food supplies, led them to revolt under their chieftain Fritigern. By now another group of Goths, the Greuthingi, had crossed the Danube and joined Fritigern's forces to create a single army, some 200,000 strong.

Alarmed, the Roman emperor Valens marched from Constantinople with 50,000 men – virtually the entire eastern Roman field army. When he encountered the Goths near Adrianople, Valens chose to attack, even though reinforcements sent by his western colleague Gratian were only three days' march away. The main force consisting of Gothic cavalry was away foraging, and Fritigern used negotiations to buy time, forming his wagons into a circle to protect the remaining warriors. However, on 9 August, a group of Roman cavalry attacked, leading their infantry to surge forward. This left the Roman infantry exposed when the Gothic horsemen returned and joined the battle. The Roman cavalry were thrown back and the infantry, exposed by the surrender of units of Thracians, were surrounded and cut to pieces. Valens himself was among the two-thirds of the army that perished at Adrianople, in Rome's worst defeat since Cannae (see pp.26–27). His successor Theodosius was forced to allow the Goths to settle in the Balkans, threatening the very existence of the eastern empire.

THE **BARBARIAN INVASIONS**

From the mid-3rd century CE, Roman frontiers on the Rhine and Danube came under strain from Germanic barbarians migrating west and south. Border troops struggled to contain these incursions and after Adrianople, when the Goths invaded Italy in 401 CE, the frontiers began to collapse. Goths, Alans, and Vandals surged across the Rhine in 407 CE, occupying most of France, Spain and North Africa. A succession of weak emperors failed to recapture the lost provinces, and in 476 CE the last western Roman emperor was deposed by his own army commander.

▶ **The Ludovisi battle sarcophagus** from the 3rd century CE depicts a battle between the Romans and Dacian barbarians.

➤ **BATTLE FOR TERRITORY** This scene from the *Grandes Chroniques de France*, a collection of illuminated manuscripts detailing the history of France, shows Frankish forces routing the Arab invaders in 732 CE, thought to be at the Battle of Tours.

Tours

732 CE ■ CENTRAL FRANCE ■ FRANKS VS. UMAYYAD CALIPHATE

UMAYYAD INVASION OF GAUL

Following the Arab conquest of Spain and the province of Septimania (north of the Pyrenees), from 719 CE Arab emirs installed themselves in several southern French towns. However, political instability in the region led Abd ar-Rahman, the Umayyad governor of Spain, to launch an expedition to prevent Septimania falling into the hands of the Frankish ruler Charles Martel.

In 732 CE Abd ar-Rahman advanced northwards towards the monastery of St Martin at Tours. Charles Martel deployed his 30,000-strong force on the road between Poitiers and Tours, blocking the progress of Abd ar-Rahman's army, which was roughly double the size. The Franks formed a compact phalanx, its flanks protected by the rivers Vienne and Chail, and weathered several attacks by the Arab light cavalry. A counter-attack by Frankish horsemen under Duke Eudo against the enemy camp led some Arab units to withdraw in order to defend the plunder stored there. This rapidly accelerated into the panicked flight of the whole army, during which Abd ar-Rahman was killed while trying in vain to rally his troops. The remnants of the Umayyad army retreated over the Pyrenees.

Although a further Arab invasion took place in 735 CE, advancing as far as Avignon, the waning power of the Umayyads and the growing power of the Frankish Carolingian dynasty meant that from then on northern France was safe from Arab invasion.

THE **ISLAMIC EXPANSION**

Beginning with the era of the prophet Mohammad in the early 7th century CE and lasting until the waning of the Umayyad caliphate in the mid-8th century CE, this period saw Islamic armies rapidly invade territories in the middle east, North Africa, Asia, and Europe. At its peak, this established the largest pre-modern empire the world had seen. Previously a collection of warring tribes, the Arab peoples were united under a new religion, Islam, which gave them a shared faith and a collective identity. The conquering Arab forces relied heavily on agile light cavalry and archers.

▶ **Christian prisoners of war** with Moorish footsoldiers during the Umayyad conquest of Spain in the early 8th century.

Lechfeld

955 CE ▪ BAVARIA ▪ EAST FRANKS VS. MAGYARS

MAGYAR INVASIONS

In June 955 CE, Holy Roman Emperor Otto I, on campaign against Slavic tribes near Magdeburg, received the alarming news that a large Magyar force was bearing down upon the Bavarian city of Augsburg. Otto mustered a force of 8,000 Germans and Bohemians and rushed to Bavaria. He avoided the open Hungarian plain, where the Magyar horse-archers could decimate his army, instead taking the more protected route through the Rauherhorst forest. On hearing of Otto's approach, the Magyar commanders Lel and Bulcsú broke off their siege of Augsburg and rushed to meet him.

Part of the 25,000-strong Magyar force ambushed the German rear-guard as it entered the forest. It then set to looting Otto's baggage train, which allowed the emperor to send a detachment of Franconians back through the forest to scatter the disordered attackers. The main Magyar army lay in wait in a crescent formation to the east of the forest; they expected an infantry assault directed at their centre, which their cavalry wings could then enfold and crush. However, Otto launched cavalry attacks at the same time as the infantry moved on the Magyar centre. The Magyar right broke, their infantry were overwhelmed, and only the left wing escaped intact, to be ambushed several days later as it tried to cross the swollen Isar river. The Magyars, their main force decimated, found themselves confined to Hungary, and would never pose a serious threat to the German Empire again.

Bishop Ulrich rides next to Otto I

> ... the victory over this savage people was not without some cost in blood.

WIDUKIND OF CORVEY, *DEEDS OF THE SAXONS*, c.973 CE

◀ **ULRICH'S CROSS** This late 15th-century cross shows Bishop Ulrich of Augsburg riding alongside Emperor Otto I at the battle of Lechfeld. The bishop played a crucial role in strengthening the defences of Augsburg, which gave Otto time to come to the city's relief. Ulrich was canonized in 993 CE. He is venerated as having particular power over floods, a reference to the swollen waters that destroyed the Magyar army as it retreated.

Magyars flee the battlefield

In context

▶ **A BLOODY VICTORY**
This 15th-century illuminated manuscript shows the fierceness of the fighting at Lechfeld. The Magyars normally relied on the mobility of their cavalry, but Otto's tactics and the unusually large number of infantry commanded by Lel and Bulcsú denied them this advantage, with catastrophic consequences. The fleeing Magyar leaders were captured during the subsequent fighting at Isar and were hanged in Augsburg.

◀ **FRANKISH KNIGHTS**
Traditionally, the strength of the Frankish army lay in its infantry, particularly its axe-wielding footmen. However, the threat of horse-borne enemies such as the Lombards, Avars, Arabs, and Magyars forced the Franks to adapt. By the time of the battle of Lechfeld, the Frankish cavalry was second to none, and so brought ruin upon the Magyars. Highly disciplined, they wore little more than padded cloth for armour, which gave them freedom of movement in the melee following a charge.

Directory: Before 1000 CE

▼ KADESH
SECOND SYRIAN CAMPAIGN OF RAMESSES II

1274 BCE ▪ MODERN-DAY SYRIA ▪ EGYPT VS. HITTITE EMPIRE

In 1274 BCE, the Egyptian pharaoh Ramesses II advanced his army into Syria, intending to stem the growing influence of Hittites and to seize the strategic town of Kadesh from them. Deceived by false information from Hittite deserters, the Egyptians made a premature advance with only part of their forces, and unexpectedly encountered the 40,000-strong Hittite army led by King Muwatallis II. The Hittite chariots, heavier than those of the Egyptians, scattered their outnumbered opponents. The Hittites plundered the Egyptian camp, while the latter regrouped. The remaining Egyptian army then arrived and launched a counterattack that drove the Hittites from the field. Both sides claimed victory, but the battle was a stalemate. Neither Egyptians or Hittites secured dominance over Syria, a situation recognized 15 years later by a treaty made at Kadesh – the earliest peace treaty whose text survives.

CHAERONEA
MACEDONIAN CONQUEST OF GREECE

338 BCE ▪ CENTRAL GREECE ▪ COALITION OF GREEK CITY-STATES VS. MACEDONIA

By 338 BCE, the growing ambitions of Philip II of Macedon to make his kingdom the dominant power in Greece had forced the rival city-states of Athens and Thebes to form an alliance against him. At Chaeronea, north of Thebes, the Macedonian army of around 30,000 infantry and 2,000 cavalry met an allied force only slightly superior in number. The Macedonians lured the Athenians forward, forcing a gap between them and the Thebans. Philip's son, Alexander, then led a cavalry charge through the gap and attacked the rear of the Theban forces. Meanwhile the Macedonians counterattacked the Athenians, using the longer Macedonian spear (*sarissa*) to overwhelm their enemies. Although the Theban Sacred Band of 300 men fought to the death, the rest of their army fled. Macedonian victory was complete and Philip II soon put an end to the independence of the Greek city-states.

► ZAMA
SECOND PUNIC WAR

202 BCE ▪ MODERN-DAY TUNISIA ▪ ROMANS VS. CARTHAGINIANS

The second of three wars fought between Rome and Carthage (the Punic Wars) ended with the battle of Zama in 202 BCE. A substantial Roman force had landed in North Africa in 203 BCE, forcing Hannibal to return from his campaign in Italy. With only 12,000 veteran troops remaining, he had to recruit thousands of untrained soldiers, who marched towards Zama, 130 km (80 miles) southwest of Carthage, to intercept the Romans and their Numidian allies. Both sides had 40,000 men, and although Roman cavalry was superior the Carthaginians had 80 war elephants. Under Hannibal's orders the elephants charged the enemy line, but the Roman soldiers simply moved aside to let them through. The Numidian cavalry then drove the Carthaginian cavalry off the field, while the Roman infantry steadily pushed back enemy soldiers. With 20,000 soldiers dead, the Carthaginians were forced to surrender, bringing the Second Punic War to an end.

PHARSALUS
CAESAR'S CIVIL WAR

48 BCE ▪ CENTRAL GREECE ▪ FORCES OF POMPEY VS. FORCES OF JULIUS CAESAR

Having failed to defeat his former ally Pompey at Dyrrachium, Julius Caesar retreated with his army into Greece, pursued by Pompey's army as far as Pharsalus. Pompey's army had superior numbers yet Pompey feared his inexperienced infantry would struggle against Caesar's veterans. He shielded his infantry by a river, and sent his cavalry against what he thought was Caesar's inadequate cavalry vanguard. In fact Caesar had placed his best legion there, reinforced by light infantry who sent a hail of missiles against their attackers. Pompey's cavalry fled, and when Caesar sent in additional forces the Pompeian army collapsed: 15,000 were killed and 24,000 taken prisoner. Pompey escaped to Egypt, but was

murdered on the command of Pharaoh Ptolemy XIII. By 45 BCE, Caesar was master of the Roman world.

TEUTOBURG FOREST
ROMAN-GERMANIC WARS

9 CE ▪ MODERN-DAY GERMANY ▪ ROMAN EMPIRE VS. GERMANIC TRIBES

By 9 BCE, the Romans occupied large areas of Germany east of the Rhine. When a revolt broke out in the Balkans, the governor, Publius Quinctilius Varus, was left with only three legions to garrison these regions. Arminius, a Cherusci chieftain, convinced Varus that an uprising was being plotted and led him, along with 20,000 Roman troops, into the German forest. In reality Arminius was the revolt's ringleader and his German tribesman harried the legionary column, killing stragglers. The Romans, powerless to pursue them in the dense undergrowth, then discovered their route had been blocked by the Germans. The trapped Romans were overwhelmed by a mass of tribesman. Varus committed suicide, and most of his men were slaughtered. Although there were subsequent expeditions to Germany, the Roman frontier became fixed back at the Rhine.

AL-QADISIYYAH
MUSLIM CONQUEST OF PERSIA

636 CE ▪ MODERN-DAY IRAQ ▪ SASSANID PERSIAN EMPIRE VS. RASHIDUN CALIPHATE

The Sassanid Persian Empire (224–651 CE), once a leading world power, had been weakened by a long conflict with the Byzantine Empire and by a subsequent civil war. When Muslim Arab armies invaded from Arabia in 633 CE, they easily overran much of Persian-ruled Iraq. Then in 634 CE, the new Persian shah Yazdegerd III brokered an alliance with the Byzantine emperor to counter-attack the Arabs. However, the Byzantine army was defeated at Yarmouk (see p.43), and the Persians were left to face the Arab force alone at al-Qadisiyyah. The Persians had 60,000

Pharaoh Ramesses II of Egypt defeats the Hittite Empire at the battle of Kadesh in this reproduction of a relief of the Ramesseum temple.

This **16th-century painting** shows the Roman army defeating Hannibal at the Battle of Zama.

troops, double the Muslims' numbers, as well as war elephants, but the Muslim Arab army held out for three days of bitter fighting. On the fourth day the Persian general was killed, after which their army collapsed. The Muslim armies advanced further into Persian territory, and by 651 CE they had completed the conquest of the Persian Empire.

YARMOUK
MUSLIM CONQUEST OF SYRIA/ ARAB-BYZANTINE WARS

636 CE ■ MIDDLE EAST ■ BYZANTINE EMPIRE VS. RASHIDUN CALIPHATE

In 634–35 CE, Muslim Arab armies sent by Caliph Umar invaded Byzantine territory, conquering Damascus and threatening southern Palestine, as well as Aleppo and Antioch. The Byzantine emperor Heraclius allied with the Persian shah Yazdegerd III, but their efforts to co-ordinate an attack against the Arabs failed, and the Byzantines launched an offensive in May 636 CE without their Persian allies. The Muslim forces had been divided into four armies and when they united, the Byzantines were forced into battle at Yarmouk, on Syria's bleak Hauran lava plain. The Byzantine army was weakened by six days of fighting, and on the final day a Muslim cavalry charge broke the

Byzantines, forcing them towards the bridge over a gorge blocked by Muslim forces, where many were slaughtered. With the main Byzantine field army destroyed, Syria and Palestine fell rapidly to the Muslim Arab army, which captured Jerusalem in April 637 CE.

BAEKGANG
BAEKJE-TANG WAR

663 CE ■ MODERN-DAY SOUTH KOREA ■ YAMATO JAPAN AND BAEKJE VS. CHINA AND SILLA

In the early 660s CE, the Korean state of Silla allied with the Chinese Tang dynasty to attack the rival Korean kingdoms of Baekje and Goguryeo. The Tang-Silla alliance invaded Baekje in the southwest of the peninsula and captured the capital. The Baekje resistance appealed for help from the Japanese Yamato dynasty. In 661 CE a large Japanese fleet arrived at Baekgang on the Geum river to bolster the Baekje resistance forces, but the narrowness of the river allowed the Tang-Silla fleet to defend against the attacks of the Japanese. Finally the Tang-Silla were able to counterattack, enveloping the Japanese flanks and trapping their ships, which could not manoeuvre to escape. Around 400 Japanese ships were lost and the remaining Baekje strongholds

soon fell. Silla then launched an attack on Goguryeo, capturing its capital in 668 CE and unifying the Korean peninsula under Silla rule.

TALAS
MUSLIM CONQUEST OF TRANSOXIANA

751 CE ■ NORTHWESTERN KYRGYZSTAN ■ ARAB ABBASID CALIPHATE AND TIBETAN EMPIRE VS. CHINA

By the 650s CE, the Tang Chinese had recaptured many regions of Central Asia which had been lost when the Han dynasty collapsed in 221 CE. Although garrisoning them strained Tang resources, the Chinese continued to push westwards through Ferghana. In 751 CE, the Chinese army and their Karluk allies encountered an Arab force sent by the newly installed Abbasid caliphate to enforce loyalty on the border regions of the Islamic world. The two sides clashed at the Talas river, north of Tashkent, but when the Karluk defected to the Abbasids, the Tang were left outnumbered and isolated, and barely a few thousand troops escaped. The defeat severely dented Chinese ambitions to expand their Central Asian territories and a revolt in China in 755 CE led to the withdrawal of remaining Chinese garrisons. The Abbasid

caliphate expanded into Fergana and neighbouring regions, bringing large areas into the Islamic sphere.

EDINGTON
VIKING INVASIONS OF ENGLAND

878 CE ■ SOUTHERN ENGLAND ■ DANISH VIKINGS VS. WESSEX

In the spring of 878 CE, Alfred the Great's kingdom of Wessex stood alone against a large army of invading Danish Vikings, which had arrived in England in 865 CE and conquered every other Anglo-Saxon kingdom. Following a surprise Viking attack in January, Alfred spent months in hiding in Somerset's Athelney marshes, before summoning a local army (the *fyrd*) to fight for their land. Thousands came, and at Ethandun in Wiltshire, the Anglo-Saxons formed up in a shield wall bristling with spears. They fought the Vikings in a full-day battle until the latter fled back to Chippenham. Two weeks later, the Viking army surrendered. Their leader, Guthrum, converted to Christianity and made a treaty with Alfred dividing England into two zones: the south and west ruled by Wessex, and the north and east (the Danelaw) under Viking control.

BACH DANG
SECOND SOUTHERN HAN-ANNAM WAR

938 CE ■ EASTERN VIETNAM ■ VIETNAM VS. CHINA

In the 930s CE, Vietnam began to assert its independence after more than 1,000 years of Chinese domination. Liu Yan, the Southern Han emperor, sent a fleet to sail up the Bach Dang River and land an army in the heart of rebel-held territory. Led by general Ngo Quyen, the outnumbered Vietnamese planted sharpened wooden stakes in the riverbed that reached below the water level at high tide. When the tide began to ebb the Vietnamese sent boats into the river, provoking an attack by the Chinese fleet. As the water level dropped many Chinese ships became stuck on the stakes or sank, and the Vietnamese killed more than half of the Chinese force. Liu Yan withdrew his remaining forces from northern Vietnam, enabling Ngo Quyen to crush the opposition and declare himself ruler of an independent Vietnamese kingdom.

1000—1500

CHAPTER 2

When the English learned that their king had
met his death, they… sought refuge in flight

WILLIAM OF JUMIÈGES, *GESTA NORMANORUM DUCUM [DEEDS OF THE NORMAN DUKES]*, c.1070

▼ SAXON INFANTRY, NORMAN CAVALRY Norman cavalrymen charge at the Anglo-Saxon shield wall in a scene from the Bayeux Tapestry, a 70-m (230-ft)-long embroidery created in the 1070s to commemorate the battle of Hastings. The Normans' use of cavalry and the deployment of large numbers of archers played key roles in William's victory.

Hastings

1066 ▪ SOUTHERN ENGLAND ▪ NORMANS VS. ANGLO-SAXONS

NORMAN CONQUEST OF ENGLAND

When King Edward the Confessor died on 5 January 1066, the nobility of Anglo-Saxon England chose Harold Godwinson as his successor. Harold's ascent to the throne was strongly disputed, however, and his rivals launched invasions to pursue their claims. In September, an army led by King Harald Hardrada of Norway landed near York, accompanied by Harold's estranged brother Tostig, and routed the northern Anglo-Saxon earls. After initial victories, Hardrada was defeated and killed at Stamford Bridge by Harold, who had advanced rapidly north to meet him. By then, Harold had also received news that Duke William of Normandy had landed in Sussex. Harold force-marched his weary troops south to face the new invaders, arriving at London less than a week later. On the evening of 13 October, he occupied a hill near Hastings, close to the Norman camp.

The battle began the following morning. Arrayed with their shields interlocking to form a wall, the 7,000 Anglo-Saxons presented a formidable obstacle to the 8,000 Normans. Successive Norman charges failed, but William astutely lured sections of Harold's army downhill, where they were cut to pieces. Harold was killed at the height of the battle, and by dusk the English army was in flight. William's army approached London and, after further clashes with English forces, he received the submission of the chief Anglo-Saxon nobles on 10 December. A fortnight later, he was crowned king. The reign of the Anglo-Saxon kings of England was at an end.

CLAIMANTS TO THE **ENGLISH THRONE**

William claimed to have been promised the English throne both by Edward the Confessor and by Harold Godwinson himself, who had visited William in Normandy in 1065 (Edward had also cultivated Norman influence in England during his time as king, based on his family ties there).

Harald Hardrada based his claim on a pact made between King Harthacnut of Denmark (also known as Canute III) and Magnus, Harald's predecessor as Norwegian king: they had agreed that each would inherit the other's kingdom in the event of either of their deaths. Since Harthacnut had already ruled England in 1040–42, Harald maintained that the English crown should naturally come to him.

▶ Edward the Confessor sends Harold Godwinson to visit Duke William in Normandy, depicted in the Bayeux Tapestry.

In detail

The battle began around 9am, with William's force arrayed at the foot of the hill and Harold's army occupying a 1,000-m (½-mile)-long ridge, their shields locked together and their spears protruding to form an almost impenetrable barrier. After the Normas released an initial volley of arrows, their infantry tried to charge up the hill, but were impeded by the marshy ground and the rain of spears that came from the Anglo-Saxon shield wall. Under this attack the Bretons on William's left flank broke and retreated down the hill, to be followed by a pursuing party of Anglo-Saxons. Despite being unhorsed, William rallied the Normans and ordered a series of feigned retreats to try to entice more of Harold's men to leave the safety of the ridge, thus making themselves vulnerable to his cavalry. The tactic was of limited success, but William's archers eventually secured his victory when one of their arrows is thought to have struck Harold in the face.

The English king suffered a mortal wound, and, with Harold's brothers also dead, the leaderless Anglo-Saxon army wavered, broke, and fled. Hundreds were cut down by the Norman cavalry as they tried to escape, and by nightfall all organized Anglo-Saxon resistance ended. Some 6,000 men in total had been killed or injured.

▶ **ARRIVAL IN ENGLAND** Here the Norman fleet is shown arriving at Pevensey on the south coast. The crossing was fraught with danger, and William was delayed by bad weather for several weeks – indeed, this almost prevented the invasion from taking place. Once he reached England, he could expect no reinforcements, so he crammed his ships with horses, equipment, and men.

▲ **SIGNS AND OMENS** Here, the Bayeaux Tapestry depicts Harold being crowned king of England on 6 January 1066, the day after Edward the Confessor's death. Nervousness at possible foreign intervention, or mischief-making by Harold's exiled brother Tostig, was compounded by signs such as the appearance of Halley's comet in late April, which was considered a portent of doom.

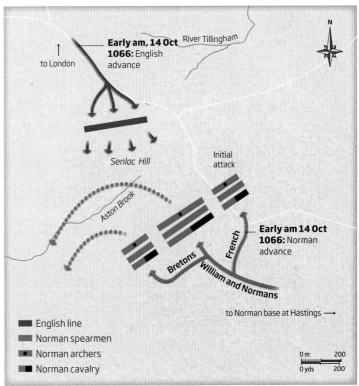

MAP OF THE BATTLE William placed the Bretons, Angevins, and Poitevins on his left flank, led by his son-in-law, Alan Fergant. He himself commanded the centre, with units from Picardy and Flanders to his right (William's forces shown in blue). The English forces consisted mainly of the *fyrd* – untrained levies raised for temporary military service – and the *huscarls*, the permanent household retainers of the Anglo-Saxon aristocracy.

THE DEATH OF HAROLD This figure with an arrow protruding from his eye (above left) is traditionally believed to be King Harold. This has been disputed, but several early chroniclers also describe the story of the fatal arrow-shot. Whatever the cause of Harold's death, the loss of royal leadership at the height of the battle proved devastating to the morale of the Anglo-Saxon army.

ARMOUR AND WEAPONS IN ACTION The Bayeux Tapestry portrays both the Anglo-Saxons and the Normans wearing three-quarter-length coats of mail armour. The mounted Normans carried thrusting javelins, while the Anglo-Saxons used kite-shaped shields and large, Danish-style axes that would have been cumbersome in the confined space of the shield wall.

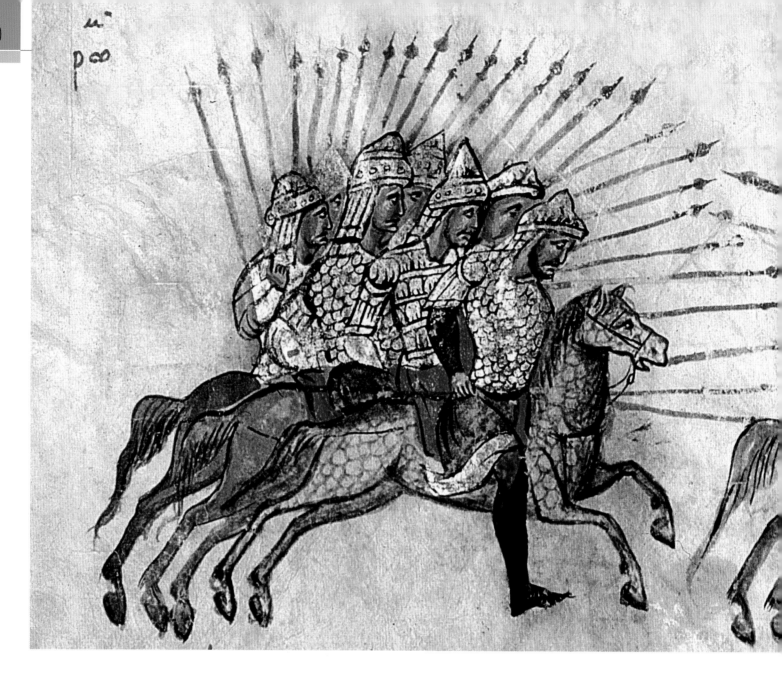

Manzikert

1071 ▪ MODERN-DAY TURKEY ▪ BYZANTINE EMPIRE VS. SELJUQ EMPIRE

BYZANTINE-SELJUQ WARS

By the 1060s, the Byzantine Empire had been ruled by a series of weak emperors and was plagued by incursions of Seljuq Turks moving west into Armenia and Anatolia. Byzantine emperor Romanos Diogenes, who ruled from 1068, sought to reclaim the initiative. He won initial victories against Seljuq Sultan Alp Arslan (see box, right), but was forced to make peace in 1069. In February 1071, Romanos sent an envoy to renew the treaty, but it was a ruse; intending to attack, he travelled east with a force of 20,000 men, half of them professional Byzantine soldiers, the remainder mercenaries or levies. After a gruelling march across Anatolia, Romanos sent part of his army to capture the fortress of Khilat, and pushed on to Manzikert with the rest. Alp Arslan's scouts had been tracking the Byzantines, and the Seljuq army lay in ambush there.

Romanos rejected Alp Arslan's peace proposals and attacked. However, the crescent-shaped Turkish line pulled back, and every time Romanos's men closed in, the agile Turkish cavalry

◀ AGE-OLD CONFLICT
This illustration from an 11th-century manuscript depicts a mid-9th-century battle between Byzantines and an invading Arab army. The Byzantines had had to defend Anatolia from Muslim incursions since the loss of Syria in the 7th century, but it was the defeat at Manzikert that signalled the loss of what had once been a Byzantine heartland.

SULTAN **ALP ARSLAN** (c.1030-73)

Alp Arslan inherited the Seljuq sultanate in 1064 after a civil war against his brother, Suleiman. He attacked Armenia, aided by nomadic Ogüz Turks, and captured the capital, Ani. This brought him into conflict with the Byzantines, who feared further Seljuk conquests in Anatolia. After Manzikert, he secured a tribute payment from Romanos and the return of Manzikert, Edessa, and Hierapolis. He then turned to the eastern Seljuq frontier, but was killed there in 1073. His son, Malik Shah I, continued making advances into Anatolia.

➤ **Alp Arslan's** fierce reputation is reflected in his name, which means "Heroic Lion". Here he is shown humiliating the defeated Romanos.

wheeled out of range. The Seljuq archers also inflicted heavy losses on the Byzantines. Finally, in the afternoon Romanos called for a retreat. His rearguard, led by a member of a rival family, deliberately pulled back too soon, and Romanos was surrounded and captured. After a week as the sultan's captive he was released, but his authority was broken. A civil war broke out in Constantinople, and Romanos was killed. As Byzantine authority fragmented, over the next decade the Seljuqs were able to conquer most of Anatolia – much of which the Byzantines were never able to recover.

Siege of Jerusalem

1099 ▪ JERUSALEM ▪ CRUSADERS VS. FATIMID CALIPHATE

FIRST CRUSADE

In 1095, Pope Urban II called for an expedition to free the Holy City of Jerusalem from Muslim occupation. A Crusader army set out, but experienced enormous difficulties in reaching its objective. The force struggled across Asia Minor, harried by Seljuq Turks, and was stretched to breaking point after laying siege to Antioch for eight months. The 12,000 crusaders who arrived on 7 June 1099 were ill-equipped to breach Jerusalem's 15-m (50-ft) walls and were running out of water. They also feared that a Fatimid army from Egypt was on its way to reinforce the garrison commander, Ifthikhar ad-Daula. A rapid assault on 13 June failed, and the crusaders settled down to lay siege: Raymond of Toulouse's Provençal troops took their position to the south by the Zion Gate, and Godfrey of Bouillon's northern French contingent faced the city's north ramparts. Six ships from Genoa arrived at the port of Jaffa, and the crusaders used their timbers to build two huge siege towers; on the night of 13 July, the crusaders wheeled these slowly into place.

At the Zion Gate, heavy fire from the defenders stopped the southern siege tower from approaching the walls, but after two days the northern siege tower reached the Damascus Gate, and scores of crusaders poured out on to the ramparts. After a brief resistance, the defenders abandoned the walls to make a last stand on the Temple Mount. Amid scenes of appalling brutality, the crusaders secured the rest of Jerusalem. The city was theirs, and remained the heart of the Crusader States in Palestine for 90 years.

In context

▲ **THE COUNCIL OF CLERMONT** In 1095, Byzantine emperor Alexius I Comnenus sent an appeal to Pope Urban II asking for help in pushing back against Muslim advances in the East. Urban's reply, at a church council at Clermont, was that Christian knights should take up arms to free Jerusalem from Muslim control. The thousands who "took the cross" in response formed the army of the First Crusade.

▶ **CITY BESIEGED** Jerusalem's defences were formidable, with 4 km (2 ½ miles) of at least 3-m (10-ft)-thick walls. The crusaders scarcely had enough men to besiege the city, and were forced to assault it. Once they breached the walls at the Damascus Gate, the final resistance took place on the Temple Mount and in the Citadel, from where Iftikhar negotiated safe passage to Ascalon.

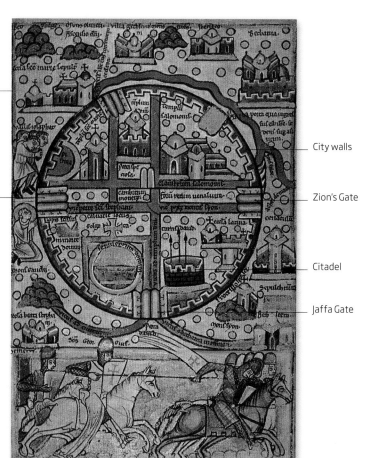

Damascus Gate

City walls

Zion's Gate

Citadel

Jaffa Gate

▲ **STORMING JERUSALEM** Here, the crusaders are shown emerging from a siege tower onto the walls and scaling ladders to make a bridgehead on the northern ramparts of Jerusalem. Once they had captured this section of the walls, thousands more crusaders poured into the city. Large numbers of defenders and civilians were massacred, and accounts speak of crusaders wading up to their ankles in blood as they seized their much sought-after prize.

Dan-no-ura

1185 ▪ SOUTHWESTERN JAPAN ▪ MINAMOTO CLAN VS. TAIRA CLAN

GENPEI WAR

In 1180, Japan was plunged into civil war. The dominant Taira clan faced an uprising by its rivals, the Minamoto, after prime minister Taira Kiyomori had installed his infant grandson Antoku on the imperial throne. After initial setbacks in this conflict – called the Genpei War – the rebels acquired a new leader, Minamoto no Yoritomo, who secured eastern Japan, and whose armies then captured the imperial capital, Kyoto, in 1183. The Taira clan fled, taking the young emperor with them, but Yoritomo's half-brother Yoshitsune forced them from their refuge on Yoshima island and pursued them with a large fleet.

At Dan-no-ura, on the straits between Honshu and Kyushu islands in southwestern Japan, the Taira fleet turned and fought. They tried to take advantage of the strong tides in the straits, which flowed eastwards in the morning and kept their enemy from approaching. Their attempts at encircling the

▲ **THE FIRST SHŌGUN** Dan-no-ura was a turning point for Minamoto no Yoritomo. After becoming leader of the anti-Taira rebellion in 1180, he survived a disastrous defeat at Ishibashiyama only to consolidate his forces and capture much of eastern Japan. After Dan-no-ura, Yoritomo exiled his half-brother, Yoshitsune, by now his most dangerous rival, and in 1192 became shōgun, beginning a line of military rulers that lasted until 1335.

▲ **CLASH OF CLANS** In this 19th-century depiction, the Taira and Minamoto fleets are shown clashing at Dan-no-ura. Despite their traditional naval superiority, the Taira were outnumbered by 840 ships to 500. This was thanks to Yoshitsune no Minamoto, who had managed to recruit hundreds of ships from towns bordering Japan's Inland Sea.

▲ **THE DEATH OF TAIRA TOMOMORI** Son of Kiyomori, Taira Tomomori won the first major battle of the Genpei War, at Uji, in 1180. His error of judgement in trying to use the tides at Dan-no-ura to outflank the Minamoto fleet led to disaster, and he was one of many Taira leaders to commit suicide by jumping into the waters. Severely wounded, he ensured his death by tying himself to a heavy anchor, shown here.

Minamoto failed when the manoeuvre took too long and the tides turned, allowing the Minamoto's ships to surround them, helped by the defection of a section of the Taira fleet. Many Taira ships were seized or sunk, and in the panic the Taira drowned the infant emperor to avoid the shame of him being captured. Taira Tomomori himself committed suicide (see right), and with the Taira leadership weakened, Yoritomo assumed the title of shōgun (the de facto ruler of the country) and established a military government at Kamakura that went on to rule Japan for a century and a half.

Hattin

1187 ▪ MODERN-DAY ISRAEL ▪
KINGDOM OF JERUSALEM VS. AYYUBIDS

AYYUBID-CRUSADER WAR

In the summer of 1187, the truce between the Crusader States of Palestine and Saladin, the ruler of Egypt, was shattered when French nobleman Raynald of Châtillon attacked a Muslim trading caravan. An incensed Saladin gathered an army of 30,000, and attacked the castle of Tiberias on the western shore of the Sea of Galilee on 30 June, aiming to lure the crusaders to come to its rescue. King Guy de Lusignan of Jerusalem had raised 20,000 men, including 1,200 knights. As Saladin hoped, Guy marched out on 3 July to break the siege.

The crusaders reached the nearby springs of Turan at noon, but from there they had to cross an arid, waterless plain. Guy pressed on, but Saladin's force cut him off from Turan, preventing any further advance. In the morning, Guy had little choice but to order a breakthrough towards the nearby twin hills of the Horns of Hattin and the springs. Several charges failed, although Raymond broke through and escaped, and the infantry fled towards the Horns, where they were massacred. Decimated by archery, the knights fought on, with Guy ordering a desperate charge at Saladin's bodyguards. In the end, tired and surrounded, the crusaders were overwhelmed and captured. With few knights left to defend it, Jerusalem fell to Saladin in early October.

The reaction in Europe was one of shock and outrage, and led directly to the Third Crusade, in which Saladin faced a new foe – King Richard I ("the Lionheart") of England. After a stinging defeat at Arsuf in 1191, and a retreat at Jaffa in 1192, Saladin conceded a number of coastal towns to the crusaders.

▶ **SALADIN VICTORIOUS** This illustration from a mid-13th century manuscript shows Saladin addressing the captive King Guy of Jerusalem. He and other noble prisoners were spared for ransom, although the truce-breaking Raynald of Châtillon was executed on Saladin's orders. Around 200 Templar and Hospitaller knights, whom Saladin viewed as dangerous adversaries, were also put to death.

In context

▲ **THE LOSS OF THE TRUE CROSS** The Crusaders' standard at the battle of Hattin was a relic of the True Cross on which Jesus Christ was said to have been crucified. It was borne by the Bishop of Acre, but was taken by the enemy: this 13th-century illumination depicts Saladin at Hattin taking the cross from the Christians.

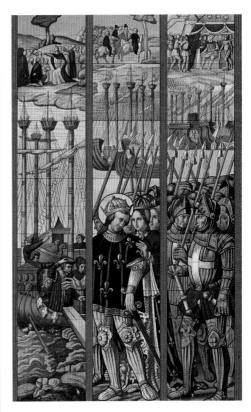

▲ **FAILURE IN THE EAST** The Crusades were a two-century-long attempt by Christian Europe to wrest Jerusalem and the Holy Lands from Islamic rule. There were nine major crusades in all, beginning in 1095, but despite briefs gains they ended in failure in 1291. The beginning of the end came in 1270, when King Louis IX of France (embarking on the Eighth Crusade, above), and much of his army, died of dysentery on arriving on the shores of Tunisia.

▲ **CHARGING TOWARDS VICTORY** Alfonso VIII is shown throwing himself
into the fray in this fresco of Las Navas de Tolosa from around the 13th century.
Although the Castilian vanguard had swept away a screen of Almohad skirmishers,
Alfonso's forces were in danger of losing the battle before Alfonso personally led
the charge, which reached Muhammad's tent and nearly captured the caliph himself.

Las Navas de Tolosa

1212 ▪ SOUTHERN SPAIN ▪ CHRISTIAN FORCES VS. ALMOHAD EMPIRE

SPANISH RECONQUISTA

By the late 12th century, the Reconquista – the reconquest of the Iberian Peninsula by the Christian kingdoms of Spain (see box, below) – had been underway for centuries. However, it met resistance with the rise of the Almohads, an Islamic movement that ruled the south from 1147. They roundly defeated Alfonso VIII of Castile at Alarcos in 1195, leading to an uneasy peace, but in 1211 raiding by the Castilians provoked the Almohad caliph Muhammad al-Nasir to seize the castle of Salvatierra, headquarters of the powerful military Order of Calatrava. The loss of this strategic position galvanized Christian opinion and inspired Pope Innocent III to summon a crusade.

The kingdoms of Aragon, Navarre, and Portugal, previously antagonistic to Alfonso, set aside their differences, and on 21 June a 13,000-strong Christian army set off south from Toledo, only to find itself blocked in mountainous terrain by a detachment of Muhammad's force. On 16 July a local shepherd guided Alfonso's troops over a hidden pass to catch the Almohads by surprise. After two days of failed negotiations, the main body of Christian forces gave battle, but were held off by the Almohad rearguard protecting the caliph's tent. In a last desperate gamble, Alfonso charged with his own rearguard; Muhammad's local Andalusian levies fled, followed by the rest of the Almohad army, which suffered heavy casualties. Muhammad died soon after the battle. The Almohad caliphate was fatally weakened both by the succession of his young son, Yusuf, and by a civil war that broke out in 1224. This gave renewed impetus to the Reconquista.

THE **RECONQUISTA**

After the Muslim conquest of Visigothic Spain in 711 CE, a few Christian strongholds in northern Spain held out. From these, new Christian kingdoms emerged in the 9th and 10th centuries to begin the Reconquista – the reconquest of the Iberian peninsula. The movement gained momentum until the capture of Toledo in 1085, and then paused until, in the aftermath of Las Navas de Tolosa, most of the cities of Muslim Spain fell: Cordoba in 1236, Valencia in 1238 and Seville in 1248. Only the emirate of Granada was left and, after the union the Crowns of Castile and Aragon gave new strength to the Christian Spanish, it, too was captured in 1492.

▲ **This altar relief** shows Abu abd-Allah Muhammad XII (Boabdil), the last Muslim ruler of al-Andalus, leaving his castle at Granada for exile in Africa.

Liegnitz

1241 ■ MODERN-DAY POLAND ■ MONGOL EMPIRE VS. POLISH DUCHIES

MONGOL INVASIONS OF EUROPE

In 1236, Mongol armies invaded the lands of the Kipchak Turks and devastated Russia, burning its principal city, Kiev. The Mongol commander, Batu, then ordered an attack on Hungary, angered by King Bela IV's sheltering of Kipchak refugees. A secondary detachment of 20,000 Mongols under leaders Kadan and Baidar embarked on a diversionary campaign against Poland. After the Mongols sacked Cracow, Duke Henry of Silesia marched to face them at Liegnitz (now Legnica), near Wroclaw, without waiting for a second army of reinforcements, led by Duke Wenceslas of Bohemia, to join him.

Henry's peasant levies, bolstered by small detachments of cavalry, mustered only half of the Mongols' numbers. The Mongols drove back his first assault, and so Henry sent his horsemen to attack. Feigning retreat, the Mongols then cut off the Polish horsemen by setting fires to their rear. Unable to see, the knights fell into disarray, and the Mongol archers devastated them with volleys of arrows. Then the Mongol cavalry charged into the European infantry, causing heavy casualties, with Duke Henry among the dead. Combined with

the defeat of Bela IV's army at Mohi two days earlier, this loss left Western Europe vulnerable to the Mongol hordes. Weeks later, however, Batu's attention drawn by the death of the Great Khan Ögodei, the Mongols withdrew eastward, and they never returned to attack Eastern Europe with such force.

THE **MONGOLS**

Previously an obscure and divided nomadic people on the east Asian steppe, the Mongols were united by Genghis Khan, who was elected their Great Khan in 1206.

Superior horsemen and archers with an unusually high level of military organization, the Mongols subjugated neighbouring states over the next 50 years, including Khwarizmia, Persia, China, and the Abbasid caliphate. The attack on Europe was only halted by the death of the Great Khan Ögodei (son of Ghengis Khan) and feuding among the Mongol nobility. Such feuds ultimately broke the Empire into separate khanates based in China, Mongolia, Russia, and Persia.

▲ **Genghis Khan**, born Temüjin, became Khan ("Universal ruler") after uniting the Mongol tribes.

In context

▲ **MOUNTED WARRIORS** This 13th-century Japanese painting, attributed to Tosa Nagata, portrays the Mongol horsemen as they may have looked at Liegnitz. Mongol military might depended entirely on its cavalry. The majority of Mongol troopers were light cavalry horse archers (as above); the rest were heavily armoured lancers.

◀ **TERROR TACTICS** After the battle at Liegnitz, the Mongols paraded Duke Henry's head on a spike around town, as depicted in this illustration from a 15th-century manuscript. It was a typical Mongol gesture, aimed at terrorizing the population, and it put an end to any further resistance.

Hic pugnat dux henricus filius sce hedwigis cum thartaris in campo qd dicitur wolstat

Hic decollat iste dux henricus fili sce hedwigis a thartaris cui anima suscepta est in celum ab angelis

◄ **MONGOL VICTORY** This 14th-century illustration shows the Mongol invaders (left) and Duke Henry's army (right) battling at Liegnitz. The European cavalry were drawn in by a feigned retreat, a typical Mongol tactic, and then cut off from the infantry, allowing Batu's archers and heavy cavalry to massacre the divided enemy.

▲ **ALEXANDER ON THE ICE** Prince Alexander is shown charging the Teutonic Knights in this illustration from a 16th-century manuscript. A minor member of the Russian ruling house of Kiev, Alexander had been summoned by the people of Novgorod to defend them from invaders including Sweden and the Teutonic Knights. He was nicknamed "Nevsky" for his victory over Sweden at Lake Neva, two years before Lake Peipus.

Lake Peipus

1242 ∎ RUSSIA-ESTONIA BORDER ∎ NOVGOROD REPUBLIC VS. TEUTONIC KNIGHTS

NORTHERN CRUSADES

Pope Innocent III authorized a crusade against the pagan peoples of the Eastern Baltic in 1198, beginning a series of Northern Crusades aimed at converting Lithuania, Latvia, and Prussia to Christianity. Just as in the Holy Land, military orders played a key role in the crusades, and from 1236 the Teutonic Knights (see right) led the campaign. As well as conducting crusades against pagans, the Knights extended their attacks to include Russian principalities, which they regarded as heretical as the Russians were Eastern Orthodox.

In 1240, the Knights launched an attack on the city of Novgorod in western Russia, and seized the key port of Pskov to the west. Although Russian ruler Prince Alexander Nevsky recovered the town, in spring 1242 the Knights renewed their attack. Alexander lured the Knights' 2,500-strong army onto the frozen waters of Lake Peipus, where the ice made it hard for them to manoeuvre, on what is now the Russia-Estonia border. Alexander's infantry held the mounted Knights in check until they were exhausted, and he then committed his cavalry to finish them off. The Knights pulled back from the melée and fled further out onto the frozen lake, where the ice broke under the weight of their horses and armour, and many drowned.

As a result of Alexander's victory, the Knights ceased their attacks on Russia, and Lake Peipus and the River Narva to the north became the boundary between the two powers' territories – a border that still exists today. Instead, the Knights concentrated their efforts on converting the pagan Prussians and Lithuanians, and expanding west towards Poland.

In context

◄ **THE ORDER OF THE TEUTONIC KNIGHTS** This German military order was established at Acre, in Palestine, in 1198, with the aim of aiding Christians on pilgrimage. In 1237 they absorbed the Sword Brothers order in Livonia, and operated primarily in the Baltic and Prussia. After the defeat at Lake Peipus, they continued to carve out a territory in Prussia and the western Baltic, establishing their headquarters at Marienburg in eastern Poland in 1309. Shown here is Heinrich von Plauen, a leader of the order.

▼ **A LANDMARK IN RUSSIAN HISTORY** This Russian stamp depicts the ice breaking beneath the Teutonic Knights at the Battle of Lake Peipus. The stamp was released in 1992 as part of the 750th commemoration of the battle and Alexander's victory, which still holds a special place in Russian history.

… God gave him the wisdom of Solomon… this Prince Alexander: he used to defeat but was never defeated.

ALEXANDER NEVSKY AS DESCRIBED IN THE *SECOND PSKOV CHRONICLE*

Ain Jalut

1260 ▪ GALILEE ▪ MAMLUK SULTANATE VS. MONGOL EMPIRE

MONGOL INVASION OF SYRIA

In 1258, the Mongol chieftain Hülegü launched an attack on Persia and the Middle East, reaching as far as Baghdad in Iraq. The city fell after a short siege; amid scenes of appalling slaughter, the last Abbasid caliph, Mutasim, was wrapped in a carpet and trampled to death. The Mongols went on to capture Aleppo, and Damascus surrendered without a fight.

The Mongols sent envoys to Qutuz, the Mamluk sultan of Egypt, demanding his submission; he refused and executed the envoys. At the time, Hülegü was preoccupied by a succession crisis in Mongolia and retreated towards Azerbaijan with the bulk of his army, closer to the Mongol homeland. His lieutenant, Kitbuga, stayed behind in command of 20,000 horsemen. Qutuz took advantage of this weakened Mongol force to cross from Egypt into Palestine. On 3 September, at Ain Jalut in Galilee, Qutuz's army encountered the Mongol horde. His general, Baybars, used the Mongol's own tactics against them: concealing the greater part of his army, he retreated with a smaller force to draw Kitbuga forwards. The Mongols fell for the ruse, but, despite being showered with Mamluk arrows, they managed to buckle the Egyptians' left wing. The Mamluks held, and when Kitubga's Syrian allies defected, the course of the battle turned in their favour. The Mongol army fled, pursued by the Mamluks – a devastating blow to their reputation for being invincible. Although the Mongols returned to Syria in 1262, and advanced towards Egypt several more times in the next 50 years, Ain Jalut marked the limit of their expansion in the Middle East.

▶ **BAGHDAD UNDER SIEGE** This 14th-century Persian manuscript shows the Mongols besieging Baghdad prior to Ain Jalut. By 1258, the Mongols had acquired sophisticated equipment from China. Accounts of the siege record 1,000 Chinese catapult operators in the Mongol army, together with siege towers, crossbows, and devices for throwing combustible missiles.

In context

▲ **MONGOLS IN BATTLE** This illustration from a 14th-century chronicle shows Mongols and Turks fighting during the Mongol invasion of the Seljuk sultanate in Turkey in 1256, just before the attack on Baghdad. The discipline and agility of the Mongol warriors on horseback (right) played a key role in their victories, but the fighting style of the Seljuks (left) was similar and almost as effective, as demonstrated at Ain Jalut.

▶ **ARMOURED WARRIORS** This Mamluk armour from the 16th century shows the high-grade chain and plate that offered protection against the Mongols' light arrows. Mamluk bows outranged those of the Mongols, and could deliver heavy, armour-piercing arrows at close range.

Crécy

1346 ▪ NORTHERN FRANCE ▪ ENGLAND VS. FRANCE

HUNDRED YEARS' WAR

On 13 July 1346, Edward III of England landed at La Hogue in Normandy on the north coast of France, determined to pursue his claim to the French crown. He had previously invaded in 1337 and won a naval victory over the French at Sluys in 1340, but had failed to capitalize on these conquests due to a lack of money, and having diverted resources to put down uprisings on the Scottish border. This time, however, Edward brought a larger force of around 15,000 men.

Edward's army sacked the city of Caen on 26 July and seized a large quantity of treasure, before moving decisively southwards. Blocked by the French army under Philip VI within striking distance of Paris, the English king instead headed north, crossing the Seine and the Somme, all the while pursued by the French defenders. Then, on 26 August at Crécy, in Ponthieu (now the province of Picardy in northern France), Edward turned his forces towards his pursuer and fought. Deployed along a 500-m (1,640-ft)-long ridge, his soldiers fired volley after volley of arrows, disrupting a series of French mounted charges, which became more disorganised as casualties mounted. This continued until Philip VI was utterly defeated, and a large number of French noblemen lay dead upon the field. The following month, Edward lay siege to Calais: as a result of the decimation of his forces, Philip could not send reinforcements, and Edward took the city in August 1347. The English then occupied large stretches of land in northern France, which they would go on to hold for over a century.

KING **EDWARD III** (1312–77)

Edward III became king in 1327 after his mother Isabella, daughter of Philip IV of France, deposed her husband, Edward II. Roger Mortimer, Isabella's lover, initially took power, but Edward III overthrew him. Edward made the first of several invasions of Scotland in 1329, which distracted him from his claim to the French throne inherited via his mother. After Crécy, the territorial concessions he extracted from the captive Philip VI were too much for the French nobility, who rejected them. The latter half of Edward's reign was marked by decline. The Black Death in 1348 was followed by economic troubles, and after unsuccessful campaigning in France in the 1360s–70s, he lost most of his territorial gains there.

➤ **This later portrait** of Edward III dates from the early 17th century.

➤ **LONGBOWS BATTLE CROSSBOWS AT CRÉCY**
In this illustration from Jean Froissart's early-15th-century account of the battle, English longbowmen arrayed ahead of the main English line face off against Genoese crossbowmen. A Genoese soldier is shown struggling to reload his weapon while a French knight ploughs through the crossbowmen's disordered ranks.

In detail

After crossing the river at the Somme via a secluded ford, the English army marched to Crécy. There, on the morning of 26 August, Edward formed up his army on a forward position across a long ridge, accompanied by his 16-year-old son, Prince Edward of Wales. The French army arrived around midday; it was at least twice the size of the English force and included 5,000 Genoese crossbowmen. Against the advice of his nobles, Philip VI of France ordered an attack. The crossbowmen stood to the front of the French force, but their strings were wet with rain, reducing their rate of fire. As a result, they suffered heavy casualties from the English longbowmen's arrows.

Impatient, the French knights charged, and became entangled with the crossbowmen as they floundered up the muddy, corpse-strewn slope. Although some reached the English ranks, they were rapidly cut down. Throughout the day and into the night, the French made 15 increasingly desperate charges. trying and failing to break the English lines. Five English ribaulds (an early form of cannon) fired into the melee, scattering the cavalry. Finally, deep into the night, Philip fled. Behind him he left around 2,000 knights and men-at-arms dead on the field, and the French royal banner captured.

▼ **ORDER OF BATTLE** The English formed up in three divisions, or "battles", with Edward, Prince of Wales, in the van together with the Earl of Northampton, and Edward III commanding the reserve in the rear. A line of archers screened each battle. The French set the Genoese crossbowmen in front, with three battles of heavy cavalry behind them, the rearmost led by King Philip himself.

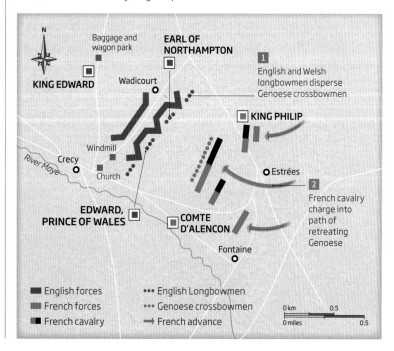

Baggage and wagon park

EARL OF NORTHAMPTON

KING EDWARD

Wadicourt

1 English and Welsh longbowmen disperse Genoese crossbowmen

KING PHILIP

Windmill

Crecy

River Maye

Church

Estrées

2 French cavalry charge into path of retreating Genoese

EDWARD, PRINCE OF WALES

COMTE D'ALENCON

Fontaine

■ English forces   ••• English Longbowmen
■ French forces   ••• Genoese crossbowmen
■ French cavalry   → French advance

0 km   0.5
0 miles   0.5

▲ **ENGLISH INVADERS AND FRENCH FORCES** This 16th-century French Illumination depicts the battle at Crécy, with Edward III's fleet in the background. Edward III's army consisted of 15,000 men and longbow archers, while Philip VI fielded an army of 12,000 mounted knights and Genoese crossbowmen.

Visor protects
exposed face

Rivetted leather band
fixes aventail to helmet

◀ **BASCINET AND AVENTAIL** This bascinet, a helmet with a pointed top, is typical of the head protection worn by French knights at Crécy. The visor, which first appeared around 1330, gave better protection and comfort for the wearer. The chain aventail protected the vulnerable neck area.

THE **HUNDRED YEARS' WAR** (1337-1453)

English kings had held land in France since William I took the English crown in 1066, and acquired more through Henry II's marriage to Eleanor of Aquitaine in 1152. When Charles IV of France died without a male heir in 1328, Edward III tried to claim the French throne, being the closest male relative. However, the French nobility awarded the throne to Charles's cousin, Philip of Valois. Edward was forced to pay homage to Philip in 1329 for his lands in Aquitaine. This affront, and Philip's declaration in 1337 that Aquitaine was forfeit, led to war.

▲ **This 19th-century illustration** depicts the recovery of Aquitaine by the French during the Hundred Years' War.

▲ **LONGBOWMEN IN FORMATION** Here, the French army (left) is shown arriving with the Oriflamme - the red-and-gold royal standard that was lost in their defeat - while the English longbowmen (right) prepare to unleash a volley. Edward selected the battleground at Crécy, occupying the higher ground, which forced the French into an disadvantageous assault.

▲ **DEFEAT OF THE TEUTONIC KNIGHTS** In this late 19th-century painting of Grunwald by Jan Matejko, Jagiello is shown at the heart of the battle. Initially he positioned himself behind his troops on the left flank, but as the Knights' charge buckled his line, he joined the melee with his last reserves, keeping the Polish-Lithuanian hopes alive until Vytautas came to his aid.

Grunwald

1410 ▪ NORTHERN POLAND ▪ POLAND-LITHUANIA VS. TEUTONIC KNIGHTS

POLISH-LITHUANIAN-TEUTONIC WAR

In 1409, war broke out between the Teutonic Knights (see p.63) and the Polish-Lithuanian Union when King Wladyslaw II Jagiello of Poland supported a revolt in Teutonic-held Samogitia, in Lithuania (see box, below). After some initial skirmishes, Jagiello brokered an agreement with his cousin Grand Duke Vytautas of Lithuania for a joint invasion of the Teutonic lands. In early July 1410, their combined 39,000-strong army crossed the Vistula, heading for the Teutonic Order's headquarters at Malbork, in northern Poland. Near the villages of Grunwald and Tannenberg, the Knights' army, led by Grand Master Ulrich von Jungingen, intercepted them and joined battle, despite being half their size.

On the right wing, Vytautas's Lithuanians charged prematurely, only to be fiercely repelled by the Teutonic Knights. The Lithuanians retreated, and some of the Knights gave chase in a rare breach of discipline, becoming mired in woods and marshes; as a result, their army was unable to break the Polish right wing, although it was close to collapse. The Polish king held on, and when the Lithuanians regrouped, they surrounded the Knights. Amid a desperate struggle, the Grand Master was killed and the remaining Knights retreated to their camp, where in a final, desperate defence, the elite of the Teutonic Order fought to the death. After the battle, Wladyslaw unsuccessfully laid siege to the Teutonic castle at Malbork, and the powers agreed peace in 1411. The Knights gave up some of their land and their power was diminished, leaving Poland-Lithuania unchallenged in the western Baltic.

KING **WLADYSLAW II JAGIELLO** (c.1352/1362-1434)

Born Jogailo, Wladyslaw became Grand Duke of Lithuania in 1382, and was crowned King of Poland in 1386 after marrying Jadwiga, heiress to the Polish throne. The union of the two countries created tensions between the King and the Teutonic order – after Wladyslaw converted to Christianity, they were denied the option of calling a crusade against him – and his cousin Vytautas, who rebelled in 1389. The land he won at Grunwald, although small, provoked further discontent among the nobles; he clashed with the Knights again in 1422, resulting in Poland-Lithuania taking control of Samogitia. This set the scene for the rebellion that started the war.

▶ **This portrait of King Wladyslaw II Jagiello** was painted in 1790 and is part of the collections of Muzeum Narodowe, Warsaw.

Agincourt

1415 ▪ NORTHERN FRANCE ▪ ENGLAND VS. FRANCE

HUNDRED YEARS' WAR

In 1415, Henry V of England invaded France in pursuit of a claim to the French throne that he had inherited from his great-grandfather, Edward III (see p.66). Landing near Harfleur on 13 August 1415 with a 12,000-strong army, he spent six weeks capturing the town, and lost half of his force to injury or disease in the process. He then decided to march to Calais, but the French under Constable d'Albret blocked the English from crossing the Somme, and Henry was forced 64 km (40 miles) south to find a ford. At Agincourt, on a stretch of road fringed by muddy fields, a French army of around 20,000 men again blocked his way.

Henry tempted d'Albret to attack by advancing slightly; the English longbowmen then sent volley after volley into the advancing French cavalry. The horses became stuck in mud, many wounded by arrows, and their dismounted riders in heavy armour could barely move in the churned-up ground. The French charge descended into chaos, and the few knights who made it to the English line were cut down at close quarters by a mass of archers armed with axes and knives. Thousands of knights and men-at-arms were killed, and the remnants of the French army retreated in disorder. Although Henry returned to England soon after his victory, he used the ensuing political instability in France to secure a treaty at Troyes in 1420. This made him heir to the French throne by marrying Charles VI's daughter, Catherine, and legitimized his occupation of much of northern France.

LONGBOWMEN AT WAR

Longbowmen played a key role in several critical English victories during the Hundred Years' War. The English longbow, which was 2 m (6 ft) long and made of yew, required enormous strength to pull, and in 1363 Edward III decreed that all able-bodied males should be trained in its use. A competent bowman could fire 10 shots per minute, reaching targets up to 250 m (820 ft) away. Thousands accompanied the English army – many of them Welsh – presenting a terrifyingly effective force. By the time Agincourt took place, their 30-arrow quivers often included armour-piercing arrowheads that could penetrate metal plate.

▲ **This 18th-century illustration** depicts longbowmen in the 14th century, around the time of the Hundred Years' War.

▲ **THE BATTLEFIELD AT AGINCOURT** This French illuminated manuscript from the 15th century shows the English and French archers at Agincourt with cavalry massed behind them. Towards the end of the battle, the French attacked the English baggage train, where French prisoners were being held. To prevent them from rejoining the battle, Henry executed hundreds of captives – sparing only those who were worth the highest ransoms.

Iron sounded on iron, while volleys of arrows
struck helmets, plates and cuirasses.

THOMAS WALSINGHAM, *ST ALBANS CHRONICLE*, c.1420-22

▲ **HUSSITE TABOR** As shown in this illumination, the Hussites compensated for their lack of trained troops with a system of defensive wagons, or tabors, chained together into a fortified circle. From within the circle, Hussite artillery could fire at enemy formations. Even if opposing troops penetrated it, they faced hails of missiles from the wagons and the dangers of a melee in a confined space.

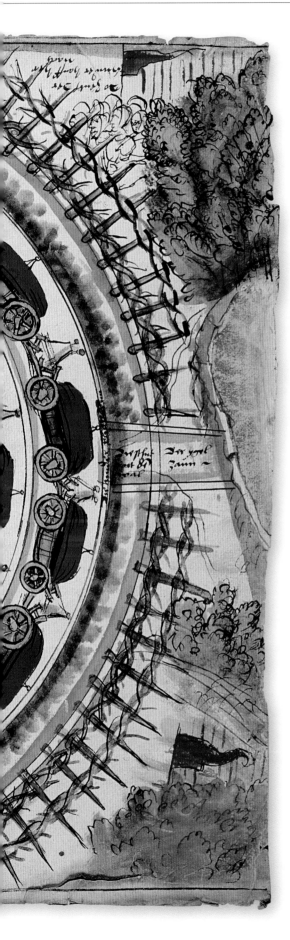

Kutná Hora

1421 ▪ MODERN-DAY CZECH REPUBLIC ▪ HUSSITES VS. CATHOLIC FORCES

HUSSITE WARS

In December 1421, Jan Žižka, leader of the radical wing of the Hussite religious reformist movement, was encamped with his army at Tabor, 80 km (50 miles) south-east of the Bohemian capital, Prague. The Hussite movement, which rejected the hierarchy and ritual of the Roman Catholic Church, had grown in strength after their founder, Jan Hus, was burned at the stake in 1415. Sigismund, the Bohemian ruler who inherited the throne in 1419, was slow to resist the Hussites, and was unable to rouse much support even when Pope Martin V launched an anti-Hussite crusade in 1420.

On 21 December 1421, Sigismund approached Kutná Hora with a royalist army of 50,000 men. Largely composed of mercenaries, his army should easily have been able to beat the Hussites' force of 12,000 mostly untrained peasants. Furthermore. the royalist commander Pippo Spano had secured the betrayal of the town of Kutná Hora from its local militia.

Žižka formed up most of his troops behind a circle of war wagons linked by chains. Seeing that the royalist army had encircled him, he formed the wagons into a column, supported by carts mounted with field cannon, and charged them straight towards Sigismund and Spano's lines. This mobile artillery blasted through the encircling royalists's line, allowing the Hussite army to escape. Sigismund chose not to pursue, wrongly believing that capturing the abandoned Hussite encampment was a victory. Throughout the rest of December, Žižka's forces launched a series of harrying raids on Sigismund's defences, and within months the king was forced to evacuate Bohemia.

THE **HUSSITE WARS** (1419-34)

The execution of religious reformer Jan Hus led to a state of near civil war in Bohemia. King Sigismund's Catholic followers were expelled from Prague, and from 1420 he launched a series of five crusades to crush the Hussites. They made little headway against the able leadership of Jan Žižka and his successor Andrew Prokop, as the Hussite wagon forts and mobile artillery defeated a series of royalist armies. An agreement at Basle in 1433 granted recognition to the moderate Hussites, causing the reformists to divide. The Utraquist moderates defeated the Taborite radicals at Lipany in 1434, bringing the Hussite wars to an end.

▶ **A Hussite force composed of cavalry** and infantry clashes with a largely mounted crusader army during the Hussite wars.

Siege of Orléans

1428-29 ▪ NORTH-CENTRAL FRANCE ▪ FRANCE VS. ENGLAND

HUNDRED YEARS' WAR

The siege at Orléans represented a turning point for the French in the Hundred Years' War. The English had returned to France in force early in 1428, intent on enforcing Henry V's claim to the French throne, affirmed by the Treaty of Troyes in 1420. They had pushed along the Loire Valley and formed garrisons on the south side of the river opposite the strategic city of Orléans on the north bank and, on 12 October, they isolated it.

The English made initial attacks on the city with some success, and on 23 October, led by the Earl of Salisbury, they took Les Tourelles, a fort that guarded a river crossing into Orléans; however, Salisbury was fatally wounded the next day. Over the next month the siege faltered, but the arrival of the Earl of Shrewsbury in December reinvigorated the English. They defeated French relief forces at the Battle of the Herrings on 12 February 1429, and by the spring Orléan's starving garrison was close to surrender.

The English had never completely cut off Orléans, however, and some reinforcements trickled in. The French were ultimately saved by Joan of Arc, a peasant woman who had persuaded the Dauphin (heir to the French throne), Charles, to entrust her with leadership of a new relief force. On 30 April, Joan and her army forced their way into the city, and on 4 May broke out to join up with more reinforcements. The English were caught between the two groups; the French drove them out of several key positions, and the English lost Les Tourelles on 7 May. Shrewsbury's army retreated, and the French celebrated an unexpected victory. For the time being, central France had been saved, and the Dauphin was crowned King Charles VII of France in Reims in July.

◄ **HAND-TO-HAND FIGHTING NEAR ORLÉANS** This 15th-century miniature is from *Le Jouvencel*, a semi-autobiographical account of experiences in the Hundred Years' War by John V of Bueil. Nicknamed "the plague of the English", Bueil was a military companion of Joan of Arc's in her military campaign at Orléans. Here he depicts fighting between the French and English near the city.

In context

▲ **JOAN OF ARC PLEADS WITH THE DAUPHIN** A young peasant woman from Champagne, Joan of Arc claimed that she heard God calling her to go to the Dauphin, Charles, to help to save France. This 15th-century tapestry depicts her arriving at court in March 1429 to ask the Dauphin to allow her to take a force to Orléans. Her success made her a target for the Dauphin's enemies.

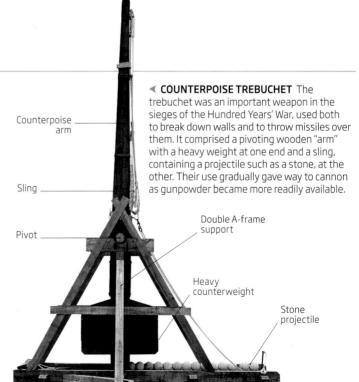

Counterpoise arm

Sling

Pivot

◄ **COUNTERPOISE TREBUCHET** The trebuchet was an important weapon in the sieges of the Hundred Years' War, used both to break down walls and to throw missiles over them. It comprised a pivoting wooden "arm" with a heavy weight at one end and a sling, containing a projectile such as a stone, at the other. Their use gradually gave way to cannon as gunpowder became more readily available.

Double A-frame support

Heavy counterweight

Stone projectile

Fall of Constantinople

1453 ▪ NORTHWESTERN TURKEY ▪ BYZANTINE EMPIRE VS. OTTOMAN EMPIRE

BYZANTINE-OTTOMAN WARS

By 1453, the once-great Byzantine Empire, which had endured for around 1,000 years, consisted of little more than the city of Constantinople, and small pieces of land in the Peloponnese and along the southern shore of the Black Sea. The Ottoman Turks had been seizing Byzantine lands since the late 13th century, and had conquered Anatolia, overrun the Balkan provinces, and were surging towards the Danube and Constantinople. Despite this threat to one of Christendom's great historic cities, the Byzantines responded weakly; even after a Polish–Hungarian crusade ended in disaster at the Black Sea port of Varna in 1444, they sent little aid.

In 1451, a new young sultan, Mehmed II, ascended to the Ottoman throne. He was determined to take Constantinople, which, situated at the junction of Europe and Asia, was the obvious capital city for the Ottoman realm that spanned both continents. In 1452, he built the fortress of Rumeli Hisar on the Bosphorus strait to prevent Christian relief forces from reaching the city via the Black Sea. Having cut off the city, he then assembled an army of 75,000-80,000 men, a fleet of around 100 ships, and an artillery train with several huge siege cannon constructed by the Hungarian engineer Urban.

Mehmet's army laid siege to Constantinople on 5 April. The city's walls were relatively well maintained and the 8,000 defenders were well prepared to weather the attack; they also had small detachments of reinforcements from western Europe. However, the powerful Ottoman artillery bombardments weakened the walls, and their ships

SULTAN **MEHMED II** (1432-81)

Mehmed II first became sultan in 1444 when his father Murad II abdicated, but he was deposed in 1446 when the Janissaries (the elite infantry of the Sultan's household) restored Murad to the throne. Mehmed's second reign began in 1451 and lasted for 30 years. After capturing Constantinople, he campaigned in Anatolia and the Balkans, where he conquered Bosnia and Albania and besieged Belgrade. An energetic administrator, he conciliated his Christian subjects by recognising the Greek Orthodox Church, and gave the Ottoman Empire a centralized bureaucracy and legal system.

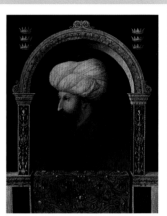

▲ **Mehmed II** was 21 years old when he brought an end to the Byzantine Empire.

breached the naval defences in the Golden Horn inlet (see opposite and p.80). Constantinople eventually fell to an assault on 29 May. Emperor Constantine was killed, and after three days of looting, Mehmed entered the city and declared it his new capital. Although the remnants of the Byzantine Empire struggled on until the capture of its last stronghold, Trebizond, in 1461, the fall of Constantinople effectively marked the end of the empire.

▶ **THE SIEGE** This 15th-century miniature depicts Mehmed II directing his troops towards the strongly defended land walls of Constantinople. The Ottoman encampment is shown to be on the opposite side of the Golden Horn, the waterway that was key to the Ottomans' capture of the city.

The blood flowed in the city like rainwater in the gutters after a sudden storm, and the corpses of Turks and Christians… floated out to the sea…

NICOLÒ BARBARO, WITNESS TO THE FALL OF CONSTANTINOPLE, 1453

In detail

As the Ottoman army closed in on Constantinople, defenders arrived from Italy, including 700 men under the Genoese soldier Giovanni Giustiniani, who then oversaw the city's defence. A chain was extended across the Golden Horn – the waterway on the city's northern side – to prevent the Ottomans from threatening the lightly-defended sea walls. However, the Ottomans built a log road across Galata, on the eastern side of the Horn, and rolled their fleet along it to reach the water, forcing Giustiniani to divert his troops from the defence of the city's landward walls.

Despite damage inflicted by Urban's giant cannon and a series of assaults, the defenders resisted, and on 25 May Mehmed opened negotiations for the city's peaceful surrender. The Byzantines rebuffed his offer, and early on 29 May the Ottomans launched a final attack: Turkish irregular troops advanced first, then the elite Janissaries assaulted a damaged section of the north-western walls. At a critical moment, Giustiniani was wounded and left his post; the Ottomans then found an undefended gate, the Kerkoporta, and poured in. As the Ottomans fanned through the city, the Emperor was killed and the Byzantines' defence collapsed. Some of the defenders escaped to their ships, and, accompanied by some Genoese and a few imperial vessels, slipped past the Ottoman fleet. Most of the remaining defenders were massacred or sold into slavery.

▶ **CITY DEFENCES** This 16th-century fresco in Moldovita monastery, Romania, depicts the Siege of Constantinople. It shows the strength of the city's walls, which had resisted numerous sieges. Emperor Constantine XI is shown patrolling the heavily garrisoned landward walls, which lacked the protection of the Golden Horn.

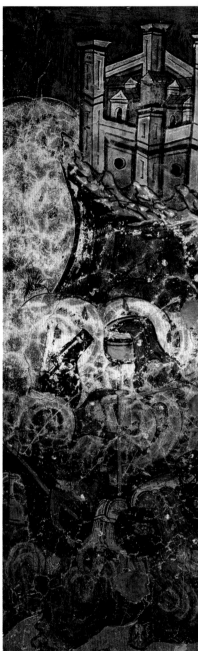

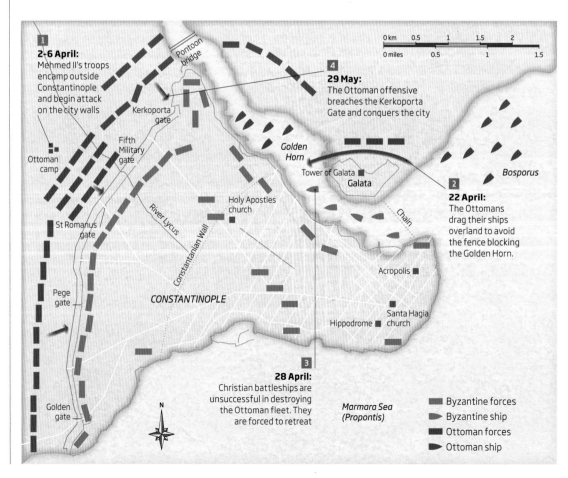

1 2–6 April: Mehmed II's troops encamp outside Constantinople and begin attack on the city walls

Kerkoporta gate

Pontoon bridge

Fifth Military gate

Ottoman camp

St Romanus gate

River Lycus

Holy Apostles church

Constantianian Wall

Pege gate

CONSTANTINOPLE

Golden gate

N

3 28 April: Christian battleships are unsuccessful in destroying the Ottoman fleet. They are forced to retreat

Marmara Sea (Propontis)

0 km   0.5   1   1.5   2
0 miles   0.5   1   1.5

4 29 May: The Ottoman offensive breaches the Kerkoporta Gate and conquers the city

Golden Horn

Tower of Galata
Galata

Chain

Bosporus

2 22 April: The Ottomans drag their ships overland to avoid the fence blocking the Golden Horn.

Acropolis

Santa Hagia church

Hippodrome

◾ Byzantine forces
▶ Byzantine ship
◾ Ottoman forces
▶ Ottoman ship

◀ **CONSTANTINOPLE, 1453** The city was protected by one of the most complex systems of defensive walls ever built. Constructed by Constantine the Great 1,000 years earlier, these walls protected the city from a landward attack from the west, and three possible seaward attacks. Before Mehmed's army arrived, a chain barrier was also extended across the Golden Horn. The Ottomans bypassed the chain by dragging their ships overland – and their artillery breached the walls.

◄ **ELITE SOLDIERS**
Ottoman Janissaries (see p.93) prepare for an assault on the walls of Constantinople. An elite corps of troops, the janissaries were recruited by the devşirme system, by which young Christian boys from the Balkans were removed from their families, converted to Islam, and trained in military skills from a very early age. They were loyal to the sultan in person, rather than to the Ottoman nobility.

▲ **CANNON FIRE** The Ottomans were equipped with massive cannon, or bombards, which fired huge stone balls at the walls of Constantinople. These weapons were provided by Urban, a Hungarian engineer who had previously offered his services to the Byzantines. However, the cannon took hours to reload and the Ottomans had only limited ammunition. As a result, most of the damage to Constantinople was inflicted by smaller artillery pieces.

Directory: 1000–1500

LEGNANO
GUELPH AND GHIBELLINE CONFLICT

1176 ▪ NORTHERN ITALY ▪ LOMBARD LEAGUE VS. HOLY ROMAN EMPIRE

In the late 12th century, northern Italy was divided by fighting between the Guelphs, supporters of the Papacy, and the Ghibellines, supporters of the Holy Roman Emperor. In 1167, the major cities of Lombardy formed a league, with papal approval, to defend themselves against Emperor Frederick Barbarossa, who engaged in five campaigns to combat them. After failed peace talks in May 1176, Frederick led his 3,000-strong army around Milan to meet with reinforcements from Germany at Lake Como. The Lombard League deployed 3,500 men to intercept him north of the city at Legnano, where they positioned themselves around the Carroccia, Milan's sacred battle wagon. The fierce battle that ensued was evenly matched until eventually the Lombard League's cavalry regrouped and attacked, scattering the Imperial army. The Imperial cause in Lombardy was damaged, and in 1183 Frederick had to concede self-government to the cities there.

XIANGYANG
SONG-YUAN WARS

1268 ▪ CENTRAL CHINA ▪ MONGOLS VS. SONG FORCES

In 1267, Kublai Khan, the Mongol Great Khan, turned his attention to conquering southern China. His key objectives were the twin fortresses of Xianyang and Fancheng; these controlled the Han river, which fed into the Yangzi, in the heart of the Song empire. Despite their huge forces, the invading Mongols were thwarted by the defenders' ability to resupply the fortresses' garrison using hundreds of river junks. The Mongols' attempts to build ramparts in the river to dam it failed, as did outright assault, and the siege dragged on for five years. Finally, Kublai Khan obtained heavy siege catapults from his nephew, the Ilkhan of Persia. The projectiles hurled by these catapults broke down Fancheng's wall within a few days and it fell to a Mongol assault. Seeing the battle was lost, the Song commander of Xiangyang surrendered. With the fall of both fortresses, the way into southern China was clear and Song morale collapsed. By 1279, Kublai Khan had completed his conquest of southern China.

▼ COURTRAI
FRANCO-FLEMISH WAR

1302 ▪ MODERN-DAY BELGIUM ▪ FRANCE VS. FLANDERS

In 1302, the towns of Flanders were in revolt against five years of French occupation. To quell this uprising, Philip IV of France sent an 8,000-strong force to Courtrai, north of Tournai, where the Flemish were besieging a castle. The Flemish militia, armed with pikes, crossbows, and *goedendaegs* (pikes with a club mounted on the end) took position in an area of marshes and small streams. When the French knights charged, they became bogged down in the marshes and were knocked from their horses by the Flemish *goedendaegs*. The remaining knights retreated and the French infantry fled, pursued by the victorious Flemish. Over 1,000 French soldiers died, including many knights whom the Flemish chose not to keep for ransom. The encounter became known as the "Battle of the Golden Spurs" for the quantity of valuable spurs looted from their corpses, and showed that drilled foot-soldiers could overcome mounted knights; however, later French victories denied Flanders its independence.

BANNOCKBURN
FIRST WAR OF SCOTTISH INDEPENDENCE

1314 ▪ SOUTHERN SCOTLAND ▪ SCOTLAND VS. ENGLAND

Robert the Bruce took the Scottish throne in 1306 and led a military campaign to drive out the English, who had gained control of many areas of Scotland following Edward I's invasion in 1296. By 1314, Stirling Castle, the only remaining English stronghold, was under siege by the Scots, and Edward II led an army of around 2,500 cavalry and 15,000 infantry to defend it. The English army was met by an 8,000-strong force of Scots (mainly infantry) in the New Park, south of the town. The battle lasted for two days – English cavalry charges were unable to penetrate the Scottish formations of spearmen, and when the English pulled back they fell victim to pits and ditches that the Scots had laid in the marshy ground. A hasty retreat by the English saw 34 barons killed, along with thousands of soldiers. Stirling Castle fell and the English never recovered their positions in Scotland, ultimately having to recognize Scottish independence in 1328.

POITIERS
HUNDRED YEARS' WAR

1356 ▪ CENTRAL FRANCE ▪ ENGLAND VS. FRANCE

In 1355, an eight-year truce in the Hundred Years' War between England and France expired. While Edward III attacked northern France, his son Edward, the Black Prince, led a force of 8,000, including around 2,500 longbowmen, north from Aquitaine on a raid into central France. The French army, led by King John II, crossed the Loire to intercept the English, and the two armies met just east of Poitiers. Outnumbered by the French, the English army positioned themselves on a narrow front protected by a marsh and stream. An initial French charge faltered under a series of volleys from the longbowmen and the retreating knights were forced into hand-to-hand combat. They attacked again, but the

Shown here in a 15th-century illumination, the Battle of Courtrai saw the victory of an all-infantry Flemish army over a French mounted army.

English led a surprise advance and the French army disintegrated. Many French knights were captured, including King John. A weakened France was forced to agree to a treaty in 1360 expanding English holding around Aquitaine and Calais.

LAKE POYANG
RED TURBAN REBELLION

1363 ■ EASTERN CHINA ■ MING DYNASTY VS. HAN DYNASTY

The Mongol Yüan dynasty of China had collapsed by the early 1360s, and three principal contenders for power emerged: the Han, the Wu, and the Ming. The Ming arose out of a smaller rebel group, the Red Turbans, and in 1363 their leader Zhu Yuanzhang began consolidating his power around the Ming capital, Nanjing. When the Han attacked the Ming-held town of Poyang using a fleet of large warships positioned on the adjacent lake, Zhu sent what reinforcements he could. The Han commander failed to block the lake entrance, allowing a Ming fleet in, but the smaller Ming ships struggled to surround and board the Han vessels. Instead the Ming used fire ships to attack the Han fleet, burning many ships. The Han retreated and much of their fleet was destroyed trying to flee the lake. Poyang was soon relieved by land and Zhu, with Han power broken, emerged as the dominant force in China, declaring himself emperor in 1368.

KOSOVO
OTTOMAN WARS IN EUROPE AND SERBIAN-OTTOMAN WARS

1389 ■ MODERN-DAY REPUBLIC OF KOSOVO ■ SERBIAN-BOSNIAN ARMY VS. OTTOMANS

The Ottoman Turks had made significant advances in the Balkans in the 1370s–80s, absorbing Bulgaria and taking the important Serbian town of Niš. Serbia itself had been weakened by civil wars, but in 1388 the ruler of the northern part, Prince Lazar, defeated the Ottomans, provoking their leader, Sultan Murad I, to retaliate. The Ottoman army of up to 40,000 men paused at Kosovo, where Lazar had a force just over half the size, including reinforcement troops from another Serbian nobleman, Vuk Branković. Ottoman archers rebuffed an initial

Serbian charge, but the Serbs still forced the Ottoman centre back. The Ottomans then launched a full counter-attack which destroyed the Serbian centre: Lazar was killed and Branković withdrew from the field with the surviving Serbian forces. Losses on both sides where vast, but Serbia, with fewer resources, was unable to resist subsequent Ottoman advances: it became an Ottoman vassal in 1390, and finally lost its independence altogether in 1459.

CASTILLON
HUNDRED YEARS' WAR

1453 ■ SOUTHWESTERN FRANCE ■ FRANCE VS. ENGLAND

In 1435, the English were abandoned by their Burgundian allies, leaving them to continue the Hundred Years' War against France alone. By 1451, the French under Charles VII had recaptured all their lost territory except for the city of Calais, but in October 1452 the Earl of Shrewsbury seized Bordeaux with an English force of 3,000 and advanced inland. The French countered by besieging the strategic town of Castillon, where the English confronted them on 17 July 1453. Although reinforcements had doubled the size of the English army, the French had built a temporary defensive fortification with over 300 field guns. When Shrewsbury impetuously gave the order to charge, he and his men were destroyed by waves of cannonballs. With their commander dead, the English retreated and were slaughtered by the advancing French. Bordeaux fell to the French soon afterwards, leaving England again in possession of just Calais and bringing the Hundred Years' War to an end.

MURTEN
BURGUNDIAN WARS

1476 ■ WESTERN SWITZERLAND ■ OLD SWISS CONFEDERACY VS. BURGUNDY

The steady advance of the Duchy of Burgundy's army down the Rhine in the 1460–70s brought it in conflict with the fiercely independent Swiss cantons (allies of the Holy Roman Empire). In 1474, war broke between the two sides, and Charles the Bold, Duke of Burgundy, led a series of invasions into Swiss territory. Burgundy's army was defeated by the Swiss Confederate army at

Depicted here in a 16th-century miniature, Nancy was the final and decisive battle that ended the Burgundian Wars.

Grandison in March 1476, but during the following June, Charles led an attack on the town of Murten. The Swiss cantons assembled a force of around 25,000 soldiers armed with pikes to relieve the siege. The Burgundians were caught by surprise, and though they had occupied the side of a hill with artillery the Swiss pike formation pushed forward and forced the Burgundian army into retreat during which thousands were killed. Charles fled with his remaining troops back to Burgundy.

▲ NANCY
BURGUNDIAN WARS

1477 ■ EASTERN FRANCE ■ OLD SWISS CONFEDERACY VS. BURGUNDY

In 1477, Charles the Bold, Duke of Burgundy, laid siege to the strategic city of Nancy in Lorraine. The region, formerly under his control, had broken away under Duke René. Charles led a mixed force of Burgundians, Italians, and Dutch, while Duke René countered with 20,000 troops, half of them Swiss mercenaries. The outnumbered Burgundians tried to reduce their disadvantage by positioning themselves along a narrow front protected by a stream and thick woods. But the Swiss phalanx advanced, pushing the Burgundian left wing back and, crucially, displacing their artillery. Although Charles tried to redeploy troops to plug the growing gaps, the Swiss superiority in numbers overwhelmed the Burgundian army which collapsed.

Charles was killed, making René's victory complete, and the Duchy of Burgundy fell apart - one portion went to the Austrian Habsburgs, and the remainder was taken over by Louis XI of France.

BOSWORTH FIELD
WARS OF THE ROSES

1485 ■ CENTRAL ENGLAND ■ HOUSE OF LANCASTER VS. HOUSE OF YORK

The Wars of the Roses, fought between rival claimants to the English throne the Houses of York and Lancaster, seemed to have ended in 1471. However, the controversial accession of the Yorkist Richard III in 1483 reignited the conflict. Many nobles flocked to support exiled Henry Tudor, the remaining Lancastrian candidate. In August 1485, Henry landed at Milford Haven in Wales. He advanced into England, and while he gathered reinforcements Richard rushed to head him off. At Bosworth, near Leicester in central England, the two armies met. Although Richard's army was larger, contingents under the Earl of Northumberland and Lord Stanley remained slightly apart from the main force. When an attack by Henry's army put Richard's line under pressure, the king ordered Northumberland to join him, but the Earl refused. Stanley allied with the Lancastrians and led to a Yorkist retreat, during which Richard was unhorsed and killed. Henry was crowned and later married Richard's niece Elizabeth of York to unite the Yorkist and Lancastrian dynasties.

1500–1700

CHAPTER 3

Siege of Tenochtitlán

1521 ▪ VALLEY OF MEXICO ▪ AZTEC EMPIRE VS. SPANISH EMPIRE

SPANISH CONQUEST OF THE AZTEC EMPIRE

The Aztec Empire began in 1428 as an alliance of three city-states in what is now central Mexico, but by the time the treasure-seeking Conquistadores of Spain arrived in 1519, the lake city of Tenochtitlán was dominant. In August some 600 Spanish, led by Hernán Cortés, marched on the city, finding many local allies along the way who were disaffected with Aztec rule. Cortés's army was welcomed into the city, where the Spanish took the Aztec emperor Moctezuma II hostage. For several months the Spanish ruled the city until a revolt sent them fleeing.

After building alliances in the Aztec hinterlands and gathering local forces, Cortés returned to Tenochtitlán to lay siege. A fleet of specially built ships supported his soldiers fighting their way across the three main causeways that linked the city to the edge of Lake Texcoco. Already ravaged by smallpox, the Aztecs finally collapsed to the Spanish forces' superior weapons and command structure after 79 days of resistance on 13 August 1521. Tenochtitlán was sacked and its monuments destroyed, bringing an end to the Aztec Empire and establishing Spanish rule in Central America and Spanish as the *lingua franca* of the region.

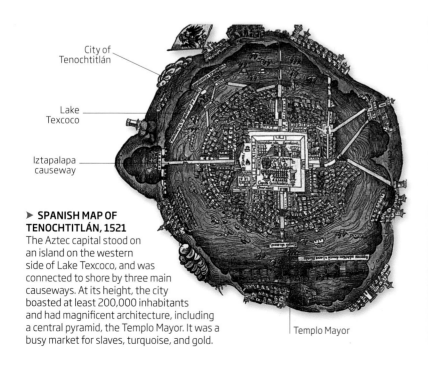

City of Tenochtitlán

Lake Texcoco

Iztapalapa causeway

Templo Mayor

▶ **SPANISH MAP OF TENOCHTITLÁN, 1521**
The Aztec capital stood on an island on the western side of Lake Texcoco, and was connected to shore by three main causeways. At its height, the city boasted at least 200,000 inhabitants and had magnificent architecture, including a central pyramid, the Templo Mayor. It was a busy market for slaves, turquoise, and gold.

> # I and my companions suffer from a disease of the heart which can be cured only with gold. 〞

HERNÁN CORTÉS TO THE ENVOYS OF MONTEZUMA II, EXPLAINING
THE MOTIVES OF HIS CONQUEST, 1519

▼ **CAUSEWAY FIGHTING** In the battle to force their way across the causeways, the Spanish were supported by 13 boats, each carrying 12 oarsmen, 12 crossbowmen and musketeers, and a captain. The Aztecs' padded cotton armour and reed shields were useless against guns and crossbow bolts, while Spanish artillery battered the city walls. Even so, the Aztecs successfully repelled the Conquistadores' initial attacks.

CONQVISTA DE MEXICO POR CORTES. Nᵒ 7

▲ **HABSBURG VICTORY** This painting illustrates a key moment in the battle: the encirclement of the French cavalry by the Imperial mixed forces of arquebusiers, Landsknechts, and cavalry. It is copied from a tapestry cycle presented to Emperor Charles V in 1531, celebrating what was his first military victory.

Pavia

1525 ▪ NORTHERN ITALY ▪ EMPIRE OF CHARLES V VS. KINGDOM OF FRANCE

FIRST HABSBURG-VALOIS WAR

In the late Middle Ages northern and central Italy were battlegrounds of warring city-states. After decades of fighting, Florence, Milan, and Venice emerged dominant, agreeing a peace treaty in 1454. The treaty held until 1494, when France, which had a claims to certain Italian territories, invaded Italy, beginning a series of conflicts in which various European powers fought over the country. The decisive battle came in October 1524, when, having marched into Lombardy and occupied Milan, Francis I of France laid siege to the city of Pavia, which was controlled by forces loyal to the Habsburg Empire of Charles V.

Pavia's defenders held out through the winter. During this time imperial reinforcements arrived and took up positions opposite the French, who began building fortifications that threatened to encircle them. In order to prevent this, and after weeks of skirmishing, imperial forces led by Fernandino Francesco d'Avalos, Marquis of Pescara, marched under cover of darkness for several kilometres north to ford the stream, and then back towards the exposed French left flank. Francis I responded with a cavalry charge, but his horsemen obscured his cannon, which failed to strike the enemy. Francis also left his infantry unsupported, fatally exposing them to the oncoming Habsburg attack, while his cavalry suffered heavy losses to Pescara's arquebusiers. The French army was virtually annihilated, and a large part of the French nobility was slaughtered. Francis I was captured and held in Spain for a year, where he eventually signed a treaty with Charles V, giving up all French claims to Italy.

EUROPEAN **MERCENARIES**

European armies of the late Middle Ages swelled their ranks with mercenaries. At the battle of Pavia, Francis I enrolled a battalion of Swiss mercenary pikeman, who were valued for their discipline and skill. The rivals to the Swiss in professional soldiering were the German Landsknechts, who fought for anyone who paid them and also favoured the pike. At Pavia, Landsknechts on both sides: the South German military leader Georg von Frundsberg led a battalion of imperial Landsknechts to victory against the renegade Black Band Landsknechts who fought for the French.

▶ **As well as being experts** in the use of the pike and two-handed sword, Landsknecht soldiers were also known for wearing flamboyant costumes.

Panipat

1526 ▪ NORTHERN INDIA ▪ MUGHALS VS. LODI DYNASTY AND AFGHANS

MUGHAL CONQUESTS

Ibrahim Lodi, who had ruled the Sultanate of Delhi since 1517, was unpopular with his nobility due to his repressive policies. Daulat Khan Lodi, the Governor of Punjab, eventually reached out to Zahir ad-Din Muhammad – better known as Babur, the ruler of Kabul – for help. In response, Babur set out in force in November 1525, crossing the Indus River with an army 12,000 strong. Local allies and mercenaries recruited en route swelled this army to around 20,000 men. Lodi, meanwhile, had gathered an army of 50,000 or more and advanced slowly north from Delhi, eventually camping near Panipat in present-day north India.

Babur reached Panipat on 12 April 1526, and for eight days the two armies faced each other without making a decisive move. Finally, in an attempt to goad Lodi into attacking him, Babur ordered a night-time cavalry raid. This was repelled, but it had the desired effect: believing his opponent to be weak, the next day Lodi advanced his army onto the fields of Panipat.

Lodi's most fearsome weapons were several hundred war elephants, which had played a major role in defeating previous Mongol invasions. However, Babur had something that these invaders did not: cannons. Their sound terrified the elephants, which panicked and trampled Lodi's men; his forces were also encircled by cavalry and entangled in Babur's defences. Lodi died on the battlefield, and Babur took Delhi, where he founded the Mughal dynasty. His descendants ruled India for 330 years.

In context

▲ **EMPEROR BABUR** A Timurid prince descended from the Mongol leaders Timur and Genghis Khan, Babur inherited a small Central Asian kingdom. Struggling against the Safavids and the Uzbeks, he captured and lost Samarkand three times before moving south to Kabul in Afghanistan. There he dreamed of a new empire east of the Indus. The invitation to oust Lodi gave him his opportunity.

▼ **WAR ELEPHANTS** Elephants had been used in war in India since at least the 4th century BCE. Later, they were used in south-east Asia and Mediterranean countries – most famously by Alexander of Macedonia. Specially trained and often protected by armour, they were mainly used to charge the enemy's troops, break their ranks, and spread panic and terror. Panipat was the first time that artillery and guns had been used against elephants. The results were devastating, and the use of elephants in warfare swiftly declined.

◄ **BABUR'S TACTICS**
Vastly outnumbered, Babur won by superior tactics. He protected the flanks of his army with trenches covered by branches. In the centre, he defended himself with carts tied together with ropes, and between these he placed his cannon and riflemen. This forced Lodi to fight on a narrower front, which greatly constricted his movements. As seen in this Mughal painting, Babur then attacked Lodi's flanks, using horsemen wielding deadly composite bows.

▶ **VICTORY AT HAND** This 16th-century Turkish miniature from Topkapi Palace in Istanbul depicts Hungarian troops (left and above) and Ottoman forces (centre and right) at the Battle of Mohacs. The Ottomans skillfully deployed artillery and elite Janissaries to overwhelm the Hungarian force.

Mohács

1526 ▪ SOUTHERN HUNGARY ▪ OTTOMAN EMPIRE VS. KINGDOM OF HUNGARY

OTTOMAN CONQUEST OF EUROPE

The Ottoman sultan Suleiman came to power in 1520, and soon began expanding his empire into Europe. After capturing Belgrade in 1521, he turned his attention to the kingdom of Hungary.

Meanwhile, King Francis I of France, who had recently been defeated at the Battle of Pavia in 1525 by the Habsburg Empire (see pp.88–89), had formed a Franco-Ottoman alliance with Sulieman against the Holy Roman Emperor Charles V. Francis asked his ally Suleiman to wage war on Charles V: this request aligned neatly with Suleiman's own ambitions, as the road to the Habsburgs lay across Hungary. The country itself was weakened by political disunity, and many Hungarian nobles failed to heed the call of its king, Louis II, to mobilize against the enemy.

On 29 August 1526, a Hungarian force consisting of fewer than 30,000 men with 50 cannon waited on swampy plains near the town of Mohács, Hungary, to meet an Ottoman force of 55,000–70,000 men with 200 cannon, headed by Suleiman himself. The initial charge of the Hungarian cavalry caused serious casualties to the Ottomans, but the Hungarians were then torn apart by Turkish cannon fire. As the Hungarians fell back, they were encircled by the fast-moving Ottoman light cavalry. The Hungarians were annihilated, and King Louis was thrown from his horse and killed as he tried to escape.

The defeat effectively ended the existence of an independent Hungary at the time, as it was absorbed into Suleiman's Ottoman Empire. The Turks, meanwhile, continued their advance into central Europe, which would take them all the way to the gates of Vienna.

In context

▲ **SULEIMAN THE MAGNIFICENT** During Suleiman's reign as sultan from 1520 to 1566, the Ottoman Empire was at its most powerful. The sultan personally led armies that conquered Belgrade, Rhodes, and most of Hungary, and annexed much of the Middle East and North Africa. As well as his military leadership, he was a great patron of culture and instituted major legal reforms. Indomitable until the end, Suleiman died of illness while campaigning in Hungary.

▶ **TURKISH JANISSARY** Translated as "new soldier", the Janissaries were elite forces that were the Ottoman sultans' household troops and the first modern standing army in Europe. They were strictly disciplined and forbidden to marry because their loyalty was to the sultan only. In battle, the Janissaries' main mission was to protect the sultan and hold the centre against enemy attack.

Great Siege of Malta

1565 ▪ MALTA ▪ OTTOMAN EMPIRE VS. KNIGHTS HOSPITALLER, MALTESE MILITIA, AND SPANISH EMPIRE

OTTOMAN-HABSBURG WARS

The small but strategically crucial central-Mediterranean island of Malta was a potential obstacle to the westward expansion of the Ottoman Empire. It was controlled by the Knights Hospitaller, a Christian military order founded in Jerusalem in the early 12th century, with headquarters on Malta since 1530. In 1560, the Ottoman navy won a decisive victory over a Christian Alliance fleet in the battle of Djerba, off the coast of Tunisia, after which it was only a matter of time before the Muslim empire's attentions were turned to Malta. Accordingly, in 1565, the Ottoman sultan Suleiman sent an invasion fleet of around 180 fighting ships carrying some 40,000 men to besiege the 700 knights and 8,000 soldiers of Malta. Their goal was to seize the island and use it as a base for futher assaults on Europe. In anticipation, the Knights of Malta had ordered the construction of two new defensive forts and the strengthening of a third. The Ottoman armada arrived off Malta in May 1565 and anchored at Marsaxlokk on the south-east coast of the island.

Led by Jean Parisot de Valette, Grand Master of the Hospitallers, for three months the Maltese repulsed repeated attacks, buying enough time for a Christian relief force to arrive. The invasion failed, in part because the time-consuming attack on Fort St Elmo (see below) could have been bypassed. The Ottomans' reputation of invincibility was shattered, and their advance into the western Mediterranean was halted.

Visual tour

KEY

▲ **FORT ST ELMO** The Ottomans first attacked Fort St Elmo. In anticipation, the Knights Hospitaller had placed heavy artillery in the fort. The defenders held off the Ottomans for several weeks, inflicting heavy losses before the fort was eventually reduced to rubble.

▶ **FORT ST MICHAEL** From Marsamxett, the Ottomans moved 100 vessels across Mount Sciberras to the Grand Harbour, from where they launched an attack on Fort St Michael. However, they sailed too close to Fort St Angelo, whose cannons destroyed the fleet.

◀ **BAY OF MARSAMXETT** After capturing Fort St Elmo, the Ottomans anchored their fleet at Marsamxett, where they decapitated the Maltese knights and floated their bodies across the bay on mock crucifixes. In response, de Valette beheaded all of his prisoners, loaded their heads into cannon, and fired them into the Ottoman camp.

▼ **BIRGU** After failing at Fort St Michael, the Ottomans surrounded and bombarded the town of Birgu. They breached the walls, but then retreated, mistakenly believing that Christian reinforcements had arrived from Sicily.

▲ **MALTA BESIEGED** This illustrated map of the Siege of Malta from the Vatican collection shows all the different phases of the battle in one painting. The central peninsula is Mount Sciberras, with Fort St Elmo at its tip. The body of water to the left is the Bay of Marsamxett, while to the right stands the Grand Harbour, where two other forts – St Michael and St Angelo – are under siege.

Lepanto

1571 ■ IONIAN SEA ■ HOLY LEAGUE VS. OTTOMAN EMPIRE

OTTOMAN-HABSBURG WARS

After their defeat at Malta (see pp.94–95), the Ottoman Turks waged a campaign to acquire the Venetian-controlled island of Cyprus. The Holy League, representing the Christian interests of Venice, the Papacy, Spain, Genoa, Malta, and Savoy, responded by sending a fleet from Messina in Sicily – but not before the Turks had captured the Cypriot cities of Nicosia and Famagusta. Learning that the Ottomans were in the Gulf of Patras, near Lepanto (modern-day Nafpaktos) in Greece, the Christians set course for a confrontation. Under the command of Don Juan of Austria, the Christian fleet numbered some 212 fighting vessels; the Ottoman force, led by Ali Pasha, was slightly larger.

On the morning of 7 October 1571, the two fleets engaged. Although fewer in number, the ships of the Holy League had more cannon, and included six vast galleasses, a new kind of gun-carrying galley developed by the Venetians. In addition,

> ### ALI PASHA (c.1510-71)
>
> Entrusted with the "Banner of the Caliphs" – a huge standard with the name of Allah embroidered on it 28,900 times – statesman Ali Pasha commanded the Ottoman forces at Lepanto. In the early stages of the battle, his flagship, *Sultana*, rammed the Christian flagship, *La Real*, commanded by Don Juan of Austria. Smashed together, the decks of the two ships formed a single battlefield. Twice the Spanish troops of *La Real* were repulsed from the *Sultana*. In their third, successful assault, Ali Pasha was killed.
>
>
>
> ▲ **This German woodcut** of 1571 shows Ali Pasha as he was in life, and with his head on a pike following Lepanto.

◀ **FLEETS LINED UP** This painting by Giorgio Vasari, completed in 1572, shows the Christian and Ottoman fleets on the brink of battle. Six huge Christian galleasses dominate the centre, while figures depicting Spain, Venice, and the Papacy stand at bottom left.

most Holy League ships were rowed by free men, as opposed to Ottoman ships, whose slaves had little interest in fighting for their masters. After hours of fierce combat, the Holy League prevailed in what was the last major engagement between oar-powered vessels in the Western world. It provided a boost to European morale, but quarrels between the Christian powers eventually led to Venice ceding Cyprus to the Ottomans in 1573.

▶ **ORDER OF BATTLE** The Holy League fleet advanced in four squadrons, with Don Juan of Austria commanding the centre. The Ottomans were ranged in a crescent across the bay, with Ali Pasha at the centre. The battle was almost lost when ships led by Uluch Ali (Ottoman left), nearly outflanked the Christians, but a Spanish squadron averted disaster with a timely intervention.

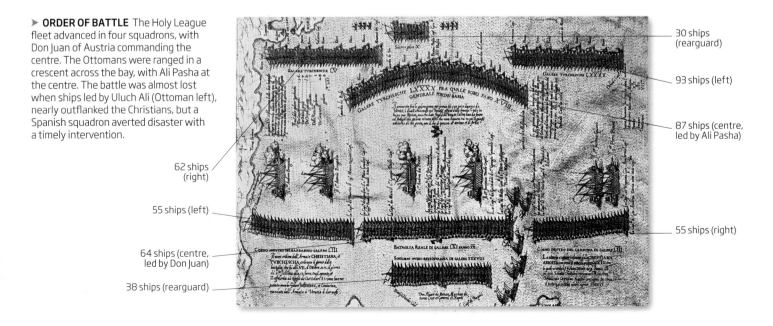

30 ships (rearguard)

93 ships (left)

87 ships (centre, led by Ali Pasha)

55 ships (right)

62 ships (right)

55 ships (left)

64 ships (centre, led by Don Juan)

38 ships (rearguard)

► **ODA-TOKUGAWA FORCES TAKE ON THE TAKEDA** This painted screen shows the way in which the Odo-Tokugawa generals used both wooden palisades and the landscape itself to break up the Takeda cavalry charges. It also shows the disciplined ranks of musketeers, who were trained to loose devastating volleys at the charging enemy.

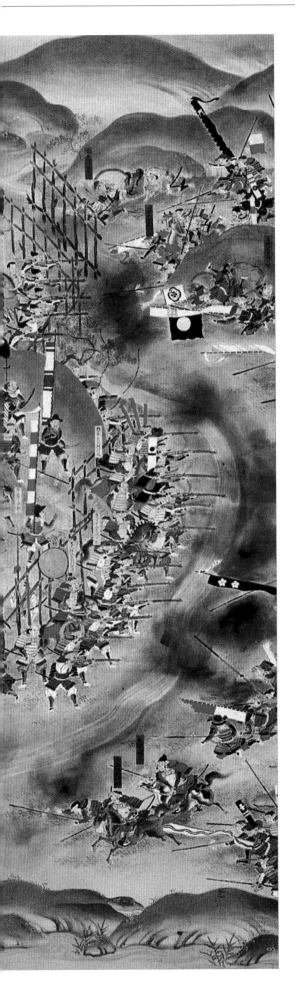

Nagashino

1575 ▪ SOUTHERN JAPAN ▪ ODA-TOKUGAWA ALLIANCE
VS. TAKEDA CLAN

SENGOKU PERIOD

At the height of Japan's Sengoku (or Warring States) Period, Takeda Katsuyori, the ruler of Japan's eastern provinces, tried to unify the country. To succeed, he had to take Kyoto, the capital, which was then controlled by Oda Nobunaga. To get there, however, he had to cross territories controlled by Tokugawa Ieyasu, an ally of Nobunaga's.

On 16 June 1575, a 15,000-strong army commanded by Takeda attacked the Tokugawa fortress of Nagashino. The attack was swiftly repulsed, and so the invaders decided to starve the defenders out. However, a messenger managed to ride from the castle for help. In response, the Tokugawa assembled an army, which joined with that of the Oda Nobunaga clan.

The combined force of 38,000 marched to Nagashino's aid. The armies met on the Shitaragahara plain, near Nagashino, on 28 June. Although outnumbered, the Takeda's strong cavalry had a fearsome reputation. To counter this, the Oda-Tokugawa built a palisade and positioned their front line behind a stream to disrupt any charges. Oda Nobunaga, an innovative tactician, had also trained his *ashigaru* (foot soldiers) in the use of matchlock muskets arrayed in three ranks, rotating their fire to allow constant reloading. As a result, successive waves of Takeda cavalry were cut down, and the invading force was routed. This use of concentrated gunfire volleys to defeat cavalry – a quarter of a century before it was first used in Europe – marked a turning point in modern warfare. It also aided Oda Nobunaga's rise to become the most powerful figure in Japan.

THE **SENGOKU PERIOD** (c.1467-c.1603)

The Sengoku Period was a period of political upheaval in Japan. Lasting from the Onin War of 1467–77 through to the end of the 16th century, it was a time in which the country was divided between numerous feudal warlords who fought constant wars for land and power. Eventually, Oda Nobunaga (1534–82) conquered many other warlords, and so began the process of unification. The process continued under Tokugawa Ieyasu (1542–1616), who defeated all opposition in 1600, and established the Tokugawa Shogunate, which ruled until the Meiji Restoration in 1868.

▶ **A portrait** of the shogun Tokugawa Ieyasu, the founder of the Tokugawa dynasty, depicted here in court dress.

Spanish Armada Campaign

1588 ▪ NORTHWESTERN EUROPE ▪ ENGLAND AND DUTCH REPUBLIC VS. UNION OF SPAIN AND PORTUGAL

ANGLO-SPANISH WAR

The root of the conflict between Spain and England in the 16th century was religious: King Philip II of Spain was a devout Catholic, and Elizabeth I of England was a Protestant. Indeed, Philip had been married to Elizabeth's half-sister, the Catholic Queen Mary I, who had died without an heir and left Philip with a claim to the throne of England. To add insult to perceived injury, the Spanish were enraged by raids on

their ships by English privateers, and by Elizabeth's military support for the Protestant rebels in the Spanish Netherlands. As head of the most powerful empire of the age, Philip was determined to bring the English monarch to heel.

In the spring of 1587, Elizabeth's spies learned that a large invasion fleet was being assembled in Spain, and so she dispatched Sir Francis Drake to make a preemptive strike. Some 30 Spanish vessels were destroyed off Cadiz, but this only delayed the inevitable. The Spanish quickly recovered, and in May 1588 Philip II sent out one of the largest fleets

▲ **THE SPANISH ARMADA IN THE STRAIT OF DOVER**
This near-contemporary painting shows the English flagship, *Ark Royal*, leading the attack on the Spanish fleet. A signal beacon burns on a headland in the background: this was part of an early-warning system that conveyed, via hilltop fires all along the southern English coast (see p.102), the news that the Spanish ships had been spotted.

ever assembled – an armada of 130 ships – on a mission to remove Elizabeth. The plan was that the Armada would sail eastwards through the English Channel to pick up a 30,000-strong army gathered on the Flemish coast, and then invade England. However, the strategy was undone by a combination of poor Spanish tactics, determined English resistance, and superior English cannons. The Spanish were forced to abandon the attack, and, while sailing home, they incurred further loses in storms off the coast of Ireland. Only around 60 ships eventually made it back to Spain.

SIR **FRANCIS DRAKE** (1540-96)

To the English, Sir Francis Drake was a hero. He was knighted by Queen Elizabeth I for his achievements, notably his circumnavigation of the globe in 1577-80. That voyage is likely to have begun as a raid on Spanish ships in the Atlantic, for Drake was foremost a privateer who made his living by plundering ships. This had the approval of his queen – so long as his targets were enemy ships. Indeed, much of Elizabeth's wealth derived from gold taken from Spanish ships in the Caribbean. Drake was vice-admiral in command of the English fleet when it engaged the Spanish Armada. At the time, King Philip II of Spain was offering 20,000 ducats (today, millions of pounds or dollars) for Drake's capture.

▲ **Born in Devon** around 1540, Drake went to sea at an early age. He remained a privateer until his death in 1596.

In detail

As the Spanish Armada advanced along the English Channel, it was twice engaged by the English fleet, first off Plymouth, then off Portland, both to little effect. Then, on 6 August 1588, the Armada anchored off Calais to await the arrival of a ground force led by the governor of the Spanish Netherlands, the Duke of Parma. At midnight on 7 August, the English sacrificed eight ships by filling them with tar, setting them on fire, and sending them towards the Spanish. Although otherwise ineffective, these fireships scattered the Armada, and the English closed in for battle. Near the small Flanders port of Gravelines, a few miles east of Calais,

the two sides engaged. The smaller and more maneuverable English ships tried to draw Spanish fire while staying out of range, then darted in quickly, firing broadsides of their own. Five Spanish ships were lost and many more were damaged. The following day, the Armada retreated north, pursued by the English fleet, which aimed to prevent the Spanish from joining up with the Duke of Parma's army.

Seeking to capitalize on the victory, Elizabeth I launched an Armada of her own the following year. Command by Sir Francis Drake, it attacked the port cities of Corunna and Lisbon, but suffered heavy losses for little gain. England and Spain finally agreed peace in 1604.

◀ **LIGHTING A BEACON** This 19th-century illustration shows the lighting of one of the warning beacons on the south coast of England, used to send the alert that the Spanish Armada has been sighted, with another beacon fire on the horizon. It is said that the news took just 12 hours to travel from the south coast to the northern city of York.

▶ **BATTLE AND ROUTE** The English fleet pursued the Armada as far north as Scotland, which the fleeing ships rounded before heading south into the North Atlantic. However, due to stormy weather and navigational errors, many ships were wrecked on the Irish coast – at the cost of more lives than were lost in combat.

▼ **ENGLISH AND SPANISH SHIPS** At 20m (100ft) in height, the British flagship *Ark Royal* (left) was one of the tallest ships of the English fleet – but it was dwarfed by the Spanish galleons (right), which rose to over 55m (180ft). However, the English vessels were faster, more maneuverable, and had guns specifically designed for use aboard ship. These guns, and the superior seamanship of the English sailors, foiled the Spanish invasion.

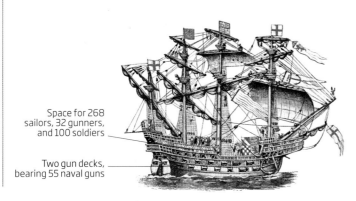

Space for 268 sailors, 32 gunners, and 100 soldiers

Two gun decks, bearing 55 naval guns

Elevated deck: Spanish galleons stood high in the water, making them vulnerable to gunfire

Three gun decks, bearing 40 conventional guns

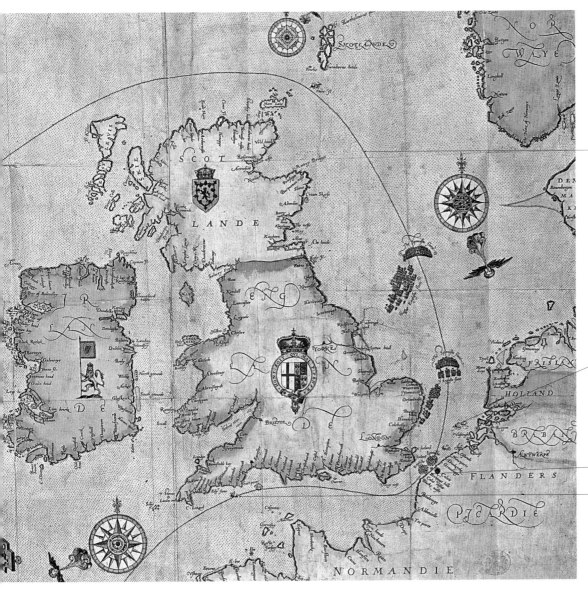

4
Mid-August:
The Armada continues north, taking the long way home, with the English in close pursuit.

3
8-9 August:
The fighting continues at Gravelines. Many Spanish ships are badly damaged, one is sunk, and several run aground. While English fleet run low on ammunition, the wind changes, forcing the depleted Spanish fleet to sail north

2
7 August:
The English fleet sends fireships against the Armada anchored at Calais. The Spanish ships scatter. Drake's ships attacks but the Spanish hold them off and regroup.

1
30 July-6 August:
The Armada sails up the English Channel in a defensive crescent formation, which is difficult for the English to disrupt.

◄ **THE ARMADA PORTRAIT** The victory over Spain cemented Elizabeth I's role as the warrior queen, as celebrated in this official Armada Portrait. Her right hand rests on Spanish territories in the New World. Despite the defeat of the Armada, the threat of invasion from the Spanish Netherlands remained. As a deterrent, 4,000 soldiers were stationed to defend the Thames Estuary. On 19 August, Elizabeth I travelled to Tilbury to address her army, arriving on horseback and in armour.

▶ **ALONSO PÉREZ DE GUZMÁN, 7TH DUKE OF MEDINA SIDONIA** King Philip II had appointed Medina Sidonia to command the Armada, despite his lack of experience, and his reputation sufered as a result. Although he was criticized at the time following the Spanish defeat, historians have noted that he performed his duties with some courage.

Hansando

1592 ■ SOUTHERN KOREA ■ KOREA VS. JAPAN

JAPANESE-KOREAN WAR

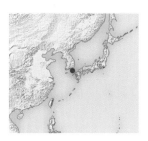

In 1592, the Japanese army invaded Korea (see box, below). However, the Korean naval fleet remained active, threatening Japanese lines of supply and reinforcement, so the Japanese warlord Wakizaka Yasuharu sailed south with 73 ships to find and destroy the Korean fleet. Korean admiral Yi Sun-Shin tracked the progress of the Japanese and located them at anchor in the Kyonnaeryang Strait.

Yi sent six ships to lure the Japanese into open water. Wakizaka gave chase, unwittingly leading his fleet into a trap: Yi had organized his 56 ships into an enveloping U-shaped formation known as a "crane's wing". As the Japanese ships advanced into this formation, they became targets for the Korean cannon to their front and on both sides. Half of the Japanese ships were large, multi-decked *atakebune* warships filled with fighting men ready to board the enemy, but the Koreans kept them at a distance with cannon fire and volleys of arrows. The Koreans deployed several turtle ships – heavily armoured warships with immense firepower and spiked roofs designed to prevent boarding (see below). The Koreans drew their formation tighter, preventing the Japanese ships from manoeuvring, and used incendiary weapons to set them alight. Some 47 Japanese ships were destroyed, 12 were captured, and only 14 escaped. Unable to secure the seaborne supply of its army, the Japanese evacuated Korea by early 1594.

THE **IMJIN WAR** (1592-98)

Japan invaded Korea twice in the late 16th century. Japanese leader Toyotomi Hideyoshi had ambitions to conquer China, and Korea was a stepping stone towards this. In 1592 he shipped a large army to Pusan, the nearest Korean port across the Tsushima Strait. His land forces made rapid progress north, capturing most of the Korean peninsula, but their seaborne supply lines were vulnerable. The Japanese fleet lacked larger gunpowder weapons, while the Koreans had the most advanced shipborne cannons in Asia, copied from China and improved.

▶ **Korean turtle ships** were highly effective in the Imjin War. They were armed with cannon and covered with spiked armour.

▼ **CONFERENCE ON THE CONQUEST OF KOREA**
This 19th-century Japanese woodblock print shows the ruler of Japan, Toyotomi Hideyoshi (centre), presiding over a war council concerning the invasion of Korea in 1592. Hideyoshi was the warrior leader who had unified war-torn Japan just two years earlier, ending the turbulent and fractured Warring States period. Buoyed by this achievement, he planned to conquer China and India.

> The remaining Japanese… rowed their boats fast and fled in all directions.

YI SUN-SHIN DESCRIBES THE END OF THE BATTLE IN HIS WAR DIARY, 1592–98

White Mountain

1620 ■ MODERN-DAY CZECH REPUBLIC ■ HOLY ROMAN EMPIRE VS. PROTESTANT UNION

THIRTY YEARS' WAR

In 1617, Ferdinand II was crowned King of Bohemia. A devout Catholic, he set about removing religious freedoms from his largely Protestant subjects. In 1618, a mob of Protestants threw two Catholic lords and their scribe out of a high window in Prague by way of protest. This Defenestration of Prague, as it became known, triggered the Bohemian Revolt – an uprising of Protestant estates against their Catholic overlords, which Ferdinand, now established as Holy Roman Emperor, set out to quash in 1620. Under the command of Johann Tserclaes, Count von Tilly, Ferdinand's Imperial army engaged the Bohemian army led by Christian of Anhalt, and pushed it all the way back to the outskirts of Prague, where the Bohemians made a stand. They settled on a low plateau known as White Mountain, which lay on the road to Prague. Here, Christian of Anhalt deployed his 23,000 troops against a 25,000-strong imperial army. Both armies employed large numbers of mercenaries.

It was winter, conditions were bitterly cold and wet, and the battle was over in just an hour. The Bohemian army was in tatters, with 4,000 men dead or wounded, but the Imperial forces suffered only around 700 casualties. Prague fell, the revolt collapsed, and Bohemia and the Czech lands were reabsorbed into the Holy Roman Empire.

In detail

▲ **IMPERIAL LEADER** Prior to White Mountain, Ferdinand was King of Bohemia and Hungary, and became Holy Roman Emperor in 1619, effectively ruling central Europe. In trying to impose religious unity on his domains, he initiated the Thirty Years' War, one of the most destructive conflicts in history, resulting in perhaps as many as 8,000,000 dead.

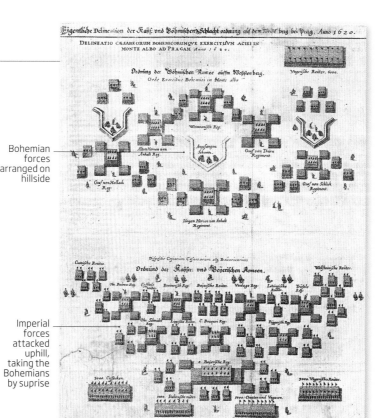

Bohemian forces arranged on hillside

Imperial forces attacked uphill, taking the Bohemians by suprise

◄ **ARMIES IN FORMATION** This map from 1662 shows the initial deployment of troops on both sides. Elevated on the hillside, the Bohemians had the better position. However, the first attack by the Imperial forces sent the Bohemian army into a retreat.

▲ **UPHILL BATTLE** This contemporary painting shows the Catholic imperial cavalry attacking the Bohemian Protestant army holding the high ground on White Mountain. Smoke hangs over the centre of the battlefield, where matchlock muskets are being fired. Both armies are deployed in classic Renaissance style: pike squares surrounded by "sleeves" of musketeers.

They could have **fought another day**, they could have **still fought for Prague.**

JAN VELINGER, "THE BATTLE OF WHITE MOUNTAIN", RADIO PRAHA

Breitenfeld

1631 ■ EASTERN GERMANY ■ SWEDISH-SAXON ARMY VS. HOLY ROMAN EMPIRE

THIRTY YEARS' WAR

The first great battle of the modern age – between the Holy Roman Empire and a Swedish-Saxon army – took place in the 13th year of the Thirty Years' War. It pitted modern tactics against old, and mobility and firepower over massed ranks. After crushing the Bohemian Revolt (see pp.106–107), the Holy Roman Emperor Ferdinand II used his Imperial army to enforce Catholic rule throughout Germany up to the Baltic coast. This alarmed King Gustavus II Adolphus of Sweden, who responded by leading his troops across the Baltic and into Germany as a self-styled "Protector of Protestantism". The rapacious behaviour of the Imperial army – particularly its

sacking and destruction of the German city of Magdeburg in spring 1631 – helped Gustavus to gain allies, and in September that year a combined Swedish-Saxon army advanced on Leipzig, which had fallen to Ferdinand's forces.

When the Swedes and Saxons reached the Lober River, which ran across the Leipzig plain, they saw the wall of pikes wielded by the 31,000 soldiers of the Imperial army, around a mile away on a brow of raised ground near the village of Breitenfeld. The combined Swedish-Saxon forces numbered around 41,000. The battle commenced, and six hours later some 27,000 Imperial soldiers were dead, wounded, or captured, against the loss of only 5,500 combined Swedish-Saxon troops. The victory was won by superior tactics, and marked the arrival of Sweden as a major European power.

▶ **BATTLE AT THE CROSSROADS** At the bottom-left of this intricate illustration from *Theatrum Europaeum* (a German history book) shows the crossroads at which Gustavus's forces clashed with Ferdinand's army. Along the flat field, ranks of soldiers stand in formation.

KING **GUSTAVUS ADOLPHUS** (1594-1632)

By the time Gustavus Adolphus became king at 16, he had already helped to lead the armies of his father, Karl IX, and inherited three ongoing wars: with Poland, Denmark, and Russia. He invested time and money on shaping the Swedish army into a well-equipped and highly disciplined force, which he led from the front and was formed from paid soldiers rather than conscripts. Well-educated and intellectually curious, he made significant reforms in administration, economics, and trade, modernizing not just Sweden's military but the state as a whole.

▲ **Gustavus Adolphus made** Sweden one of the great powers of Europe and earned himself a reputation as a master strategist.

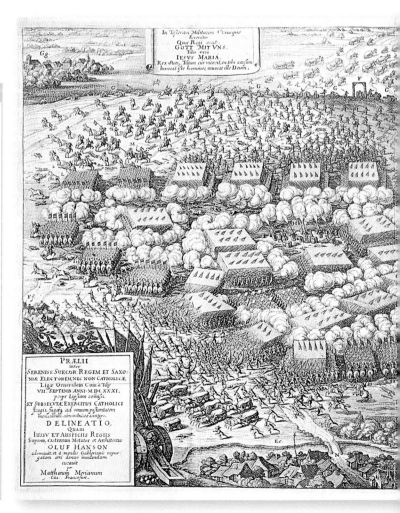

Visual tour

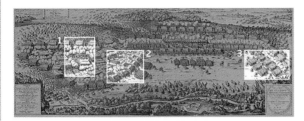

KEY

▶ **THE IMPERIAL ARTILLERY** Both sides had artillery, but the Swedes' was lighter and quicker to load and fire. The imperial artillery was so cumbersome that the Swedes and their allies could easily move out of its line of fire. Later in the battle the Swedes manoeuvred the Imperial infantry into a position where they were vulnerable to fire from their own cannon.

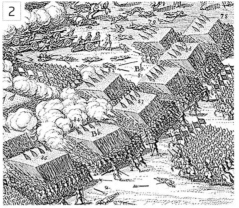

◀ **BRIGADES VS. BATTALIONS**
The Imperial forces were organized in 17 large battalions of up to 2,000 men, each a battle square of pikemen protected by small numbers of musketeers. By contrast, the Swedes were organised into smaller, more mobile units, with ranks of musketeers at the front and pikes behind. This arrangement allowed them to unleash sustained volleys that struck down the Imperial troops who could not get close enough to engage with their pikes.

▶ **THE CAVALRY ROUTED**
The Imperial cavalry attempted to outflank the Swedes and Saxons, but they were unaware of Gustavus's reserve brigades. Instead of charging into the Swedes' rear they found themselves between ranks and caught in a lethal cross-fire. The horsemen were cut down by volleys of grapeshot. The Imperial attack came apart and the survivors fled the field.

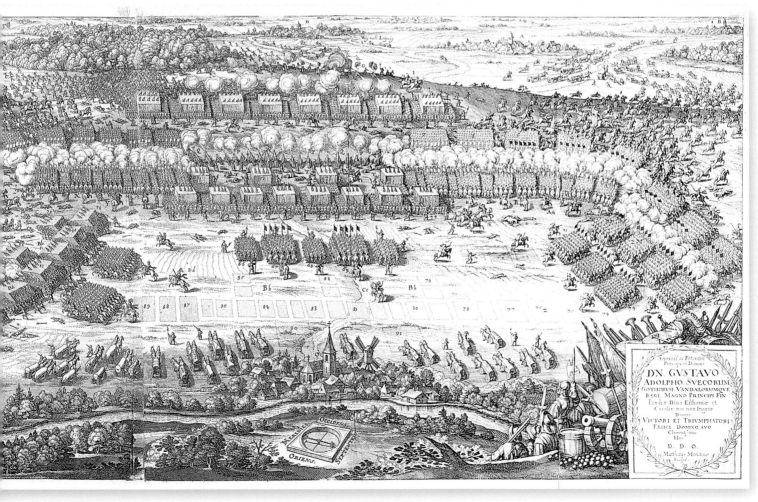

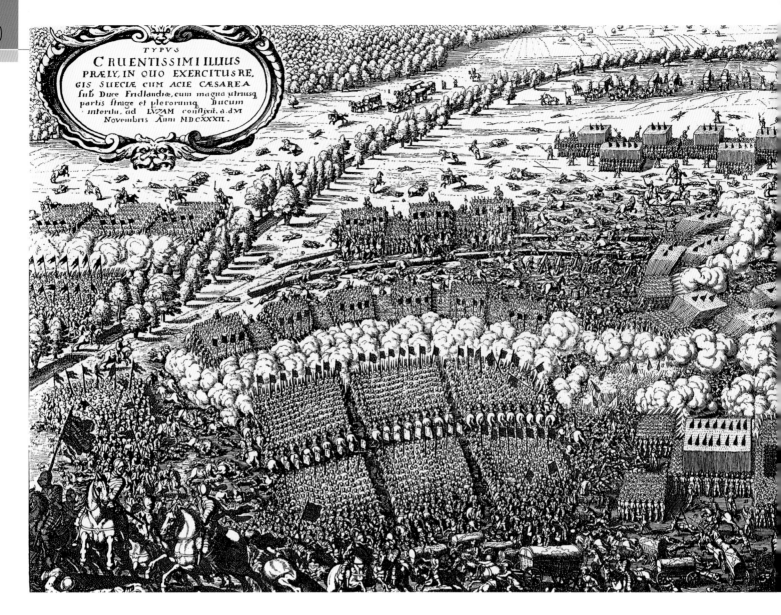

Lützen

1632 ■ EASTERN GERMANY ■ SWEDISH (PROTESTANT) ARMY VS. IMPERIAL (ROMAN CATHOLIC) ARMY

THIRTY YEARS' WAR

After victory at Breitenfeld in 1631 (see p.108), the allied forces of the Protestant Union and Sweden, led by Swedish king Gustavus Adolphus, were in the ascendancy in northern Europe. He and his allies had advanced south to Bohemia (in the present-day Czech Republic) before being pushed back by the Imperial Roman Catholic army under Albrecht von Wallenstein.

In September 1632, Wallenstein's forces invaded Saxony, threatening the Protestants' lines of communication. However, as winter approached, Wallenstein decided that the campaign season had ended and split his army, sending part of it on a

separate mission under the command of Count Pappenheim. On hearing this, Gustavus Adolphus decided to attack, hoping to gain the element of surprise. However, his advance met a small Catholic force at the Rippach stream, a few miles south of Lützen, who held them off. Alerted to the enemy's approach, Wallenstein recalled Pappenheim and his men, and they set up a defensive position along the Lützen–Leipzig road. On the morning of November 16, the Protestant army advanced towards the Catholics through heavy fog. The battle was ultimately a victory for the Protestants and ended the Catholic threat to Saxony. However, it came at a cost: Gustavus Adolphus was killed in the fighting and the Protestant cause lost one of its most able leaders.

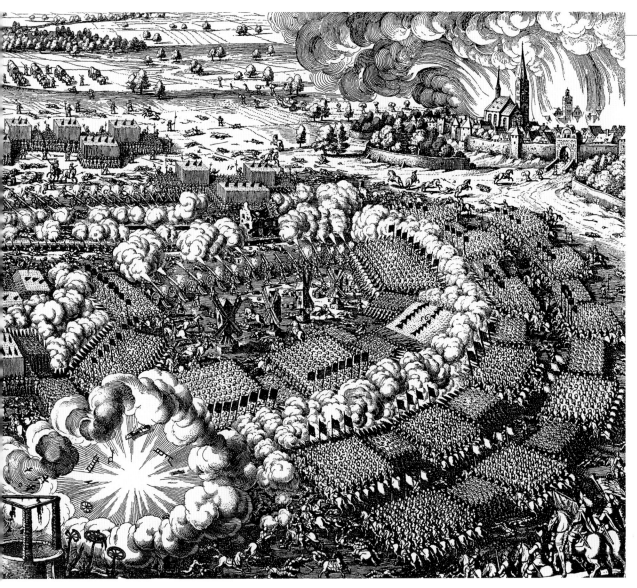

◄ **CLASH OF ARMIES**
This engraving from 1633 shows several phases of the battle at the same time; the Imperial forces are seen at the bottom. The battle began with the Protestant cavalry charging the Imperial army's left flank, while the infantry attacked at their centre and right. The Swedish infantry were initially repulsed, but on a second assault they captured the hill and all of the Catholic artillery. The situation deteriorated rapidly and Wallenstein began retreating.

In context

▲ **DEATH OF THE KING** In the early afternoon, Gustavus Adolphus led a charge into the fray, but in the confusion that followed he was separated from his men. He was shot several times, stabbed, and fell from his horse. His troops were unaware of his death until they saw his riderless horse. When his body was eventually found it was secretly evacuated from the field on an artillery wagon.

Bullet hole from the battle

Elk-hide leather

► **THE KING'S ARMOUR**
Gustavus's buff coat was stripped from his corpse and taken to Vienna as a trophy. His body was taken in procession through northern Germany to Sweden, where he was finally buried in 1634. His horse's hide was mounted on a wooden model and is now kept at Sweden's Royal Armoury.

Marston Moor

1644 ▪ NORTHERN ENGLAND ▪ PARLIAMENTARIANS VS. ROYALISTS

ENGLISH CIVIL WAR

In 1644, almost two years after the start of the civil war in England (see box, right), the struggle between King Charles I and parliament reached a decisive point. York, a Royalist stronghold in the north of England, came under siege from a combined Parliamentary and Scottish army led by Thomas Fairfax and the Earl of Leven. King Charles ordered his nephew, Prince Rupert of the Rhine, to march with his Royalist army to the relief of the city. Rupert, who had recently captured Liverpool, marched his army across the Pennines and took the Parliamentary forces by surprise, causing them to break off the siege and face the new threat.

The Royalists positioned their forces on Marston Moor, around 11 km (7 miles) from York. The Parliamentarians gathered on a ridge overlooking the moor, setting the stage for one of the largest battles ever fought on English soil. The Royalists had around 4,500 cavalry to the Parliamentarians' 7,000, and 12,000 Royalist foot soldiers were outnumbered

by 20,000 or so Parliamentary and Scottish infantry. After initial artillery exchanges, Prince Rupert's commanders persuaded him to delay his attack until the next day due to the late hour and poor weather. However, under cover of a thunderstorm that evening, the Parliamentary army mounted a surprise cavalry attack led by future English ruler Oliver Cromwell. The intense battle lasted just two hours; more than 4,000 Royalists were killed and 1,500 taken prisoner, and Prince Rupert fled south. The Parliamentarians emerged victorious, and went on to take control of both the city of York and the north of England.

THE **ENGLISH CIVIL WAR** (1642–51)

The English Civil War was fought between the Parliamentarians (known as "Roundheads" because of their cropped hair) and the Royalists (known as "Cavaliers"). The goal of the Roundheads was to institute Parliamentary rule in England, as opposed to the absolute rule of the monarchy supported by the Royalists. The war began in 1642, and although King Charles I was executed in 1649, it continued with the Royalists joining an alliance of convenience with the Scots, until their final defeat at Worcester on 3 September 1651. The monarchy was abolished and replaced with the Commonwealth of England ruled by Oliver Cromwell.

▲ **This illustration** from a 17th-century military handbook depicts a Cavalier (left) and a Roundhead (right).

◀ **TURNING THE TIDE** This 19th-century painting depicts the close combat between cavalry and infantry during the battle. The superior Parliamentarian numbers and bold tactics helped overcome the Royalists, leading to the first major victory of the war in favour of the rebels. The Parliamentarians claimed their forces suffered only around 300 casualties from the fighting, although the real number is likely to be higher.

▼ **THE BATTLEFIELD AT MARSTON MOOR** Royalist forces from York were late to the battlefield, and were still deploying in the early evening when the Earl of Leven ordered a surprise Parliamentarian attack: cavalry led by Oliver Cromwell attacked the Royalist's right flank. On their left wing, the Royalist cavalry held back a second Parliamentary cavalry charge and then charged at the Scottish infantry. Cromwell responded by turning to attack Goring's Royalist cavalry to their rear, and the Parliamentary infantry crushed the Royalist centre.

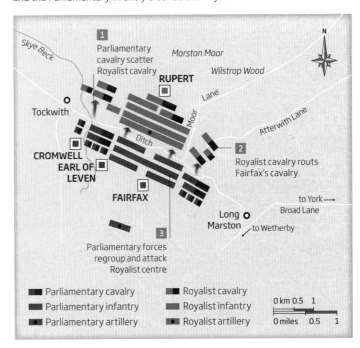

1 Parliamentary cavalry scatter Royalist cavalry

2 Royalist cavalry routs Fairfax's cavalry

3 Parliamentary forces regroup and attack Royalist centre

Skye Beck · Marston Moor · Wilstrop Wood · RUPERT · Moor Lane · Tockwith · Atterwith Lane · Ditch · CROMWELL · EARL OF LEVEN · FAIRFAX · to York → · Broad Lane · Long Marston · to Wetherby

■ Parliamentary cavalry
■ Parliamentary infantry
■ Parliamentary artillery
■ Royalist cavalry
■ Royalist infantry
■ Royalist artillery

0 km 0.5   1
0 miles   0.5   1

▲ **PARLIAMENTARIANS' TRIUMPH** Oliver Cromwell leads his New Model Army into battle at Naseby, as depicted in this hand-coloured copper engraving. When Prince Rupert's cavalry left the battlefield, Cromwell's army made a disciplined charge, first against the remaining Royalist cavalry and then their infantry, all but destroying both. Within a year of the Battle of Naseby, King Charles I surrendered to the Scots, who later handed him over to the Parliamentarians.

Naseby

1645 ▪ CENTRAL ENGLAND ▪ PARLIAMENTARIANS VS. ROYALISTS

ENGLISH CIVIL WAR

This battle was a turning point in England's civil war between the Royalists under King Charles I and the Parliamentarians led by Oliver Cromwell (see p.113). Despite winning several battles in 1644–45, the Parliamentary forces had yet to achieve the decisive victory that would settle the conflict. To strengthen their cause, in January 1645 Parliament founded the New Model Army – a red-uniformed, professional, full-time force that was capable of being deployed anywhere in England, Scotland, or Ireland.

In May 1645, the Royalists captured the city of Leicester in central England, and Thomas Fairfax and Oliver Cromwell led the New Model Army to meet them. The two sides met south of the city near Naseby on 14 June. The Royalists, led by King Charles but commanded by his nephew Prince Rupert of the Rhine, took the high ground on one side of a valley. When the Parliamentarians moved to take the higher, less boggy ground, the Royalist cavalry charged. Their initial attack was successful, but when the Royalists continued in pursuit of fleeing Parliamentarians, Cromwell unleashed his cavalry. By the time Prince Rupert's cavalry returned to the field, it was too late. The Royalists forces had been routed and King Charles had fled. In the aftermath, Cromwell retook Leicester and the Royalist strongholds in the south and west.

Prince Rupert, commanding the Royalist cavalry

Thomas Fairfax leading the Parliamentarian infantry

King Charles I with the Royalist forces

Oliver Cromwell, who attacks the Royalist cavalry from the right

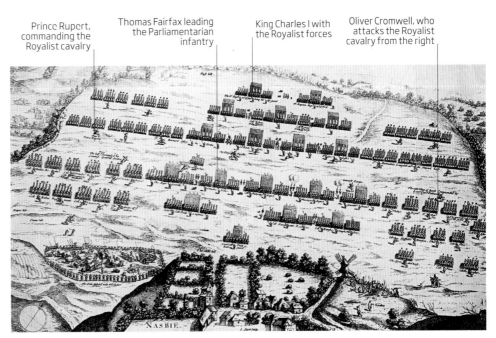

▲ **THE BATTLE PLAN** This 17th-century engraving by Robert Streeter depicts the two armies lined up along the valley, each with their infantry in the centre and cavalry at both flanks. The land between the forces was waterlogged, so Cromwell advised Fairfax to move to higher ground. As he did so, Prince Rupert's cavalry on the right flank attacked and broke through the cavalry on the Parliamentary left, then took off after them.

Raid on the Medway

1667 ■ SOUTHEASTERN ENGLAND ■ DUTCH REPUBLIC VS. ENGLAND

SECOND ANGLO-DUTCH WAR

In the second half of the 17th century, the English and Dutch were engaged in a battle for naval supremacy to control the riches of newly discovered territories in the Americas and southeast Asia; however, most battles were fought in the North Sea and the English Channel. The two fleets had previously clashed during the First Anglo-Dutch War (1652-54) and hostilities resumed in 1665 with the Second Anglo-Dutch War (1665-67). Several Dutch victories weakened the English fleet and depleted the country's finances. The English king, Charles II, began peace talks in May 1667, but Dutch leader Johan de Witt decided to inflict a final humiliating defeat on the English to end the war swiftly and gain the upper hand in the negotiations.

In June, he ordered a raid on the English fleet, which was laid up in dock. Led by his brother Cornelis de Witt and the skilled admiral Michiel de Ruyter, around 80 Dutch ships sailed up the Thames Estuary and captured the fort at Sheerness on the southeast coast of England. The ships proceeded up the Medway river to Upnor, where they breached the defensive chain of sunken "blockships", and destroyed an unprepared English fleet. The raid was a huge success and one of the worst defeats the Royal Navy ever suffered. The Dutch sank 15 English ships of the fleet, and captured a prize vessel, the *Royal Charles*, and a frigate, *Unity*, which they towed back to Holland. The two nations made peace, with the Dutch taking the upper hand. However, the English secured consolation territories in Africa and North America – including a small settlement known as New Amsterdam, but later named New York.

LIEUTENANT-ADMIRAL **MICHIEL DE RUYTER** (1607-76)

Born in the Dutch coastal town of Vlissingen, de Ruyter first went to sea as a young boy, and became one of the greatest admirals in Dutch history. He swiftly rose up the ranks to be named merchant captain in 1635, and later served as part of the Dutch fleet fighting the Spanish in 1641. De Ruyter is best known for his role in the Anglo-Dutch Wars, in which he won many major victories, serving as vice admiral and later as lieutenant-admiral. His successes during the Third Anglo-Dutch War saved the Dutch Republic from invasion. He died in 1676 after being wounded in battle against the French outside Sicily.

▶ **Michiel de Ruyter** was admired for his military prowess; the admiral was also loved by his sailors, who affectionately named him *Bestevaêr* ("Grandad").

▼ **THE DUTCH NAVY TAKES THE MEDWAY** The Raid on the Medway was a successful attack by the Dutch Navy on English battleships at a time when most of the latter were laid up, virtually unmanned and unarmed, in the fleet anchorages off Chatham Dockyard and Gillingham in Kent. This painting by Dutch artist Jan van Leyden shows two English battleships ablaze, and the captured *Royal Charles* (centre) flying Dutch flags.

> A dreadful spectacle as ever Englishman saw and a dishonour never to be wiped off.

JOHN EVELYN, AN EYEWITNESS TO THE DUTCH RAID, IN HIS DIARY, 1667

Siege of Vienna

1683 ▪ EASTERN EUROPE ▪ CATHOLIC ALLIANCE ARMIES VS. OTTOMANS

OTTOMAN-HABSBURG WARS

The Ottomans had first laid siege to Vienna in 1529 under Suleiman the Magnificent, but the defenders fought them off, bringing an end to a century of Ottoman expansion. In the aftermath, Vienna strengthened its fortifications.

By the late 17th century, the Habsburg-Ottoman borderlands in Hungary had enjoyed prolonged peace with the Ottomans under the terms of the 1664 Treaty of Vasvár. Ottoman rule extended west as far as Hungary, and the mainly Protestant Hungarians preferred the religious freedom they had under the Ottomans to the oppressive rule of their Roman Catholic Hapsburg neighbours. The Habsburgs broke the treaty in 1682 by advancing into Hungary, so the Hungarians turned to Constantinople for help. The Ottoman Grand Vizier, Kara Mustafa Pasha, advanced towards Hungary at the head of an army of more than 100,000, bolstered by Hungarian and Crimean Tatar soldiers.

Kara Mustafa arrived at the Habsburg capital of Vienna on 14 July 1683 and laid siege. Kara Mustafa sent the traditional demand for surrender, but the military governor, Ernst Rüdiger Graf von Starhemberg, refused. Meanwhile, the Holy Roman Emperor Leopold I, who had fled Vienna, desperately petitioned the French, then the Germans and the Poles, to come to the aid of his city.

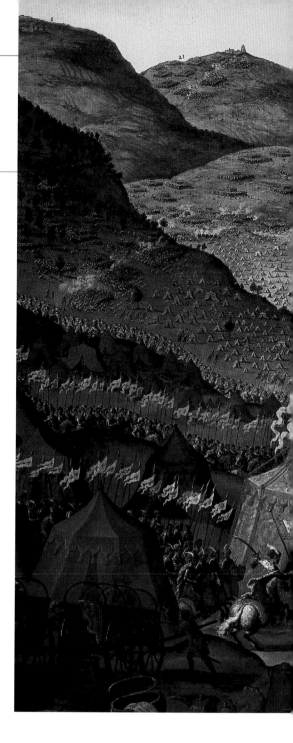

➤ **BATTLE OF KAHLENBERG** At the start of the second Siege of Vienna there had been some 15,000 defenders in the city. This 17th-century painting by Frans Geffels depicts the scene at the beginning of the battle that saved the city. The Christian relief armies are gathered on the hills; the vast Ottoman forces dominate the foreground.

Visual tour

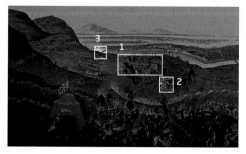

KEY

➤ **WELL-DEFENDED CITY** Anticipating an Ottoman attack, the Viennese blocked the city gates, reinforced the walls, erected bastions that served as firing positions for the defending troops, and raised an inner rampart. They levelled the buildings around the city, leaving an empty plain that would expose attackers to defensive fire.

1

◀ **OTTOMAN TACTICS** To protect themselves from defensive fire, the Ottomans dug long lines of trenches toward the city, left. They also built tunnels under the walls and filled them with large quantities of gunpowder, which they detonated to break down the fortifications. By early September, parts of the walls were destroyed and the Ottoman army nearly entered the centre of the city on 8 September.

▶ **ARRIVAL OF RELIEF FORCES** By the time the Ottomans entered Vienna, only a third of the defending garrison could still fight and its munitions were nearly exhausted. The city's only hope was the long-awaited Christian relief armies, seen here crossing the river Danube. They gathered on the hills overlooking the city and the battle began on 12 September.

In detail

In response to Emperor Leopold I's plea for help (see p.118), Pope Innocent XI helped fund a Catholic alliance. The Dukes of Bavaria and Saxony sent troops, as did Portugal, Spain, Venice, and King Jan III Sobieski of Poland. Together, this host of more than 70,000 troops marched towards Vienna. The city was on the verge of falling to the Ottomans when the armies crossed the River Danube. They mustered on the Kahlenberg hill overlooking Vienna and used bonfires to signal their arrival to the besieged city.

The battle began early on the morning of 12 September. The Ottomans attacked first in an attempt to disrupt the placement of the alliance's cannon. The Catholic forces countered, advancing, according to one Turkish chronicler, "as if an all-consuming flood of black pitch was flowing down the hills". The well-disciplined Imperial forces quickly took several key positions and by midday, after only eight hours of fighting, the Ottoman army had suffered significant losses. In the early afternoon, the Polish infantry advanced on a new front, squeezing the Ottoman army between Polish and Imperial forces. This set up the battle for the decisive blow – a massed charge by 18,000 predominantly Polish cavalry led by King Jan III Sobieski. This was largest such charge in history. It destroyed the Ottomans' lines, and they fled the battlefield. After only 15 hours of battle, Vienna was liberated.

▶ **FATE OF THE OTTOMAN LEADER**
The Grand Vizier Kara Mustafa Pasha, depicted here in a 17th-century portrait, oversaw the two-month-long siege of Vienna. His failure to capture it cost him his life. On 25 December 1683, on the orders of Sultan Mehmet IV, the Janissary corps executed Kara Mustafa Pasha by strangulation with a silk cord, while he was staying in the palace at Belgrade.

▼ **LIBERATION OF VIENNA** This contemporary painting depicts the famous charge of lancers led by King Jan III Sobieski. Less than three hours later, the Imperial forces had won the battle and Vienna was saved. The Ottomans fled leaving all their possessions, which were later looted by the Polish army. The king wrote to his wife saying: "Ours are treasures unheard of... tents, sheep, cattle and no small number of camels... it is victory as nobody ever knew before".

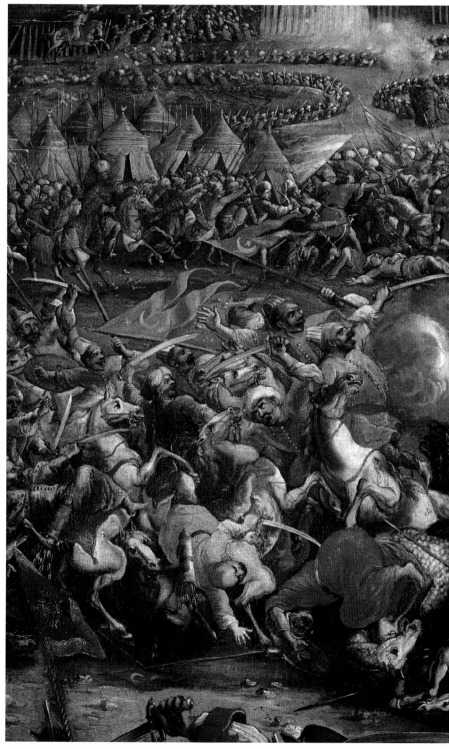

➤ **WINGED HUSSARS' ARMOUR** The lancers of this Polish elite mounted military unit, known as the Hussars, had distinctive wings, attached to their heavy armour. They charged at full gallop in a knee-to-knee formation, carrying 4.5–6 m (15–20 ft) lances. The sight terrified the enemy's horses and shook the confidence of adversaries on the battlefield.

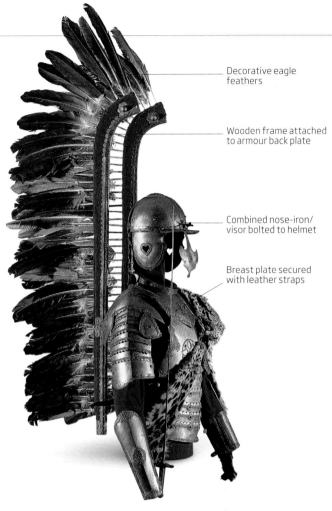

Decorative eagle feathers

Wooden frame attached to armour back plate

Combined nose-iron/ visor bolted to helmet

Breast plate secured with leather straps

KING **JAN III SOBIESKI** (1629–96)

Born in Ukraine, Jan III Sobieski was king of Poland and Lithuania from 1674 until his death. As the highest ranking of all the military leaders who assembled to come to the rescue of Vienna, Sobieski took command of the entire relief force of about 70,000 men. It was the cavalry charge he led that finally broke the Ottoman Turks, so he was hailed as the saviour of not just Vienna, but of all Christendom. However, he offended his allies by leading a victory march into the city before the Holy Roman Emperor Leopold I arrived, and allowing his soldiers to loot the Ottomans' encampment.

▲ **The conquering king** Jan Sobieski was hailed throughout Poland. This statue by Tadeusz Barącz is in the city of Gdańsk.

Directory: 1500–1700

King Francis I's tomb at the Basilica of St Denis bears carvings depicting his victory at Marignano.

▲ MARIGNANO
WAR OF THE LEAGUE OF CAMBRAI

1515 ▪ NORTHERN ITALY ▪ KINGDOM OF FRANCE VS. OLD SWISS CONFEDERACY

In 1515, a French army led by 21-year-old King Francis I fought the Swiss at Marignano, southeast of Milan, during the Italian Wars (1494-1559), a series of battles between the European powers for control of Italian city-states including Milan. On 13-14 September, Francis's 38,000 armoured lancers, infantry, and German *landsknecht* mercenaries fought 22,000 Swiss pikemen and halberdiers (armed with a halberd, a pike with an axe-head). Over two days the elite Swiss soldiers charged the French artillery, aiming to seize the guns. The French struggled to defend themselves, and only gained an advantage on the second day with the arrival of Venetian allies. The battle ended in a decisive victory for the French, who then captured Milan.

CAJAMARCA
SPANISH CONQUEST OF PERU

1532 ▪ PERU ▪ SPAIN VS. INCA EMPIRE

At Cajamarca, on 15 November 1532, a force of 128 Spaniards destroyed an army of 80,000 Incas without a single loss of Spanish life. Led by the explorer Francisco Pizarro, the conquistadors had ventured deep into the Inca king Atahuallpa's lands and requested to meet him in the walled city of Cajamarca. The king left his army outside the city and entered the main square with an unarmed retinue of 7,000 men. Meanwhile, the Spanish, armed with hand-weapons and firearms, hid themselves around the square. A small number met with the king. Following Pizarro's instructions, they demanded that the Incas become Catholic and accept Charles V, the Holy Roman Emperor, as their ruler. When Atahuallpa refused, the Spanish opened fire. The stunned Incas, who had never encountered guns, were killed in their thousands; those who survived fled in panic, as did the Incan army outside the city. King Atahuallpa was captured and later executed. This marked the start of the conquest of Peru.

ALCACER QUIBIR
MOROCCAN-PORTUGUESE CONFLICTS

1578 ▪ NORTHERN MOROCCO ▪ KINGDOM OF PORTUGAL VS. SULTANATE OF MOROCCO

The presence of the Ottomans in Morocco was seen by the Portuguese as a potential threat, leading to clashes between Christian Portugal and Muslim Morocco. In 1576, the Portuguese king, Sebastian, allied with the deposed Moroccan sultan Abu Abdallah, who was engaged in a civil war to recover the throne from his uncle, Abd al-Malik. In 1578, Sebastian led an 18,000-strong army to Morocco, where Abu Abdallah joined him with an additional 6,000. Abd al-Malik had rallied his countrymen against the invaders, raising a force of 50,000. The armies met near the town of Alcacer Quibir. Although less well-equipped, Abd al-Malik's army had superior numbers, which it used to encircle the Portuguese soldiers. After four hours of heavy fighting the Portuguese army was defeated. Sebastian, Abu Abdallah, and Abd al-Malik were all killed during the fighting; their deaths gave this battle its nickname – the Battle of the Three Kings.

IVRY
FRENCH WAR OF RELIGION (1562-98) AND ANGLO-SPANISH WAR

1590 ▪ NORTHERN FRANCE ▪ KINGDOM OF FRANCE VS. CATHOLIC LEAGUE

Henry of Navarre, a Protestant, became King Henry IV of France in 1589, but due to his religion he had little support. He faced a strong challenge from the army of the Catholic League, which was supported by Philip II of Spain. Henry gained support from Elizabeth I of England, who provided funding and reinforcements. Henry's army met the League near Ivry. The battle opened with an exchange of artillery fire before a mass cavalry charge. The armies were evenly matched in number, but Henry's army charged close to the enemy and fired pistols before attacking with swords, a tactic that proved more effective than the Catholic League's use of lances. Once the League's cavalry had been overpowered, Henry's army defeated their infantry. Although the League was destroyed at Ivry, Henry still had to convert to Catholicism in 1593 before he could enter Paris in 1594 and consolidate control of the country.

SACHEON
JAPANESE INVASION OF KOREA

1598 ▪ MODERN-DAY SOUTH KOREA ▪ JAPAN VS. KOREAN AND CHINESE FORCES

Japan invaded Korea twice in the 1590s intending to conquer the Korean peninsula, but were forced to withdraw both times. During the autumn of their second invasion (1598) the Japanese leader Toyotomi Hideyoshi died, and when the Chinese entered the war in support of Korea, the Japanese retreated. To hinder their withdrawal, the Koreans and Chinese launched attacks on the Japanese coastal fortresses, which were protecting the evacuation. The castle fortress of Sacheon was of key importance to the Japanese as it formed a vital link in their communications. In October, a Chinese army of 36,000 arrived to lay siege, using battering rams and cannon against the fortress gate; inside, the defenders used catapults to hurl firebombs at their enemy. In a daring move, the Japanese commander, Shimazu Yoshihiro, led his army out to fight the Chinese and defeated them, ending the siege.

SEKIGAHARA
SENGOKU PERIOD

1600 ▪ CENTRAL JAPAN ▪ EASTERN JAPAN VS. WESTERN JAPAN

The Battle of Sekigahara changed the course of Japanese history. The death of leader Toyotomi Hideyoshi, who had waged war on Korea and China, left Japan under the rule of his five-year-old son. To fill the power vacuum, two main rival factions emerged: a western coalition of generals led by Ishida Mitsunari; and leading military figure Tokugawa Ieyasu, who controlled much of eastern Japan. Their battle took place in the small mountain valley of Sekigahara, central Japan. Ishida arranged his forces at the western end, with additional forces commanded by general Kobayakawa Hideaki on the northern slopes ready to attack the enemy flank. However, at a crucial moment, Kobayakawa turned against his leader and commanded his troops to attack Ishida's army. This defection decided the battle for Tokugawa who became master of Japan, founding the last shogunate (military dictatorship) that ruled for the next 268 years.

ROCROI
THIRTY YEARS' WAR AND FRANCO-SPANISH WAR

1643 ■ NORTHEASTERN FRANCE ■ KINGDOM OF FRANCE VS. KINGDOM OF SPAIN AND THE HABSBURG EMPIRE

Although the Thirty Years' War had originated in Bohemia as a Catholic-Protestant conflict, it spread into Europe as a general battle for power between countries. By 1635, France had declared war on Spain and the Habsburg Empire. In 1643, the Spanish army advanced through the Ardennes into northern France where it met French forces outside the fortress town of Rocroi. On 19 May, the battle began with a failed French cavalry charge followed by a successful Spanish counter-attack. The French cavalry then swept around behind the Spanish, dispersing their cavalry and leaving their pikemen and infantry badly exposed. After two hours of fighting the Spanish surrendered. France's victory was a major factor in forcing the Habsburgs to make concessions that in 1648 led to the Peace of Westphalia, a series of treaties that would end the Thirty Years' War and conclude the European Wars of Religions.

YANGZHOU
MASSACRE DURING THE QING DYNASTY

1645 ■ EASTERN CHINA ■ QING VS. MING

The events at Yangzhou took place as the newly enthroned Qing dynasty in Beijing sought to establish its control over all China. Officials still loyal to the deposed Ming had set up an rival administration in China's old capital city of Nanjing. In retaliation for this act of defiance, the Qing sent an army led by the military general Prince Dodo. The route to Nanjing took the army via Yangzhou, a city also loyal to the Ming. Prince Dodo's Qing army laid siege, but the city was well defended with cannon mounted on the city walls. The Qing suffered heavy casualties until, after a number of days, they finally managed to breach the walls and take the city. In revenge for the losses inflicted on his army, Prince Dodo executed the general who had overseen the defence of the city. He then ordered his own men to carry out a mass slaughter of the inhabitants of Yangzhou. Virtually the entire population of the city was wiped out in a bloody massacre that lasted for 10 days. After learning of the fearful punishment that had been inflicted on the people of Yangzhou, Nanjing surrendered without a fight.

SOLEBAY
THIRD ANGLO-DUTCH WAR

1672 ■ SOUTHEAST ENGLAND ■ ENGLISH AND FRENCH NAVIES VS. DUTCH NAVY

The Third Anglo-Dutch War, part of the naval conflicts between England and the Dutch Republic, opened with a surprise attack on an Anglo-French fleet. On 28 May, a frigate sailed into Solebay (now Southwold Bay), having sighted the Dutch fleet two hours away. The Anglo-French fleet was at Solebay to refit and in danger of being caught unprepared, just as the English fleet had during the Dutch Raid on the Medway (see pp.116–17). The English fleet of around 71 ships, commanded by the Duke of York and the Earl of Sandwich, was hastily put to sea, while the French fleet diverted to fight from a distance. The Dutch arrived with 61 warships and engaged in battle with the English fleet about 16 km (10 miles) off the coast. The Duke of York had to transfer ships twice as his flagships were taken out of action, and Sandwich was killed. Both navies lost two ships each and the battle ended inconclusively, the Dutch and the English each claiming victory. The Third Anglo-Dutch War would end in 1674, by which stage England had established its naval supremacy.

THE BOYNE
WILLIAMITE WAR

1690 ■ NORTHEASTERN IRELAND ■ WILLIAMITE FORCES VS. JACOBITE FORCES

Despite having taken place in Ireland, this battle was fought between two English kings – one Catholic, and one Protestant. The Catholic ruler, James II, had been deposed by his Protestant son-in-law, William of Orange. James fled to France and then Ireland where he sought to regain the crown, and his army soon controlled the entire island except for two Protestant strongholds in the north. In June 1690, William landed in Ireland to confront James. The two opposing armies met at the River Boyne, north of Dublin. James's army of untrained peasants, reinforced by 6,000 French troops, was poorly equipped. William's army comprised professional soldiers from Holland, Denmark, and England, and exiled French Huguenots (Protestants). The Williamite army overpowered the Jacobites and James fled to France, ending the threat of a Catholic resurgence in England.

▼ ZENTA
GREAT TURKISH WAR AND OTTOMAN-HABSBURG WARS

1697 ■ MODERN-DAY SERBIA ■ HABSBURG EMPIRE VS. OTTOMAN EMPIRE

After defending Vienna in 1683 (see pp.118–21), Habsburg Austria won several victories over the Ottomans, only to suffer several defeats by the mid-1690s. In 1697, the Ottoman Sultan Mustafa II and his army arrived at Belgrade, and Prince Eugene of Savoy, commander-in-chief of the Habsburg army, engaged them in battle. Eugene's army advanced on the Ottomans as they crossed the Tisa River near Zenta. Taken by surprise, the Ottoman army were put in disarray by an artillery bombardment. The Habsburg cavalry charged, forcing the Ottomans to retreat towards the bridge where the Habsburg infantry intercepted them, cutting off their escape. The battle was a decisive Habsburg victory: thousands of Ottomans were killed and much of their treasure was seized. The victory ultimately led to the 1699 Treaty of Karlowitz, which signalled the end of Ottoman dominance in Europe.

The Holy League defeated the Ottoman Empire at the Battle of Zenta, depicted in this contemporary painting of the battlefield.

1700—1900

CHAPTER 4

Blenheim

1704 ▪ BAVARIA ▪ GRAND ALLIANCE VS. FRANCO-BAVARIAN ARMY

WAR OF THE SPANISH SUCCESSION

In 1701, Britain, Austria, and the Dutch Republic formed a Grand Alliance to counter the expansionist policies of French king Louis XIV. In 1704, fearing a French attack on Vienna, the Duke of Marlborough led a British army into Bavaria, where he joined up with an Austrian army led by Prince Eugene of Savoy. French and Bavarian forces under the Duc de Tallard , meanwhile, were encamped by the Danube – and with superior numbers (60,000 to Marlborough's 52,000) did not expect to be attacked.

On 13 August Tallard was astonished to see massed Allied troops advancing towards him across the plain. The two armies joined in fierce battle on the flanks, with Prince Eugene engaging the mostly Bavarian units on the Allied right, and the British attacking Blenheim village on the left. Repeated infantry assaults on the village failed, but as French reserves were drawn into the struggle, the French centre weakened. Marlborough threw his forces into a major attack to the west at Oberglau, where the French were routed. Seeing the battle lost, the Bavarians fled the field. The French continued to defend Blenheim, but surrendered in the evening. Franco-Bavarian casualties were around 30,000, including many who drowned fleeing across the Danube. French military supremacy was shaken, ultimately leading to Louis' defeat.

▼ **BLENHEIM, 1704** This plan shows the position of the two armies at the start of the battle (boxes with a diagonal slash indicate cavalry). The Franco-Bavarian army was drawn up in a strong defensive position behind the marshy River Nebel, the River Danube anchoring its right flank. While Prince Eugene engaged the Bavarians to his right, Marlborough's troops crossed the Nebel, broke through the French line at Oberglau, and finally captured Blenheim.

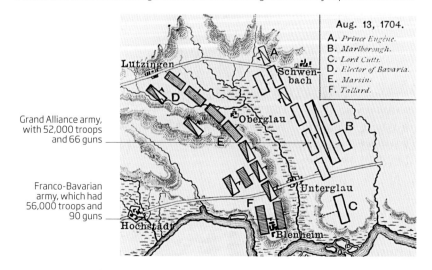

Aug. 13, 1704.

A. *Prince Eugène.*
B. *Marlborough.*
C. *Lord Cutts.*
D. *Elector of Bavaria.*
E. *Marsin.*
F. *Tallard.*

Grand Alliance army, with 52,000 troops and 66 guns

Franco-Bavarian army, which had 56,000 troops and 90 guns

▲ **SCENES FROM THE BATTLE** Three panels painted by contemporary artist Louis Laguerre show (from left to right): the Grand Alliance army attacking across the Nebel at the start of the battle, including grenadiers in their mitre caps; the fleeing French floundering in the River Danube at the battle's end; and Prince Eugene commanding the Allied army amid the carnage on the right wing.

Give my duty to the Queen, and let her know
her army has had a glorious victory.

THE DUKE OF MARLBOROUGH, DESCRIBING THE BATTLE IN A LETTER TO HIS WIFE, 13 AUGUST 1704

… study Charles XII… to be cured of the madness of the conquering.

VOLTAIRE DESCRIBES THE AMBITION OF THE SWEDISH KING IN *HISTORY OF CHARLES XII*

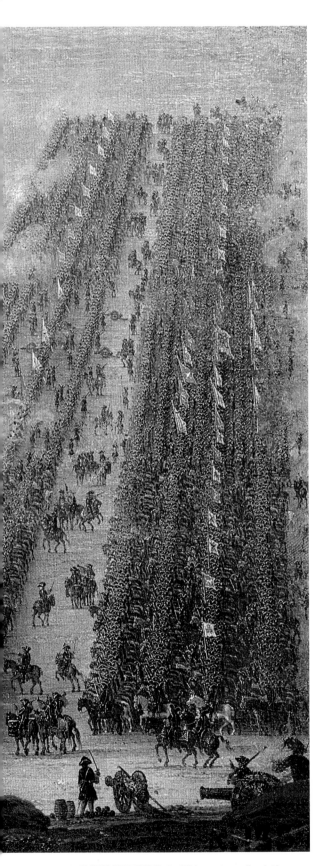

▲ **CLASH OF ARMIES** An 18th-century oil painting depicts the Russian and Swedish armies at Poltava. The cannon and musketry created clouds of gunpowder smoke that obscured the battlefield, making it difficult for commanders to observe the course of the battle. The Russians outnumbered the Swedish, fielding around 50,000 troops against 25,000. The defeated Swedes suffered some 10,000 casualties.

Poltava

1709 ▪ CENTRAL UKRAINE ▪ RUSSIA VS. SWEDEN

GREAT NORTHERN WAR

At the start of the 18th century, the Swedish empire was the dominant power in the Baltic; however, within a few years Tsar Peter the Great of Russia began to present a threat. The ambitious Swedish King Charles XII won initial victories against Russia, but spurned the chance to negotiate peace on favourable terms.

In summer 1707 Charles invaded Ukraine, but failed to achieve a decisive victory, despite support from Ukrainian Cossacks. Pursued by Peter's army, the Swedish troops suffered from a lack of supplies and harsh weather. By the summer of 1709 Charles's position was desperate. Laying siege to the fortress of Poltava on the Vorskla River, he was wounded in the foot by a stray shot and had to hand over command to Marshal Carl Gustav Rehnskiöld. Peter dug in his army nearby, building redoubts to protect the approaches to his camp. On 8 July the outnumbered Swedes gambled on an attack. They took casualties even before the main battle began by making unsuccessful attacks on the Russian redoubts. An initial onslaught by Swedish forces drove back the Russian centre, but the advancing troops were enveloped on the flanks, and a final Russian cavalry charge completed a general rout. The remainder of the Swedish army surrendered three days later. Charles XII escaped south to the Ottoman Empire, where he was imprisoned for five years, while Tsar Peter celebrated Russia's political rise.

THE **MODERNIZATION OF RUSSIA**

As tsar from 1682 to 1725, Peter the Great transformed Russia from a backward state on the margin of Europe into a major military power. Using foreign technical expertise, he modernized his armed force, introducing Western-style uniforms and the latest military equipment, such as flintlock muskets and siege artillery. He replaced the *streltsy*, Russia's traditional military elite, with guards regiments loyal to himself. Building a modern fleet and creating St Petersburg as a new capital in place of Moscow, he shifted the focus of Russian power to the Baltic.

▲ **Peter the Great had** St Petersburg built from scratch on Baltic marshland from 1703, to serve as a port and capital city for his modernized empire.

Plassey

1757 ▪ BENGAL ▪ BRITISH EAST INDIA COMPANY VS. PRINCIPALITY OF BENGAL, FRANCE

SEVEN YEARS' WAR

In the mid-18th century, the British and French East India Companies competed for influence and trading rights along India's coasts. In 1756, a new nawab (ruler) in Bengal, Siraj ud-Daulah, turned against the British, occupying their trading post at Calcutta. In response, Britain's East India Company sent 31-year-old Colonel Robert Clive from Madras to Bengal with a force of British infantry and Indian sepoys. Clive reoccupied Calcutta and began plotting the overthrow of the nawab. In secret deals, he bought the support of leading Bengalis, most notably the ambitious Mir Jafar, a senior figure in the nawab's army.

In June 1757, Clive advanced toward the Bengali capital, Murshidabad, at the head of a 3,000-strong force, three-quarters of them sepoys. At Plassey (Palashi) on the Hooghli River he was confronted by Siraj ud-Daulah and an army of 50,000. The British were outnumbered and outgunned, as the French had sent a force of artillerymen to boost the nawab's resistance. Nonetheless, on 23 June, Clive gave battle. The outcome hung in the balance until it began to rain heavily: the British covered their gunpowder to keep it dry, but the Bengalis did not, rendering their weapons inoperative. Charging Bengali cavalry were slaughtered by British cannon and musket fire. Mir Jafar, commanding a third of the nawab's forces, stood on the sidelines as the Bengali army disintegrated. The victory set the British on the path to control of Bengal, and eventually of all India, at the expense of French influence there.

In context

▼ **THE BLACK HOLE MASSACRE** When Calcutta was seized by Bengali forces in June 1756, British personnel were locked overnight in a dungeon in Fort William. Packed together in hot, airless conditions, only 23 out of 146 survived until the dawn according to a British witness. The atrocity was used to justify British military intervention in Bengal.

▲ **FLEEING THE FIELD** At the height of the battle, Bengali nawab Siraj ud-Daulah panicked and fled the field on a camel. His flight caused the final demoralization of his forces. Ten days after the defeat, Siraj was executed on the orders of Mir Miran, son of the new nawab, Mir Jafar.

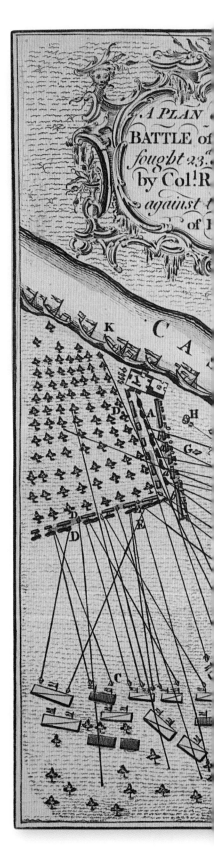

▼ **MAP OF THE BATTLE** This plan from 1760 shows the Bengali camp of the top right, with Bengali and French troops in red (infantry) and yellow (cavalry). The British forces can be seen on the left in black next to their encampment, with Bengali cannon battering their defences. The British ammunition store is shown between the British camp and the river.

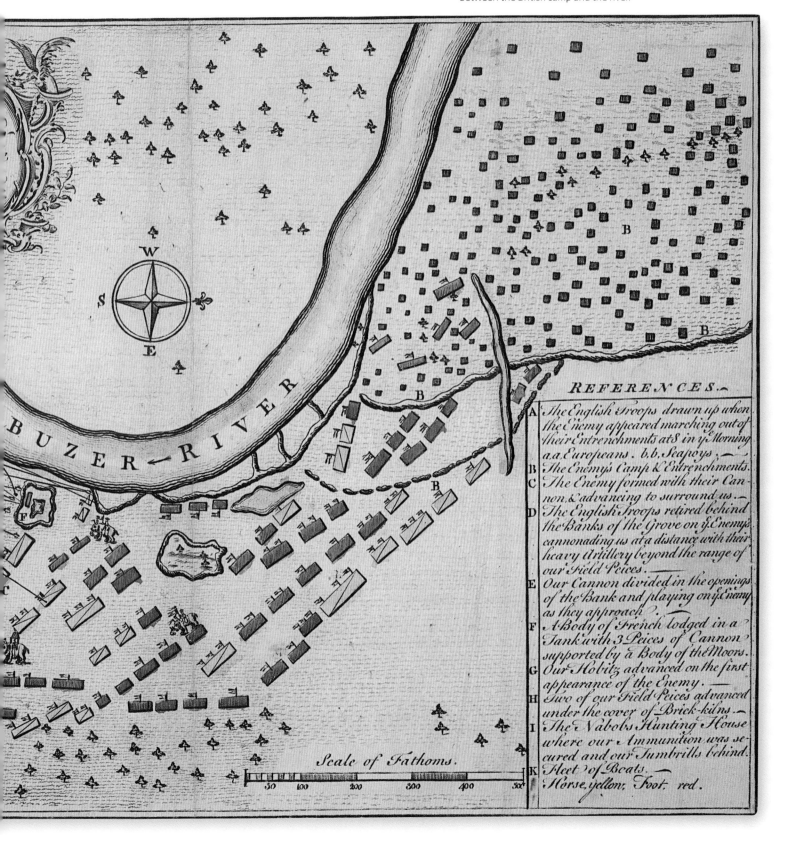

REFERENCES.

A The English Troops drawn up when the Enemy appeared marching out of their Entrenchments at 8 in ye Morning a,a, Europeans. b,b, Seapoys.

B The Enemys Camp & Entrenchments.

C The Enemy formed with their Cannon, & advancing to surround us.

D The English Troops retired behind the Banks of the Grove on ye Enemys cannonading us at a distance with their heavy Artillery beyond the range of our Field Peices.

E Our Cannon divided in the openings of the Bank and playing on ye Enemy as they approach.

F A Body of French lodged in a Tank with 3 Peices of Cannon supported by a Body of the Moors.

G Our Hobitz advanced on the first appearance of the Enemy.

H Two of our Field Peices advanced under the cover of Brick-kilns.

I The Nabobs Hunting House where our Ammunition was secured and our Tumbrills behind.

K Fleet of Boats.

Horse, yellow, Foot, red.

Scale of Fathoms.

50 100   200   300   400   50

A. Se. Maj. der König von Preussen comandiren den rechten Flügel Dero Armee. B. Fürst Moritz von Anhalt. C. General
Retzow, so den linken Flügel comandiret. D. General Ziethen, so die Cavallerie comandiret. E. 4 Regimenter Preuss. In-
fanterie, so anfänglich hinter die Cavallerie des rechten Flügels gestanden, u. selbigen unterstützet. F. der Oesterreichis.
linke Flügel, woselbst sich der General Nadasti mit seinem Corps de Reserve befand, welcher gleich anfangs auf die Preuss.
Cavallerie losging, aber bald zurück getrieben wurde, u. völlig in die Flucht sich begiebt. G. Pr. Carl v. Lottheringen. H. Gen. Daun.
I. Oest. rechter Flügel, so mit starken Batterien u. Verhacken bevestiget war. K. Gräben, worin Panduren gelegen. L. das
Dorf Borne. M. das Dorf Leuthen, welches von allen Seiten mit Redouten u. Verschanzungen umgeben war, hier währete das
Gefechte eine gute Stunde, da die tapfern Preuss. Batl. einen Angriff nach dem andern wagten, u. doch endlich Meister da-
von wurden. Die Eroberung dieses Dorfs entschied auch das Treffen, u. es ergriff so wol die feindl. Infanterie als Caval. in
gröster Eilfertigkeit die Flucht u. wurden von der Preuss. Cavall. u. besonder von den tapfern Husaren bis in die sin-
kende Nacht verfolget, eine unzählige Menge dar nieder gehauen, u. viele 1000 Gefangene eingebracht. W. Oesterr.
Bagage u. Munitions Wagen, deren der General von Ziethen den 8ten schon an 3000, nebst der sämtl. Bagage
u. den mehresten Zelten gehabt, und stunden noch alle Wege u. Felder voll. auf den Vorgrund O. ist der Angriff der 4 Sächs. Regimenter leichte Reuter abgebildet. Sonst ist noch erbeutet worden an 200 Canonen,
an 60 Fahnen u. Standarten, u. an Gefangenen hat man Abends den 7ten schon 12.500. gehabt. Der Oester.
Verlust an Todten, die auf dem Platz geblieben, erstreckt sich an 6000. hoher.
und die Menge der Blessirten noch viel höher. Der
Preuss. Verlust an Todten u. Blessirten wird überhaupt nicht
über 4000 Mann betragen.

A. Se. Maj. der König von Preussen comandiren den rechten Flügel Dero Armee. B. Fürst Moritz von Anhalt. C. General
Retzow, so den linken Flügel comandiret. D. General Ziethen, so die Cavallerie comandiret. E. 4 Regimenter Preuss. Infanterie, so anfänglich hinter die Cavallerie des rechten Flügels gestanden, u. selbigen unterstützet. F. der Oesterreichis.
linke Flügel, woselbst sich der General Nadasti mit seinem Corps de Reserve befand, welcher gleich anfangs auf die Preuss.

Leuthen

1757 ▪ MODERN-DAY POLAND ▪ PRUSSIA VS. AUSTRIA

SEVEN YEARS' WAR

In late 1757, fighting a coalition of Austria, France, and Russia, Prussia was at risk of being overrun by hostile armies. In this desperate predicament, Prussian king Frederick II (the Great) went on the attack. He routed a French and Austrian force at Rossbach in November, and then turned to meet another Austrian army under Charles of Lorraine that had just captured Breslau in the disputed territory of Silesia. With around 66,000 troops, the Austrians outnumbered Frederick's army by two to one.

On 5 December, Charles drew up his forces in a line in front of Breslau, centred on the village of Leuthen. Frederick planned to exploit his highly disciplined army's exceptional skill in battlefield manoeuvres. While feigning an attack on the Austrian right – which fooled the Austrians for hours – he shifted the bulk of his army to the other flank, using the cover of low hills to mask his movement. Marching in perfect formation, the Prussian infantry assembled at right angles to the left end of the Austrian line, with cavalry and artillery in support. The unexpected Prussian attack rolled up the Austrian line until a fierce battle was joined in Leuthen village. The Austrians belatedly succeeded in transferring troops from their right to join the fight, but a deadly Prussian artillery bombardment and a final charge by Prussian cavalry put them to flight. The victory established Frederick's reputation as one of the greatest military commanders of the 18th century, and in the aftermath of the battle the Prussians went on to capture the city of Breslau (modern-day Wroclaw in Poland).

◄ **ARENA OF WAR** This contemporary engraving depicts the mixture of formality and ferocity that characterised the fighting at the battle of Leuthen. The single day's action cost the Austrians some 22,000 casualties and the Prussians more than 6,000. In total, around one in six of the troops who took part was killed or wounded.

PRUSSIAN INFANTRY

In the first half of the 18th century, Prussia developed the most admired army in Europe. Its infantry were peasant conscripts who, via harsh discipline, were terrorized into a trained force that unquestioningly carried out any order it was given. Drilled in the complex procedure of firing flintlock muskets, the soldiers were capable of delivering four volleys per minute, which was twice that of most infantry of the period. Frederick the Great was mocked by his enemies for having his troops march on the battlefield with the same smartness and precision as on the parade ground, but that very discipline enabled him to execute his tactical schemes.

▲ **In a painting** by Daniel Chodowiecki, Frederick II of Prussia, on horseback, inspects his infantry on parade. The discipline of the Prussian infantry was one of the wonders of the age.

In detail

▶ **THE ROUTE TO BATTLE**
Wolfe's fleet of warships and
troop carriers sailed west from
its base on the Île d'Orléans. It
anchored west of Quebec on
9 September, but bad weather
prevented a landing for three
days. Until the last moment,
Wolfe kept the precise location
of the landing to himself: L'Anse
au Foulon (Fuller's Cove).

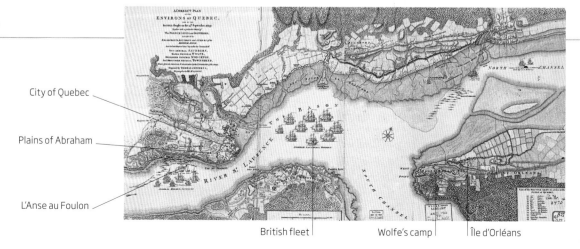

City of Quebec

Plains of Abraham

L'Anse au Foulon

British fleet | Wolfe's camp | Île d'Orléans

Plains of Abraham

1759 ▪ QUEBEC CITY ▪ BRITAIN VS. FRANCE, FRENCH CANADA

SEVEN YEARS' WAR

In 1759, during the world's first global conflict, Britain fought for control of France's North American colonies. In June, a military force under 32-year-old General James Wolfe travelled up the St Lawrence River to attack Quebec, the capital city of New France. Wolfe established a base on the banks of the river, opposite the city, but French defences organized by the Marquis de Montcalm stopped the British from crossing to the Quebec side. An attempted landing east of the city in July failed, repulsed by entrenched French troops. By September, Wolfe was in chronic ill health and knew that his fleet would soon have to withdraw to avoid the winter ice. He therefore gambled on landing troops upstream west of Quebec, where a cliff provided cover.

On the night of 12 September, more than 4,000 British troops scaled the 54-m (177-ft)-high cliff and drew up on the Plains of Abraham. Montcalm marched out of Quebec to give battle. The British lay flat to avoid French cannon fire, then rose to meet Montcalm's infantry with disciplined musket volleys. The main body of the French broke and fled, although fire from their skirmishers exploiting cover on the flanks took a heavy toll on the pursuing British. Wolfe himself was killed, and Montcalm fatally wounded during the retreat. In a major step towards British control of Canada, Quebec surrendered on 18 September.

◀ **TAKING QUEBEC** This contemporary illustration shows the different stages of Wolfe's operation: the initial night assault by British light infantry up the sheer face of the cliffs (centre left); the follow-up landings (below left), in which troops take a pathway to the top; and the confrontation between British and French soldiers on the Plains of Abraham (above left).

◀ **THE BRITISH LANDING**
The first British troops ashore in the early hours of 13 September achieved total surprise, because the French had considered the terrain too difficult for an attack and had left it only lightly defended. Wolfe's men were hardened redcoats of the regular army, whereas almost half of Montcalm's troops were colonial militia or Native American auxiliaries.

◀ **THE DEATH OF GENERAL WOLFE**
Wolfe's victory and death at Quebec made him a British military hero. Benjamin West's famous painting of the event, exhibited in 1771, helped transform the ambitious young officer into a martyr who died for his country. Wolfe died of gunshot injuries to his chest and stomach.

And **vain** was their **endeavour** our **men** to **terrify** / though
death was all **around us**, not one of us **would fly!**

CONTEMPORARY AMERICAN BALLAD ON THE AMERICAN VICTORY AT SARATOGA, 1777

Saratoga

1777 ▪ NEW YORK STATE ▪ USA VS. BRITAIN

AMERICAN WAR OF INDEPENDENCE

In 1776, the US colonies declared independence from British rule, and Britain was still struggling to regain control of its American territories the following year. British General John Burgoyne embarked on an invasion of New York from Canada, seizing Fort Ticonderoga in July and cutting a road through the wilderness to the Hudson River. Marching down the Hudson, Burgoyne's forces soon ran short of supplies. Their attack on a US base at Bennington in mid-August failed, with heavy losses; his Native American auxiliary forces deserted, and the promised support of other British forces failed to materialize. US troops under General Horatio Gates fortified a position by the Hudson at Bemis Heights, blocking Burgoyne's path, and so on 19 September the British advanced to attack the Heights.

Gates allowed General Benedict Arnold to send forward light infantry and riflemen to harass the British right flank at Freeman's Farm. Cut down by sharpshooters hidden in the woods, the British faltered, but Gates refused Arnold's pleas for a general attack. They had suffered the heavier losses, but the British held the field. After a flaming row, Gates, who remained in his entrenchments, relieved Arnold of his command. Burgoyne tried another attack on 7 October, but was again repulsed, and the Americans pushed forwards to retake Freeman's Farm. Burgoyne withdrew north to Saratoga. Surrounded and under artillery bombardment, he negotiated a surrender that took effect on 17 October. The defeat was a shattering blow to British prestige and convinced France that it should support the US revolt.

▲ **BENEDICT ARNOLD WOUNDED** Although he had officially been removed from command for insubordination, at the crucial moment of the fighting on 7 October, General Arnold appeared on horseback and led a wild charge against a redoubt held by Hessian soldiers. He was shot from his horse and seriously wounded, but the Hessians were put to flight, leaving the US forces in control of the battlefield.

WASHINGTON'S **CONTINENTAL ARMY**

When the War of Independence began, the American rebels' only armed forces were the militia of the individual colonies. In 1775 the Second Continental Congress authorised the creation of a Continental Army and appointed George Washington, a Virginian with considerable military experience, as its commander-in-chief. Washington sought to build a European-style army, drilled to fire disciplined musket volleys and to manoeuvre in formation with bayonets fixed. At Saratoga, his army was still young, and depended more on enthusiasm than strict discipline, but in 1781 it won a decisive victory over the British at Yorktown.

▶ **At the time** of the battle of Saratoga, the American commander-in-chief, George Washington, was fighting the British in Pennsylvania.

In detail

Saratoga was a battle that the British should not have fought. Faced with an enemy that was numerically superior and dug into a strong defensive position on high ground, they would have been wise to fall back northwards. However, Burgoyne had confidence in his force of British regulars and Hessians - disciplined German troops trained to fight in the European style, firing massed musket volleys and advancing into enemy fire with bayonets fixed. On the other side, Gates's troops were largely colonial militia and Continental Army soldiers, which were less formally trained, but Gates took a conventional European view of battle tactics: he intended to sit in his entrenchments, which Burgoyne would attempt to take by frontal assault. The aggressive actions of his subordinate, Benedict Arnold, subverted the plan to some extent, but to positive effect.

The heavily wooded terrain was ideal for the US riflemen, who were expert at exploiting cover, and positioned themselves on the flanks of the enemy advance. The British possessed light infantry and rifle-armed German *jaegers* (skirmishers), but failed to use them as effectively as the US force - indeed, the US riflemen's deliberate targeting of British officers was criticized by the British as assassination and not legitimate warfare. The US achieved their great victory at a cost of only around 500 casualties out of some 15,000 men. British casualties were around 1,000 out of 7,000, with the remainder captured.

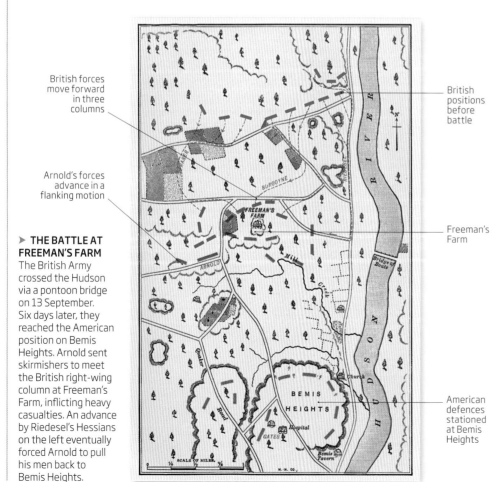

British forces move forward in three columns

Arnold's forces advance in a flanking motion

British positions before battle

Freeman's Farm

American defences stationed at Bemis Heights

▶ **THE BATTLE AT FREEMAN'S FARM**
The British Army crossed the Hudson via a pontoon bridge on 13 September. Six days later, they reached the American position on Bemis Heights. Arnold sent skirmishers to meet the British right-wing column at Freeman's Farm, inflicting heavy casualties. An advance by Riedesel's Hessians on the left eventually forced Arnold to pull his men back to Bemis Heights.

▲ **DANIEL MORGAN** A Virginian frontiersman, Daniel Morgan formed a company of volunteer riflemen at the start of the war. At Saratoga, he commanded the 500 riflemen of the Provisional Rifle Corps, who picked off British officers. Morgan ended the war as a general, winning the Battle of Cowpens in 1781.

◄ **SURRENDER OF GENERAL BURGOYNE**
The British surrendered on 17 October. As a formal gesture, General Burgoyne offered his sword to General Gates who declined it, instead inviting the defeated commander to take refreshment in his tent. According to the surrender terms, the 6,000 captured British soldiers were supposed to be shipped home, but most remained prisoners until the end of the war.

▲ **AMERICAN LONG RIFLE** Patriot sharpshooters were equipped with a long-barrelled flintlock rifle that had probably been introduced to America by German immigrants. Primarily a hunting weapon used by farmers and woodsmen, it was far more accurate than the standard infantry musket, which had a smooth (unrifled) barrel. Reputedly, a frontiersman with a long rifle could hit a turkey's head at 90 m (100 yards).

► **HESSIANS AT SARATOGA** Some 30,000 "Hessians" served in the war, and made up 40 per cent of Burgoyne's force at Saratoga. Short of troops to fight in America, Britain hired soldiers from the rulers of the German states. Many of them came from Hesse-Kassel – hence the name – and arrived as complete formations with their own officers, uniforms, and weapons. They were particularly hated by the US Patriots.

Fleurus

1794 ■ AUSTRIAN NETHERLANDS ■ FIRST FRENCH REPUBLIC
VS. COALITION ARMY

FRENCH REVOLUTIONARY WARS

Between 1789 and 1794, revolutionaries overthrew the French monarchy and installed a series of increasingly radical governments. From 1792, the revolutionaries were at war with a widening coalition of European powers, and the Austrian Netherlands (modern-day Belgium) became the chief battleground for the rival forces. In June 1794, French General Jean-Baptiste Jourdan's army besieged the Austrian fortress of Charleroi. A coalition army of Austrian, Dutch, and British troops under Prince Josias of Coburg went to break the siege. However, the garrison surrendered before the coalition army arrived, and Jourdan was able to deploy all 76,000 of his men to face Coburg's 52,000 on their arrival. Confident in the quality of his troops, Coburg advanced his army in five columns nonetheless. The French line struggled to hold in the ferocious fighting, and Prince William of Orange's Dutch troops almost broke through on the French left.

Informed of the progress of the battle by aerial observers in a hydrogen balloon, Jourdan deftly moved his reserves to shore up resistance where disaster threatened. At the climax, he sent the French cavalry forward in a charge, breaking the Austrian line in the centre of the field. Coburg ordered a withdrawal, although his losses had been far lighter than those of the French. Through this victory, France secured control of the Netherlands, and consolidated the reputation of the revolutionary army (see box) both in France and on the world stage.

FRENCH **REVOLUTIONARY ARMY**

The French Revolution initially caused chaos in France's armed forces as officers sympathetic to the monarchy fled the country or were arrested. The revolutionary government resorted to conscription, culminating in the *levée en masse* of August 1793, which enrolled all men aged 18 to 25. Training these troops and integrating them with the remains of the old royal army was a daunting task, but the revolutionary zeal of many of the new citizen-soldiers, and their large numbers, made up for their inexperience. Often led by newly promoted officers from lowly social backgrounds, the new French army dominated Europe for two decades.

▲ **French citizens** enrol for service the army during the mass conscription of 1793 ordered by the revolutionary government.

▲ **OBSERVING THE BATTLE** The battle of Fleurus saw the first use of an aircraft in warfare. The French had created an Aerostatic Corps to exploit balloon flight, the new technology pioneered in France from 1783. Observers in a hydrogen balloon tethered behind the French lines were able to make sense of the confused fighting, sending messages down a cable to their commander General Jourdan.

Marengo

1800 ▪ MODERN-DAY NORTHERN ITALY ▪ FRANCE VS. AUSTRIA

FRENCH REVOLUTIONARY WARS

General Napoleon Bonaparte made himself head of the French government as First Consul in 1799. France was still at war with the British-Austrian coalition, and to maintain his hold on power, Napoleon needed military victories. In spring 1800, an Austrian army of 31,000 under General Michael Melas besieged French forces in Genoa, northern Italy. In response, Napoleon led an army over the Alps from Switzerland through the St Bernard Pass and entered Piedmont, seizing Milan and

cutting Melas's lines of communication with Austria. Surprised by Napoleon's bold manoeuvre, Melas saw no alternative but to give battle. Having defeated the French forces in Genoa on 4 June, Melas marched to meet Napoleon's 23,000-strong army as it advanced west across the Piedmont plain.

The two armies drew up on opposite sides of the river Bormida, near the village of Marengo (today, in northern Italy). Napoleon was unaware of Melas's plan and was convinced that the Austrians would try to slip away without fighting, so detached substantial forces, including a division under General Louis Desaix, to block possible escape routes. Napoleon was

▲ **EYEWITNESS AT MARENGO** This picture was painted by Louis-François Lejeune, a French army officer who was present at Marengo. Napoleon and his staff are shown in the left foreground. Further off, Desaix is depicted being shot from his horse while leading the French counterattack. In the background, Kellerman's cavalry can be seen launching their decisive charge against the Austrian flank. Around one in five of the 54,000 men in the battle was killed or wounded.

therefore taken by surprise when the Austrians crossed the Bormida on the morning of 14 June and attacked. Fighting resolutely, the Austrians threw the French centre into disarray, and only resistance from Napoleon's elite consular guard prevented a rout. The Austrians were already celebrating victory when Desaix's division arrived at the battlefield and delivered a counterattack. Desaix was killed, but a charge by General François Kellerman's cuirassiers (heavy cavalry) broke the Austrian flank. The Austrians abandoned the field in disarray, and Melas agreed to an armistice. Austria lost Piedmont, and Napoleon was confirmed as leader of France.

NAPOLEON **BONAPARTE** (1769-1821)

Born in Corsica, Napoleon began his career as an artillery officer. Promoted to command an army after suppressing an uprising in Paris in 1795, he used success in battle as a springboard for his political ambitions, which culminated in his assumption of the title of Emperor in 1804. An aggressive, risk-taking general, he outfought all of the armies of Europe, but overreached himself by invading Russia in 1812. After a disastrous retreat from Moscow, he was overwhelmed by a hostile poltical coalition in 1814 and exiled. He returned the following year, but, defeated at Waterloo, ended his days as a prisoner of the British.

▲ **Jacques-Louis David** painted this heroic portrait of Napoleon crossing the St Bernard Pass. In reality, Napoleon traversed the pass on a mule.

Trafalgar

1805 ▪ SOUTHERN SPAIN ▪ BRITISH FLEET VS. FRENCH–SPANISH FLEET

NAPOLEONIC WARS

A fleet of 33 French and Spanish ships of the line, led by French admiral Pierre-Charles Villeneuve, left Cadiz on 19 October 1805, heading east towards the Mediterranean. Villeneuve aimed to relieve the British blockade of French ports, enabling the French to launch an invasion of Britain. The British admiral Horatio Nelson, who was blockading Cadiz with 27 ships of the line, gave chase. By 21 October the two fleets were off Cape Trafalgar, and Villeneuve began to turn back to Cadiz. Fearing his prey might escape, Nelson prepared to attack. Arranged in two groups, one led by Nelson on board *Victory*, the British warships sailed towards Villeneuve's line. Nelson issued a series of flag signals, including the famous edict: "England expects that every man will do his duty".

After braving broadsides for 40 minutes during the slow approach, Nelson's ship *Victory* crossed behind Villeneuve's flagship *Bucentaure*, raking the French ship with cannon fire that brought carnage to its crowded decks. *Victory* came under heavy fire before other British ships arrived in support, and, in the early afternoon, Nelson was shot by a sniper from the rigging of the French ship *Redoubtable*. Despite their admiral being mortally wounded, the British fared better in the fighting, and the eight French warships in the rear of Villeneuve's line, slow to turn back towards the action, took little part in the battle. By the day's end, 17 French and Spanish warships were captured, including *Bucentaure* and the Spanish flagship *Santa Ana*, and one French ship had exploded. Nelson died of his wounds, but his victory established Britain as the world's leading naval power for a century.

▶ **NAVAL TACTICS**
Traditional tactics in the age of sail saw opposing fleets lining up parallel to one another to exchange broadsides. However, Nelson often attacked at right-angles to the enemy line and cut across it, focusing his ships' fire on this point. At Trafalgar he attacked in two columns, striking between the Spanish and French fleets.

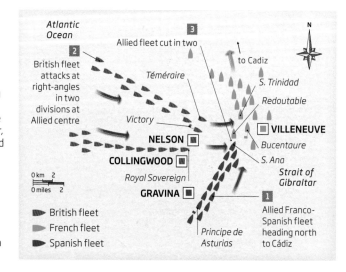

Atlantic Ocean

2 British fleet attacks at right-angles in two divisions at Allied centre

3 Allied fleet cut in two

to Cadiz

N

Téméraire

S. Trinidad

Redoutable

Victory

■ **VILLENEUVE**

Bucentaure

NELSON ■

S. Ana

COLLINGWOOD ■

Royal Sovereign

Strait of Gibraltar

GRAVINA ■

0 km   2
0 miles   2

◆ British fleet
◆ French fleet
◆ Spanish fleet

1 Allied Franco-Spanish fleet heading north to Cádiz

Principe de Asturias

▲ **CLOSE COMBAT** Nelson deliberately engaged in chaotic fighting at close range ("pell-mell"), slaughtering enemy crews as broadsides raked the decks – but at high cost to his own men, too. The French 74-gun *Redoubtable*, shown here as a dismasted hulk, lost 200 men to a single broadside from the 98-gun *Temeraire*. The ships were almost unsinkable and often fought until the enemy boarded or they surrendered.

May the great God… grant to my country…
a great and glorious victory

HORATIO NELSON, IN A PRAYER WRITTEN BEFORE THE BATTLE OF TRAFALGAR, 1805

Austerlitz

1805 ▪ MODERN-DAY CZECH REPUBLIC ▪ FRANCE VS. AUSTRIA AND RUSSIAN EMPIRE

NAPOLEONIC WARS

In 1805, Russia and Austria joined Britain in the Third Coalition against Napoleon's France. When Austria declared war in August, Napoleon was camped at Boulogne, preparing to invade Britain. He marched his Grande Armée from this encampment to southern Germany, and in October forced the surrender of the entire Austrian army at Ulm, with French troops occupying Vienna. However, Russia came to Austria's

aid, and a combined Russo-Austrian army of 90,000 men gathered northeast of Vienna. With the onset of winter, Napoleon faced severe supply problems. Reluctant to retreat to France, he gambled on tempting his enemy into giving battle. Advancing to Austerlitz with 70,000 men, he took up an apparently poor defensive position, with his right wing weak and the Pratzen Heights at his centre unoccupied.

The inexperienced Russian Tsar Alexander I, assuming personal command of his army, took the bait. Attacking on 2 December, the coalition army concentrated its effort against

◀ **FRENCH VICTORY** Captured officers and standards of the Russian Imperial Guard are presented to the victorious Emperor Napoleon after the battle of Austerlitz. The Russians and Austrians had lost almost a third of their force killed, wounded, or taken prisoner. Because of the presence of Napoleon, Alexander I of Russia, and Francis II of Austria, Austerlitz is known as the Battle of the Three Emperors.

the right of Napoleon's line and marched onto the Pratzen Heights. The French right held, thanks to the timely arrival of a corps under Marshal Davout after a two-day forced march from Vienna. In the centre, Marshal Soult led another corps uphill on to the Heights, emerging from thick fog into sunlight to overwhelm the Austrian troops on the plateau. Attacks and counterattacks raged until the French Imperial Guard finally secured the Heights. With their left wing also driven back, the coalition forces abandoned the field. Austria called for peace, and the Russians withdrew to their homeland.

WAR OF THE **FOURTH COALITION** (1806–1807)

After the battle of Austerlitz, Austria made peace, but Britain and Russia remained at war with France, and were joined by Prussia in the Fourth Coalition. In October 1806, Napoleon crushed the Prussians at Jena-Auerstedt and, after a drawn battle at Eylau, also triumphed over the Russians at the Battle of Friedland in June 1807. Napoleon imposed peace on Prussia, and made Russia his ally against Britain through the Treaty of Tilsit in July 1807.

▲ **On 14 October 1806**, Napoleon's Grande Armée defeated the Prussians on two battlefields, at Jena and at the nearby village of Auerstedt (above). The French went on to occupy Berlin 11 days later.

In detail

Napoleon's approach to warfare was often characterized by his pursuit of a decisive battle, even if this involved substantial risks. Mikhail Kutuzov, a Russian general on the coalition side at Austerlitz, understood this, and realised that the French could be defeated by avoiding battle, since Napoleon would eventually be forced to withdraw from Austria due to his precariously overextended lines of supply and communication. Kutusov, however, was overruled by Tsar Alexander I, who instead chose to attack the French right flank, which was weakly held. This was exactly what Napoleon wanted. He had massed his troops in his centre and left, intending to devastate the coalition forces by attacking the left flank.

As so often in Napoleon's battles, his plan was risky and almost foundered. The Austro-Russian forces almost broke through on the French right, and the Russian coalition forces fought an unexpectedly fierce counterattack on the French left. The hard-won success of Marshal Soult's French infantry and the Imperial Guard cavalry in the centre, however, put the coalition forces in an impossible position. Soult's men were able to turn to their right and envelop the mass of Austro-Russian troops who had pressed forward south of the Pratzen Heights, cutting the coalition army in half. Napoleon's gamble had paid off, and he emerged the victor despite having been outnumbered.

▶ **NAPOLEON'S GRAND ARMÉE** In this 19th-century painting, Emperor Napoleon visits his forces assembled at Boulogne on the Channel coast in preparation for an invasion of Britain in the summer of 1805. Known as the Grande Armée, the force was organized into six self-contained corps that could operate independently, allowing for exceptional mobility and flexibility in manoeuvre. At its peak in 1812, the Grande Armée numbered almost 700,000 men.

▼ **CAVALRY CHARGE** At the climax of the battle the cavalry of the Russian Imperial Guard, in their dazzling white uniforms, charged with sabres drawn to retake the Pratzen Heights from Soult's French infantry. A valiant attack, it was defeated through a counter-charge by Napoleon's Imperial Guard cavalry, who drove the Russian elite horsemen from the Heights, leaving the French in command of the centre of the battlefield.

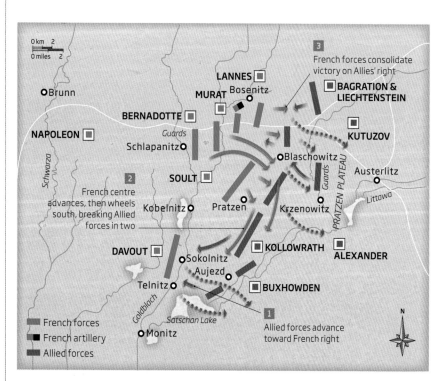

▲ **ORDER OF BATTLE** At the start of the battle, the position of the rival armies at Austerlitz was asymmetrical, with the main weight of the Russo-Austrian forces attacking the French right flank, while Napoleon's forces were concentrated in his centre and left. The marshy land around the Goldbach stream proved an obstacle to the Russo-Austrian advance, which was also blocked by the arrival of Davout's troops. Both sides used heavy cavalry as reserves.

▼ NAPOLEON'S ELITE MARSHALS

Louis-Nicolas Davout (below), one of Napoleon's "Marshals of the Empire", played a major role at Austerlitz. Napoleon created this title for his favourite generals; many of his military successes depended upon the skills of these loyal subordinates. They formed a new French aristocracy, with Davout later becaming Prince of Eckmühl.

▲ **FRANCIS HUMILIATED** On 4 December 1805, two days after Austerlitz, the proud and reserved Austrian Emperor Francis II humiliatingly submitted to meeting the upstart Emperor Napoleon to request an armistice and discuss peace terms. As a result of the defeat, Austria surrendered the territories it controlled in northern Italy, and Francis renounced the title of Holy Roman Emperor, which had given the rulers of Austria suzerainty over Germany.

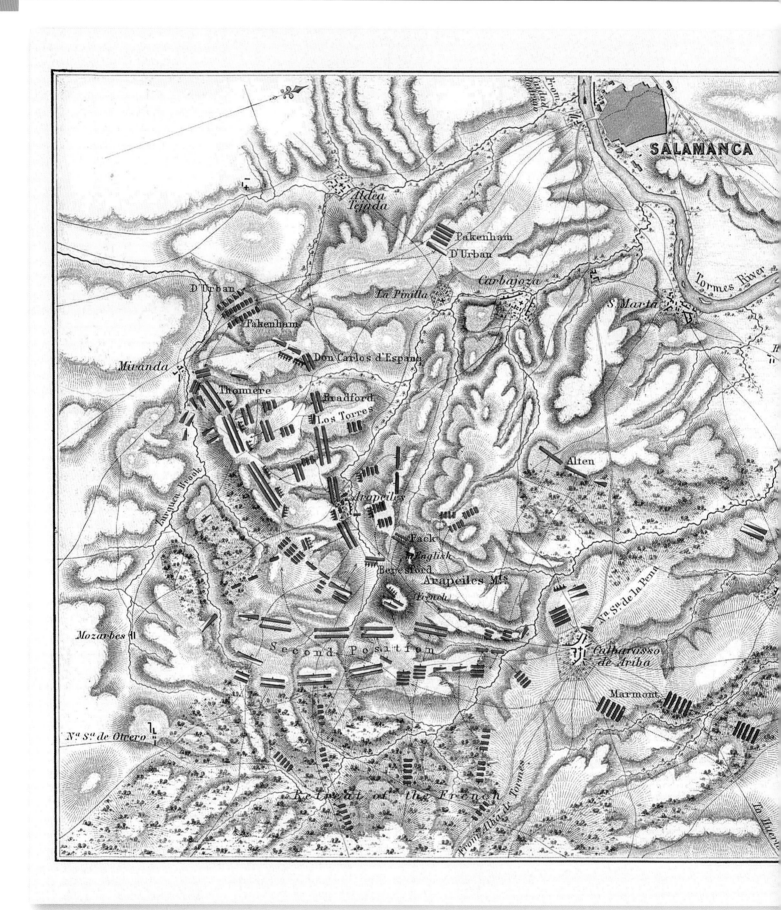

▲ **OVERVIEW OF THE BATTLE** The Anglo-Portuguese (in red) and French forces (in blue)
clashed in the ridges and valleys outside Salamanca. The French attempt to outflank the
right of Wellington's army left them overstretched and exposed to attack by British infantry.
In all, five out of eight French divisions were destroyed.

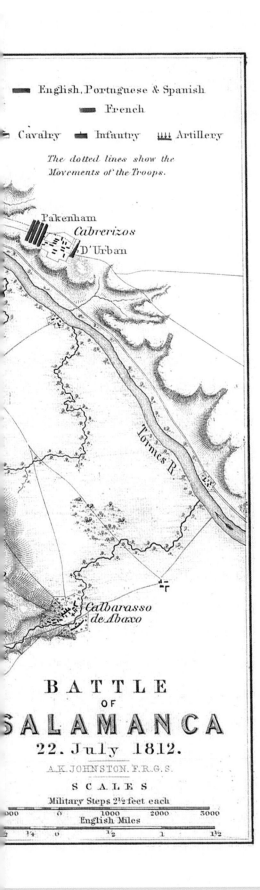

BATTLE
OF
SALAMANCA
22. July 1812.

A.K. JOHNSTON, F.R.G.S.

SCALES

Military Steps 2½ feet each

Salamanca

1812 ▪ WESTERN SPAIN ▪ ANGLO-PORTUGUESE ALLIANCE
VS. FRENCH EMPIRE

PENINSULAR WAR

Early in 1812, Viscount Wellington (who later became a duke) led an army of British, Portuguese, and Spanish troops out of Portugal into French-occupied Spain as part of the war against Napoleon in the Iberian peninsula (see box, below). In June 1812, Wellington advanced on Salamanca, which was held by French forces under Marshal Auguste Marmont. The two armies were of equal strength, with almost 50,000 men each, but Marmont was expecting reinforcements.

For days the two sides manoeuvered within sight of one another, each seeking an advantage, until on 22 July Marmont believed he saw a chance to cut off Wellington's line of retreat to Portugal. The French commander ordered his left wing to outflank the right of the British position, and so they marched westward along a ridge across the front of Wellington's army, where they became separated from the rest of the French troops. Seizing his opportunity, Wellington ordered his infantry to attack uphill at the western end of the ridge. Meeting the French marching column head-on, the British launched a bayonet charge, while their heavy cavalry, wielding sabres, inflicted devastating blows on the French left wing. Marmont was wounded by cannon fire, leaving the French leaderless but still resistent. After more fierce fighting, however, the French abandoned the field.

Wellington had won a major victory in a battle that marked a key turning point in the Peninsular War. He inflicted 14,000 losses on Marmont's army, and liberated Madrid from French control soon after, fatally weakening Napoleon's hold on Spain.

THE **PENINSULAR WAR** (1807-14)

This part of the Napoleonic Wars began when France and its ally Spain invaded Portugal, which had refused to join their war against Britain. Napoleon turned on Spain in 1808, leading to a popular uprising against the French in May. Britain sent an army to Portugal, while Spanish guerillas harassed the occupying forces. In 1811, the French were driven from Portugal, then defeated at Salamanca in 1812 and Vitoria in 1813. The war ended as allied forces invaded France over the Pyrenees, and captured Paris. Napoleon abdicated on 4 April 1814.

▲ **Spanish soliders** join the uprising against the French occupation of Madrid, 2 May 1808 ("*Dos de Mayo*" Uprising).

Borodino

1812 ■ WESTERN RUSSIA ■ RUSSIAN EMPIRE VS. FRANCE

NAPOLEONIC WARS

In June 1812, Emperor Napoleon of France invaded Russia with an army of 250,000 men. The Russians retreated, avoiding a decisive battle. By September, Napoleon was closing on Moscow but had lost almost half of his initial force to starvation, disease, and desertion. Deciding at last to stand and fight the invaders, the Russians appointed veteran Marshal Mikhail Kutusov as their commander. He took up position across the

Smolensk–Moscow road at Borodino, fortifying a line of hills with earthworks. On 7 September, Napoleon launched a series of crude frontal assaults upon the Russian line. Both sides inflicted heavy casualties on the other with cannon fire, and the two armies struggled for control of the Bagration flèches – arrow-shaped earthworks on the Russian left – and the Raevsky Redoubt, where around 20 heavy guns were located. French troops repeatedly took these strongpoints only to have them retaken by the Russians in ferocious counterattacks. By late afternoon, French troops had secured the Raevsky

▲ **CLASH OF CAVALRY** French and Russian horsemen clash at the Raevsky Redoubt, the site of the fiercest fighting at Borodino. About 250,000 men took part in the battle, with roughly equal numbers on each side. The ferocity of the attacks and counterattacks by massed infantry and cavalry led to heavy casualties, with around a third of the soldiers killed or wounded.

Redoubt and the Russian centre lay open; however, Napoleon failed to commit his last reserves, the Imperial Guard, to exploit the opportunity for total victory. Kutusov was able to withdraw his army in good order.

Losses on both sides had been exceptionally heavy, the Russians suffering 45,000 casualties, the French 35,000. Seven days later Napoleon occupied Moscow, but it was a pyrrhic victory, and soon his Grande Armée embarked on a disastrous winter retreat. His forces depleted, Napoleon lost the Battle of Leipzig in 1813, leading to his overthrow in 1814.

In context

◄ **MIKHAIL KUTUSOV** Russian general Kutusov lost an eye fighting in the Crimea in the 1770s. Considered the embodiment of Russian patriotism, he was made commander-in-chief in 1812. He attempted no manoeuvres at Borodino, letting slaughter take its course. After the battle he withdrew beyond Moscow, keeping his army intact.

The road to Moscow offers a safe route for the withdrawal of the Russian army

The Russian artillery defends the Bagration flèches

The Raevsky Redoubt commands the Russian centre

The French drive back the Russian left flank

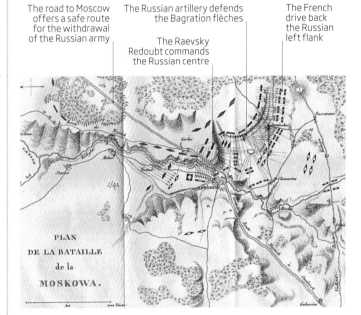

▲ **BATTLEFIELD AT BORODINO** This 19th-century engraving shows the Russian defensive line at the Kalatsha River. There was little fighting on the Russian right, where the terrain made an attack difficult. The French, meanwhile, concentrated their assaults on the centre and left, which were held by General Pyotr Bagration's 2nd Army. The extreme left of the line was weak, but Napoleon failed to exploit this.

▲ **RETREAT FROM MOSCOW** As French troops entered Moscow, a fire erupted and destroyed most of the city. Unable to force the Russians into submission, on 19 October 1812 Napoleon ordered a withdrawal to the west. Starving, frozen, and harassed by the Russian army and partisans, the French forces disintegrated. Less than 30,000 survived the retreat.

New Orleans

1815 ▪ LOUISIANA ▪ USA VS. BRITAIN

WAR OF 1812

The War of 1812 between the US and Britain officially ended on 24 December 1814, when delegates from both nations signed a peace treaty in Belgium. However, the news took time to cross the Atlantic, and so fighting continued in the US until early the following year. At that time, British troops had already landed near New Orleans, and US general Andrew Jackson was undertaking the defence of the town with a ragtag force of regular soldiers, militia, and assorted volunteers. After some initial skirmishes, the British army, led by General Edward Pakenham, launched a full-scale attack on 8 January 1815.

The US forces lined up behind primitive fortifications between the Mississippi River and a nearby swamp, and installed a battery of cannon on the opposite bank of the river. Pakenham planned to send a detachment across the river to seize the battery and fire on the US line from the flank, but the crossing was delayed. Instead, his infantry advanced in two columns. British artillery was focusing on the US battery, but the US artillery bombarded the advancing infantry; at the same time, the morning mist lifted, exposing them. Muskets and cannon shot down the advancing British, few of whom even reached the ditch in front of the US line. Pakenham was among the 300 British killed in less than half an hour. The victory gave a huge boost to patriotic feeling in the newly-founded US.

▲ **BATTLE BY THE MISSISSIPPI** The battle of New Orleans took place at the Chalmette plantation on the east bank of the Mississippi River. The few British troops that reached the ditch protecting the US lines were stranded there because ladders were brought up too late. US casualties numbered fewer than 50 dead and wounded.

In context

▲ **LAKE BORGNE** To attack New Orleans, the British had to land troops from the sea. However, their approach was blocked by five US gunboats. On 14 December, more than 1,000 British sailors and marines, rowing in longboats armed with light cannon, attacked Jones's flotilla at Lake Borgne. They captured the gunboats after a fierce fight in which 17 British and six Americans died.

◀ **GENERAL ANDREW JACKSON** Jackson's role at the battle of New Orleans made him a national hero. As a youth, he had fought the British in the American Revolutionary War, and from 1812 he led Tennessee militia in a ruthless campaign against the Creek Indians, culminating in victory at Horseshoe Bend in Alabama in 1814. He went on to serve as US President from 1829 to 1837.

Waterloo

1815 ▪ MODERN-DAY BELGIUM ▪ BRITISH, DUTCH, AND PRUSSIAN ARMY VS. FRENCH ARMY

NAPOLEONIC WARS

Having adbicated in 1814 (see p.143), Napoleon I was exiled to the Mediterranean island of Elba. However, in February 1815 he escaped to France and reassembled his army. He advanced into Belgium in June, facing the Prussian army under Marshal Gebhard von Blücher and the British under the Duke of Wellington, both supported by the Dutch. On 16 June the French defeated the Prussians at Ligny and fought a battle with the British at Quatre Bras. Wellington withdrew and took up a defensive position near Waterloo with 68,000 men, and on 18 June, Napoleon's force of 72,000 attacked. Wellington's troops fiercely defended positions at Hougoumont chateau and the farm of La Haye Sainte, and repulsed a frontal assault by French infantry columns with muskets and a cavalry charge. Blücher's army marched in, attacking Napoleon's right flank. The French cavalry charged Wellington's line repeatedly and threatened to break it, and at around 6pm, La Haye Sainte fell. The elite French Imperial Guard

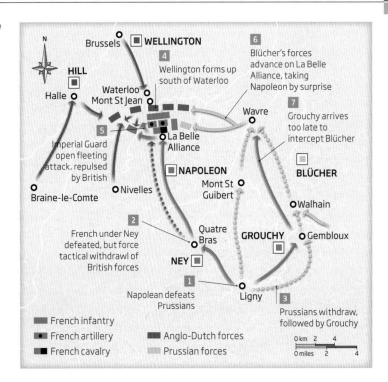

► **THE WATERLOO CAMPAIGN** Wellington drew up his forces on the Mont Saint Jean ridge to the south of Waterloo, and Napoleon centred his army at La Belle Alliance, to the south again. On 18 June, while the British and Dutch forces resisted attacks by the French, the Prussians evaded French units on the right and marched to the main scene of the battle, securing victory.

advanced, but even they were no match for the British. Wellington ordered a general attack and, as the Prussians pressed forward too, the French defeat was inevitable. However, Wellington described the battle as "the nearest run thing you ever saw in your life". Napoleon spent the rest of his life imprisoned on the remote island of St Helena.

▼ **BRITISH INFANTRY SQUARE** When attacked by cavalry, British infantry formed hollow squares with lines of bayonets on each side, as seen to the left of this 1874 oil painting by Henri Félix Emmanuel Philippoteaux. However, the formation left the soldiers vulnerable to cannon fire. Wellington's army suffered 15,000 casualties; 25,000 of Napoleon's men were killed or wounded.

Boyacá

1819 ▪ CENTRAL COLÓMBIA ▪ INDEPENDENTIST ARMY VS. SPAIN

SOUTH AMERICAN WARS OF INDEPENDENCE

Spain's South American colonies had been fighting to free themselves from Spanish rule since 1809. In 1819, the Venezuelan Simón Bolívar assembled an army of local guerrillas, including *llaneros* (cowboys), and British and Irish veterans of the Napoleonic Wars. Bolívar then led this disparate force across swamps and mountains from Venezuela into New Grenada (Colómbia), towards its capital, Bogotá. A Royalist army, commanded by Colonel José María Barreiro and roughly equal in size to Bolívar's force, attempted to stop them. The two clashed at the Vargas Swamp in central Colómbia on 25 July, then raced towards Bogotá. When Barreiro's army reached the Teatinos River, they found Bolívar waiting. The Royalists' vanguard was crossing the river at the Boyacá Bridge, exhausted from marching over harsh terrain and ill-prepared for a fight; Bolivar's *llaneros* cavalry attacked and decimated them. The rest of Bolívar's men emerged from a valley to take the main force by surprise, swiftly overcoming Royalist resistance and taking 1,800 prisoners, including Barreiro. Three days later Bolívar occupied Bogotá, and Spanish rule in New Grenada was at an end.

◄ **TURNING POINT FOR THE INDEPENDENCE MOVEMENT** Bolívar's victory at Boyacá Bridge is considered the beginning of independence from the Spanish for the north of South America. The forces engaged were quite small, with only some 3,000 men fighting on each side, and Bolívar's army suffered just 66 casualties. In this 19th-century engraving, Bolívar's *llaneros*, identifiable by their long lances, are clearly seen surrounding the Royalist army.

COMMANDER **SIMÓN BOLÍVAR** (1783-1830)

Born into a wealthy family in Caracas, Bolívar was a revolutionary and politician who fought for the independence of his native Venezuela from the Spanish. In 1813 he briefly ran the country, but his government was ousted, and Spanish Royalists took back control. His victory at Boyacá ended Spanish rule in New Grenada. In 1821 he won the Battle of Carabobo, which led to Venezuelan independence. He went on to campaign successfully for the liberation of both Ecuador and Peru. His dream was to unite Spanish-speaking South America into a single country, but his vision was never realized, and he died disillusioned in Colómbia aged 47.

➤ **Simón Bolívar** was nicknamed "El Libertador", or "the Liberator" because of the role he played in South America's struggle for independence.

Balaklava

1854 ■ CRIMEAN PENINSULA ■ BRITISH, FRENCH, AND TURKISH ALLIANCE VS. RUSSIA

CRIMEAN WAR

In March 1854, Britain and France joined the war between Russia and Ottoman Turkey in the Black Sea, lending their support to the Turks. During September 1854, an Anglo-French expeditionary force landed in Crimea and laid siege to the Russian port of Sevastopol. On 25 October, in an attempt to disrupt the siege, the Russian army attacked the main British supply port, Balaklava.

First, the Russians seized the high ground to give their artillery a commanding position, then they advanced across the plain towards the port. However, the Scottish infantry of the 93rd Highland Regiment blocked their path, drawn up in line – described in British accounts as the "Thin Red Line". The Highlanders held off two Russian cavalry charges with disciplined volley fire. The Heavy Brigade cavalry counterattacked, charging uphill to drive the Russians back. Unfortunately for the British, this was not the end of the battle. Observing the action from a hilltop, the British

commander Lord Raglan saw the Russians carrying off some captured artillery and issued an order for the Light Brigade cavalry to retake the guns. The message became jumbled in transmission – the Light Brigade's commander, Lord Cardigan, misinterpreted it and sent his men on a frontal charge against a Russian artillery battery. Almost half of the 660 cavalrymen were killed, wounded, or taken prisoner, and the British fell back on their defences in front of Balaklava, allowing the Russians to claim a victory. Sevastopol held out under siege for a further 11 months.

In detail

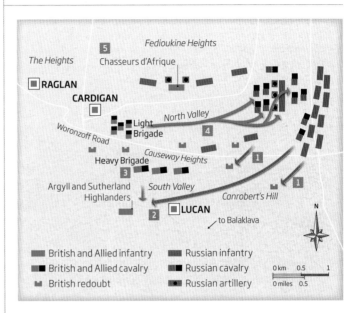

▬ British and Allied infantry	▬ Russian infantry
▬ British and Allied cavalry	▬ Russian cavalry
◣ British redoubt	▬ Russian artillery

▲ **ATTACK AND COUNTERATTACK** The battle began with the Russian seizure of the high ground from the Ottoman troops **1**. The Russians then attacked down South Valley **2**, but were repulsed by the British **3**. However, Russian artillery fired on the charge of the Light Brigade along North Valley from both the front and flanks **4**. The French cavalry tried to protect the British cavalry by attacking Russian batteries on the Fedioukine Heights **5**.

Worm for extracting unfired charge from gun barrel

Elevating wheel for changing angle of fire

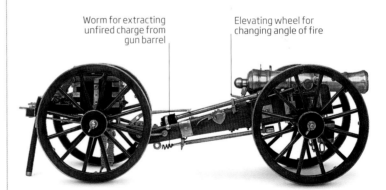

▲ **END OF AN ERA** At the time of the Crimean War, muzzle-loading smoothbore cannon like this field gun were the standard artillery for both sides. Essentially unchanged since the Napoleonic Wars, they fired solid shot or varieties of explosive shell. But a technological revolution was underway. Many infantrymen in Crimea carried rifle muskets - muzzle-loaded arms with rifled barrels - and the 1860s saw the arrival of breech-loading artillery with rifled barrels and the first machine-guns.

◀ **INTO THE VALLEY OF DEATH** This 19th-century painting by William Simpson depicts the infamous Charge of the Light Brigade, also immortalized by Alfred Tennyson in his poem. The battle hinged on two cavalry charges, the first by the British Heavy Brigade and the second by the hussars, light dragoons, and lancers of the Light Brigade. Although famous as a military blunder, the cavalry did reach the Russian lines and inflicted almost as many casualties as they suffered.

Solferino

1859 ▪ NORTHERN ITALY ▪ FRANCO-PIEDMONTESE ALLIANCE VS. AUSTRIA

ITALIAN WARS OF INDEPENDENCE

In 1859, French emperor Napoleon III formed an alliance with the kingdom of Piedmont–Sardinia, then ruled by Victor Emmanuel II, aiming to drive the Austrian Empire out of northern Italy. The French troops travelled to Italy by train – the first time an army had been mobilized by rail. The Franco-Piedmontese forces (commanded by Napoleon) clashed with Emperor Franz Joseph I's Austrian army at Magenta in northern Italy, then pursued them east towards the River Mincio. On 24 June, the allies attacked the Austrians again, catching them off guard while they prepared their own offensive. The troops on the Austrian left had spread themselves too thinly preparing to envelop the enemy, and were put under pressure by the superior allied force. In the centre of the battlefield at the village of Solferino, the Austrians hastily entrenched themselves and inflicted massive losses on the French troops, but the French managed to break through enemy lines in the early afternoon. At San Martino,

▲ **PIEDMONTESE TROOPS ATTACK AT SAINT MARTIN** The forces of the kingdom of Piedmont-Sardinia are depicted (left) during the fighting at San Martino on the northern flank of the battlefield. The Piedmontese suffered heavy losses, and felt betrayed when their ally France later made peace with Austria, but still allowed the Austrians possession of Venice. However, following the wars of independence, Victor Emmanuel II was proclaimed king of a united Italy in 1861.

on the Austrian right, Franz Joseph's armies fought off brave attacks by the determined but poorly organized Piedmontese forces. Eventually the Austrians accepted defeat and abandoned the field, their retreat covered by a rainstorm that made pursuit impossible.

Shocked by the slaughter (some 40,000 men had been killed, wounded, or gone missing), Napoleon had no wish to continue. One witness of the battle's aftermath, Swiss businessman Henri Dunant, was so horrified that in 1863 he founded what became the International Red Cross.

LOUIS **NAPOLEON BONAPARTE III** (1808–73)

Louis Napoleon Bonaparte was the nephew and heir to Emperor Napoleon I. Elected president of the French Second Republic in 1848, in 1852 he staged a coup to establish the Second French Empire, becoming Emperor Napoleon III. Family tradition compelled him to pursue military adventures, but he had none of the tactical genius of his uncle. He engaged France in the Crimean War in 1853–56 and the war against Austria in 1859. In 1870, he blundered into war with Prussia and was taken prisoner. Released in 1871, he spent his last years in exile in the UK.

▲ **This portrait of Napoleon III** was painted by German artist Franz Xaver Winterhalter in 1855.

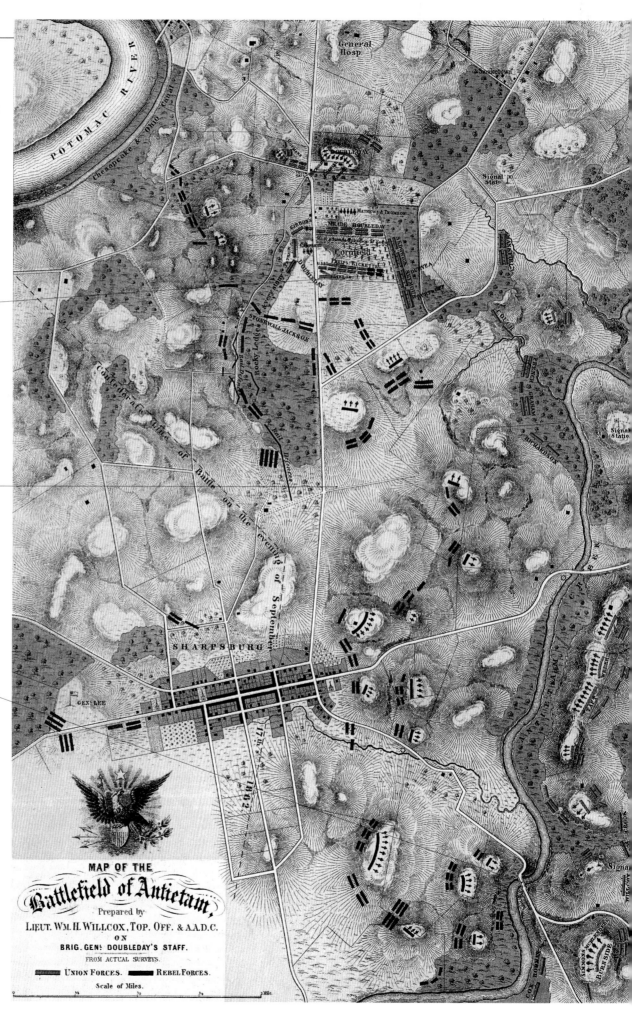

▶ BATTLEFIELD MAP OF ANTIETAM The two armies were separated by Antietam Creek, except on the Confederate left where McClellan had moved Union troops across the water before the battle. McClellan failed to capitalize on his superior numbers, or coordinate operations in different sectors of the field. This allowed Lee to move troops to wherever they were most needed.

1

6am:
Union 1st Corps advances from the north down the Hagerstown Pike; savage fighting follows in Miller's Cornfield and the West Woods, which change hands several times over the course of the battle.

2

9:30am:
Union troops cross Antietam Creek and attack the Confederate centre. Confederates positioned in a sunken lane, later known as Bloody Lane, hold out until 1pm. McClellan fails to exploit his success when the position is taken.

3

10am–1pm:
Union soldiers fight to cross a bridge over the creek, later called Burnside's Bridge. By 4pm, the Confederates are struggling to hold their position when a division arriving from Harpers Ferry drives back the Union left flank.

MAP OF THE
Battlefield of Antietam,
Prepared by
LIEUT. WM. H. WILLCOX, TOP. OFF. & A.A.D.C.
ON
BRIG. GEN! DOUBLEDAY'S STAFF.
FROM ACTUAL SURVEYS.

▬▬▬ UNION FORCES.   ▬▬▬ REBEL FORCES.

Scale of Miles.

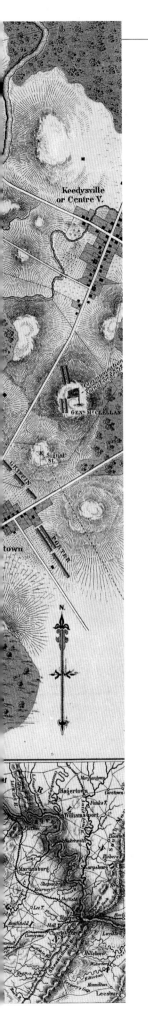

Antietam

1862 ■ NORTHEASTERN USA ■ UNION ARMY VS. CONFEDERATE ARMY

AMERICAN CIVIL WAR

In 1861, civil war broke out in the US after bitter disputes over slavery between Union states, where abolitionism was gaining popularity, and rebel Confederate states (see p.166). In September 1862, Confederate general Robert E. Lee led his army into the Union state of Maryland, and a copy of Lee's movement orders fell into the hands of Union commander General George McClellan. Learning that Lee had divided his forces into two weaker groups, McClellan saw the chance to "destroy the rebel army", as ordered by President Abraham Lincoln, but he moved too slowly to trap his opponent. Lee, after withdrawing towards Virginia, assembled his troops and joined battle on 17 September at Sharpsburg,

behind Antietam Creek. McClellan had around 80,000 men, whereas Lee had fewer than 30,000, although thousands were marching to join him.

The Union forces launched a series of attacks on the Confederate left, which resulted in numerous casualties and stalemate. Union troops broke through in the centre, but failed to press home their advantage. On the Union left, General Ambrose Burnside suffered heavy losses as his men crossed a narrow bridge under Confederate fire; in the afternoon, Union troops crossed the creek via a ford to the south. Lee's cause almost appeared lost, but a fresh Confederate division arrived, forcing Burnside's Union troops to pull back, and the savage day's fighting ended. Although he had 20,000 reserves, McClellan decided not to continue the battle the following day, allowing Lee to escape beyond the Potomac.

In context

▲ **UNION TROOPS ADVANCE ON DUNKER CHURCH** In the opening stages of the battle, the Union forces, well equipped and smartly uniformed, launched successive attacks against the left side of the Confederate line around the whitewashed Dunker Church. Between them the two sides suffered almost 23,000 casualties in the battle – the most recorded fatalities in one day's fighting in American history.

▲ **LINCOLN VISTS MCCLELLAN AT ANTIETAM** Angered by McClellan's failure to crush Lee's army, Abraham Lincoln sacked him after visiting the battlefield. Even so, the battle was a Union victory and strengthened the president's hand, allowing him to issue the Emancipation Proclamation, freeing slaves in Confederate territory.

Gettysburg

1863 ■ NORTHEASTERN USA ■ UNION ARMY VS. CONFEDERATE ARMY

AMERICAN CIVIL WAR

In June 1863, after a series of victories over the Union forces, General Robert E Lee's Confederate Army of Northern Virginia invaded Pennsylvania. On 28 June, President Abraham Lincoln appointed General George Meade to command the Union Army of the Potomac, with orders to seek out and destroy Lee's army. However. the battle of Gettysburg began by accident on 1 July when a Confederate division, raiding the town of Gettysburg in search of shoes, unexpectedly encountered Union cavalry. A firefight broke out, and the scattered elements of both armies hastened towards the fighting.

Showing their habitual aggression, the Confederates drove the Union forces back to a ridge south of the town by the end of the day. Further troops continued to arrive, some 90,000 Union and 70,000 Confederate soldiers eventually engaging. On the second day, the Confederates delivered their main assault against the left wing of the Union defences, with a subsidiary attack on the right at Culp's Hill. The Union soldiers held their ground, notably at a high point known as Little Round Top, which was defended by the 20th Maine regiment. On the third day, Lee ordered three divisions under General James Longstreet, one led by Major General George Pickett, to launch a final attack on the Union centre. This frontal assault ended in disaster, as Union firepower mowed down the advancing infantry. Content with what he had achieved, Meade allowed Lee's shattered army to withdraw without further harassment.

THE **AMERICAN CIVIL WAR** (1861-65)

By June 1861, 11 southern states had seceded from the US, forming the Confederate States of America. President Abraham Lincoln decided to use military force to maintain the Union. The Confederacy had inferior resources but won many of the early battles. However, in summer 1863, the Gettysburg disaster left the southern states facing inevitable defeat. A grinding attritional strategy masterminded by General Ulysses Grant brought the Union forces to victory in April 1865. At a cost of 600,000 lives, the war ended slavery and upheld the unity of the United States.

▶ **Abraham Lincoln,** the 16th President of the United States, led his country through its bloodiest chapter - the Civil War.

▲ **DECISIVE COMBAT** The climax of the battle came on 3 July with the massed Confederate attack known as Pickett's Charge. Fired upon by Union cannon and by infantry sheltered behind stone walls, only a fraction of the 15,000 Confederate infantrymen reached the Union line. They were then driven back by Union counterattacks in hand-to-hand fighting.

In detail

The battle of Gettysburg was lost through Confederate errors rather than won by inspired Union generalship. Fatally, General Lee lacked his most gifted commander, General Thomas "Stonewall" Jackson, who was killed at Chancellorsville in May 1863. On the first day of the battle, the Confederates, having driven the Union forces back to Cemetery Hill, failed to launch an immediate uphill assault, instead giving their enemy time to consolidate their defensive position. Had Jackson been on the field, it is possible that the Confederates would have used bolder tactics. Once the Union troops were stationed on the high ground, Lee's subordinate general, James Longstreet, urged him to outflank the enemy, and so threaten their rear and force them to withdraw without further fighting. However, Lee insisted that his superior troops could crush the Union army. Overruled, the reluctant Longstreet was slow to send his men forward on the second day. On the third day, with a heavy heart, he ordered the frontal attack known as Pickett's Charge. He was convinced that it would fail, and it did. The battle marked the high point of the last major Confederate advance northwards.

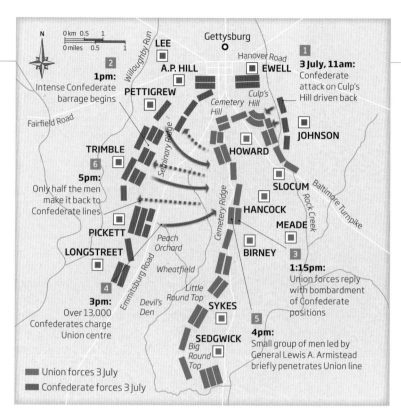

▲ **GETTYSBURG, DAY THREE** On 1 July, the fighting began to the north and west of Gettysburg – then the Union forces fell back to the high ground stretching from Culp's Hill to the Round Tops. On the second day, the Confederates attacked the Union left and right without making decisive gains. The third-day advance against the Union centre by three Confederate divisions failed because of the intensity of Union firepower.

▼ **CONFEDERATE FLAG** Union troops captured this flag of the 11th Mississippi Infantry Regiment at Gettysburg. Taking part in Pickett's Charge, the regiment was almost wiped out, losing 340 of the 393 men who took part in the action.

▼ **UNION FLAG** The Civil War-era United States flag bore 34 stars, one for each state of the Union. The 23 states that stayed loyal to the Union when the Confederacy was created contained four-fifths of America's white population, nine-tenths of its industry, and three-quarters of its railroads.

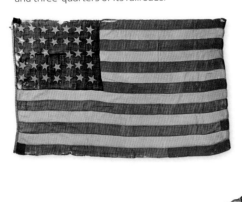

Cast bronze smoothbore barrel

Flared muzzle

Elevation screw for raising and lowering barrel

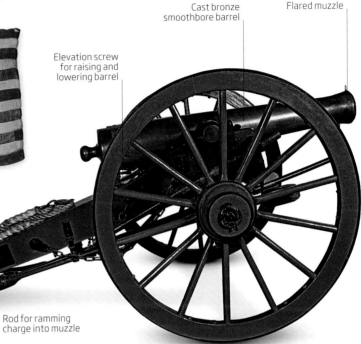

Rod for ramming charge into muzzle

▼ **UNION VOLUNTEER INFANTRY** The Union troops that fought at Gettysburg were all volunteers, mostly enlisted for three years' service in the early months of the war. They were far better equipped and supplied than their Confederate opponents, who rarely had proper uniforms and were often short of adequate footwear. This picture was taken by one of the first war photographers, Alexander Gardner.

▲ **CIVIL WAR NAPOLEON CANNON** This 12-pounder brass smoothbore cannon was the most common artillery piece of the American Civil War. It fired cannonballs and explosive shells as well as shrapnel or canister shot that sprayed iron or lead balls on advancing infantry. More than musketry, it was Union cannon fire that cut down the massed Confederate infantry in Pickett's Charge.

▲ **HOSPITAL TENT** This photograph, taken after the battle, shows an army surgeon preparing to operate on a wounded man lying on a table. The best available treatment for many wounds was amputation, but one in four amputations killed the patient. More than 3,000 Union troops and almost 5,000 Confederates lost their lives in the battle, and some 30,000 men in total were wounded.

Königgrätz

1866 ■ MODERN-DAY CZECH REPUBLIC ■ PRUSSIA VS. AUSTRIA

AUSTRO-PRUSSIAN WAR

In June 1866, war broke out between Prussia and Austria over the two nations' rival claims to leadership of the German states. Exploiting his country's excellent railway system, Prussian chief-of-staff Helmuth von Moltke rapidly moved three armies to the Austrian border, seizing the strategic initiative. Outmanoeuvred, Austrian commander Ludwig Benedek adopted a defensive position at the Elbe River, between Sadowa and Königgrätz (now in the Czech Republic). However, communication between Moltke and his armies, which relied on the electric telegraph, broke down in the lead-up to the battle, leaving his 100,000-strong Second Army still marching towards the battleground when the fighting began on the morning of 3 July. As a result, the Austrians outnumbered the Prussians at the start of the battle. The Austrians also had excellent artillery, including the latest breech-loading rifled

▲ **A HARD-FOUGHT VICTORY** This 1866 painting shows the Prussian king Wilhelm I and his entourage arriving at the battlefield after the decisive victory at Königgrätz (also known as the Battle of Sadowa). The Prussian armies had lost 2,000 killed and 7,000 wounded, but Austrian casualties were far more severe with 44,000 men dead, wounded, or taken prisoner. The victory was a decisive step towards Wilhelm I being crowned Emperor of Germany five years later.

cannon. Taking the offensive, the Prussians initially suffered heavy casualties, but in the early afternoon an Austrian counterattack broke down in the face of the Prussian infantry's rifle fire.

The belated arrival of the Prussian Second Army, smashing into the Austrian flank, settled the outcome. The Austrians withdrew in disorder, their retreat covered by brave cavalry charges that prevented a Prussian pursuit. The peace terms imposed on Austria left Prussia in control of northern Germany and poised to push for German unification under Prussian leadership.

In context

▲ **PRUSSIAN INFANTRY IN ACTION** Prussian foot soldiers were armed with the Dreyse needle gun, a breech-loading bolt-action rifle that had a higher rate of fire and greater accuracy than the Austrians' muzzle-loaded Lorenz rifles. The Prussian rifle could be reloaded by a soldier lying prone, while the Lorenz had to be reloaded standing. The Prussian infantry were also superior in training and discipline.

▲ **THE "IRON CHANCELLOR" PREVAILS** Otto von Bismarck, the architect of German unification, was on hand to observe the victory at Königgrätz. As chief minister of Prussian King Wilhelm I from 1862, Bismarck fought wars against Denmark, Austria, and France that led to the founding of the German Empire in 1871. He served as Chancellor until 1890.

Sedan

1870 ▪ NORTHEASTERN FRANCE ▪ GERMAN STATES AND PRUSSIA VS. FRANCE

FRANCO-PRUSSIAN WAR

The Prussian chief minister Otto von Bismarck provoked French Emperor Napoleon III into declaring war in July 1870. The Prussians were joined by the armies of the German states, except Austria. The French mobilization was slow and chaotic, which allowed the Prussians to seize the initiative. Their chief-of-staff, Helmuth von Moltke, outmanoeuvred the French: one army was besieged in Metz while another, led by Napoleon and Marshal Patrice de MacMahon, fell back to the fortress town of Sedan.

By 1 September, the 120,000 French soldiers were encircled inside Sedan and under fire from over 400 Prussian guns. Napoleon was ill and MacMahon wounded, so the troops were left without effective leadership. Showing outstanding courage, groups of cavalry attempted to break out, launching near-suicidal charges against the Prussian lines. These efforts failed, and Napoleon was urged to lead a final breakout attempt, but he had no interest in such a costly gesture. Instead, on the morning of 2 September, he surrendered to Prussian King Wilhelm I. He and 100,000 of his men were captured and the Second French Empire collapsed. An uprising in Paris followed, leading to the establishment of the French Third Republic. By the end of the Franco-Prussian War in May 1871, France had lost both Alsace and Lorraine to a newly united Germany and had to pay substantial reparations. The humiliating defeat stirred discontent in France.

▶ **FIGHTING AT BAZEILLES** In the opening stages of the battle of Sedan the Prussians savagely attacked the French troops on the streets of this village 3.5 km (2 miles) south of town, as seen in this 19th-century print. The willingness of French soldiers to fight to the death contrasted starkly with Napoleon's defeatism. France suffered 17,000 casualties, compared with some 9,000 on the Prussian side.

In context

▲ **THE SIEGE OF PARIS** After Sedan, the French Republican government established itself, and refused to accept defeat. The Prussians besieged Paris and fighting continued elsewhere in France; the Paris garrison made sorties, such as this surprise bridge attack, but their resistance was gradually worn down. Paris eventually fell on 28 January 1871, but was plunged into more bloodshed with the uprising of the Paris Commune only weeks later.

▲ **THE NEW GERMAN EMPIRE** On 18 January 1871, during the siege of Paris, Prussia's King Wilhelm I was declared Emperor of Germany at a ceremony held in the Hall of Mirrors at Versailles. The unification of all the German states except Austria under Prussian leadership created the most formidable military power in Europe.

ESTAMINET
DU
COMMERCE·
RESTAURANT

CRÖCHLING 1892

Little Bighorn

1876 ▪ MONTANA, MIDWESTERN USA ▪ PLAINS INDIAN WARRIORS VS. USA

GREAT SIOUX WAR

Since the mid-19th century, the US government had been moving Native Americans to reservations. However, many resisted, in particular the leaders of the Sioux Plains Indians.

In 1875, following the discovery of gold in South Dakota, the US army sent troops to move the local population. By spring 1876, angry at white encroachments on their lands, several thousand Lakota Sioux, Cheyenne, and Arapaho

tribespeople, including 1,500 to 2,000 warriors, led by the Sioux Chiefs Crazy Horse and Sitting Bull, gathered at an encampment by the Little Bighorn River in Montana. On 25 June, Lieutenant Colonel George A. Custer, leading some 600 men of US Seventh Cavalry, located the camp; although reinforcements were a day's march away, he chose to attack.

Major Marcus Reno led 140 troopers in the initial assault. The attack caught the Plains Indians by surprise, but they counterattacked, driving Reno's men back to a defensive position on a hill. Meanwhile, Custer led 210

men along a ridge to attack the camp from the other side. They were repelled as Crazy Horse's warriors swarmed uphill towards them. For a while, the troopers' rifle fire held the warriors off, but once the skirmish line broke, Custer and his men were doomed. Pursued by Crazy Horse's warriors, they were trapped on what has become known as Last Stand Hill. A final warrior charge swept over them and the few survivors were killed as they tried to flee. Reno's men and the rest of the Seventh Cavalry held out until the next day, when the Plains Indians broke off the fight – their largest victory over the US government.

In context

◄ **SIOUX LEADER** Leader of the Hunkpapa Sioux, Sitting Bull inspired the Little Bighorn gathering. During the battle, he rallied the Native American warriors and saw to the safety of the women and children, while Chief Crazy Horse went to meet the US attackers. After the battle, Sitting Bull fled to Canada. He died in 1890 at the Battle of Wounded Knee – the last major clash of the war.

▼ **PLAINS INDIAN SHIELD** An important part of a warrior's equipment, along with bows, lances, clubs, and knives, shields were decorated with symbols that endowed them with magical force, so providing spiritual assistance as well as physical protection. By the time of Little Bighorn, warriors were also using rifles and pistols bought from white traders or captured from enemies, although they still maintained traditions from pre-modern warfare.

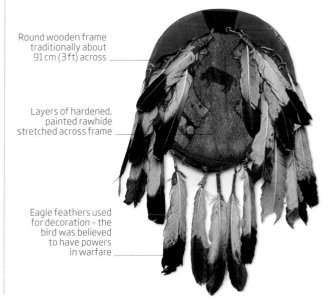

Round wooden frame traditionally about 91 cm (3 ft) across

Layers of hardened, painted rawhide stretched across frame

Eagle feathers used for decoration – the bird was believed to have powers in warfare

◄ **THE DEFEAT OF THE US ARMY** This depiction of the final stage of Little Bighorn, when the Plains Indian warriors on horseback pursued scattered US soldiers, was painted by an unknown Sioux. Both sides fought much of the battle dismounted, firing rifles from behind cover. The total US losses were 268 killed and 55 seriously wounded; the dead included two of Custer's brothers. Estimates of the number killed among the Plains warriors range from 31 to 300.

If we went to war to overthrow the military system of Zululand, in what way have we succeeded?

LADY FLORENCE DIXIE ON THE ANGLO-ZULU WAR IN *A DEFENCE OF ZULULAND AND ITS KING*, 1882

Isandlwana

1879 ▪ SOUTH AFRICA ▪ ZULU WARRIORS VS. BRITAIN

ANGLO-ZULU WAR

This war began as a campaign of colonial expansion. In December 1878, British authorities delivered an ultimatum to the Zulu king Cetshwayo (see below), requiring him to give up a group of Zulus accused of raiding British territory. He failed to comply, so in January 1879 Lord Chelmsford, British army commander in southern Africa, launched an invasion from Natal. Chelmsford divided his force into three. The central section crossed the Buffalo River, the border between Natal and Zululand, at Rorke's Drift and camped at the foot of Isandlwana Hill. Chelmsford rode off in search of the Zulu and, seriously underrating their military prowess, left his camp defended by just 1,500 men, including 800 British regulars of the 24th Foot and native infantry. Cetshwayo mobilized his army, and his lightly-equipped, barefooted warriors moved in to repel the invaders. On 22 January, 15,000 Zulu attacked the British. They adopted their traditional "buffalo-horn" formation – the main "body" delivered a frontal assault, while the two "horns" outflanked the British to the right and left. At first the British army's rifles and field guns held the frontal attack, but they were soon overwhelmed by Zulu spears – only a few men on horseback escaped. Bizarrely, a solar eclipse plunged the battlefield into darkness as the slaughter began. Six months later the British crushed the Zulus.

▲ **DOOMED BRITISH TROOPS** The British Army Redcoats are depicted making a resolute last stand against Zulu warriors armed with shields and small spears in this 19th-century painting of the battle. Some 800 British soldiers and almost 500 of the Africans fighting with them were killed – it was not a Zulu custom to take prisoners. The Zulu dead numbered between 1,000 and 2,000 men.

In context

◀ **KING CETSHWAYO** A strong military leader, Cetshwayo was the last king of the independent Zulus. Born in 1826, he took control of Zululand in 1856 after defeating his brothers in a power struggle, but was not proclaimed king until 1873, following the death of his father Mpande in 1872. A formidable presence, his dignified response to defeat won the sympathy of his British captors. He was exiled to Cape Town, then in 1882 to London. He returned to Zululand in 1883, but died in February 1884.

▶ **TRADITIONAL ZULU WEAPONRY** The Zulu warriors used these short spears, or "iklwa", and cowhide shields, or "isihlangu". Rather than throwing their spears from distance, they chose to fight at close quarters and, protected by the shields, delivered a deadly upward thrust to their enemy. Cetshwayo's men did carry firearms, but the weapons were of poor quality and they had not been properly trained to use them.

Directory: 1700–1900

CULLODEN
JACOBITE RISING OF 1745

1746 ▪ SCOTTISH HIGHLANDS ▪
JACOBITES VS. LOYALIST BRITISH ARMY

In 1745 the French were at war with Britain, and backed Charles Edward Stuart (Bonnie Prince Charlie) in trying to re-establish his Catholic family on the British throne in place of the Protestant Hanoverians. Charles landed in the Outer Hebrides in July and marched south to England with his Jacobite followers. Failing to rouse popular support, he retreated north, pursued by a loyalist British army under the Duke of Cumberland. On 16 April 1746, at Culloden Moor outside Inverness, Charles's force of Scottish Highland clansmen and Irishmen engaged Cumberland's army. The loyalists opened with heavy gunfire, inflicting severe losses on the disorganized Jacobites. When the Jacobites finally attacked, they were driven back by disciplined British troops, and within an hour the battle was over. Defeated, Charles fled to France and made no more attempts on the throne.

QUIBERON BAY
SEVEN YEARS' WAR

1759 ▪ NORTHERN FRANCE ▪ BRITAIN
VS. FRANCE

In 1759, France planned to invade Britain, aiming to end British participation in the Seven Years' War. The Royal Navy, however, had blockaded the main French fleet in Brest. In November, bad weather forced the British to raise the blockade and 21 French heavy warships set sail, pursued by 24 British equivalents, which caught up with them off Quiberon Bay, Brittany, on 20 November. A westerly gale was blowing and the French commander led his ships into the bay, believing that the British would not dare follow among the shoals and reefs in heavy seas. But the British entered the bay, and a desperate fight ensued. Two French ships sank and five others were captured or ran aground. Seven escaped into the shallow River Vilaine after throwing their guns overboard. For the loss of two ships, the British had crippled France's sea power and neutralized the threat of invasion.

SIEGE OF YORKTOWN
AMERICAN REVOLUTIONARY WAR

1781 ▪ EASTERN USA ▪ AMERICAN
CONTINENTAL ARMY AND FRANCE
VS. BRITAIN

The US had been fighting for independence from Britain since 1775, and was supported by France. In August 1781, General Charles Cornwallis led a 7,000-strong British army to Yorktown, Virginia, a port on Chesapeake Bay. They built a fortified camp and awaited reinforcements from the sea. But on 5 September, French warships defeated a British fleet off Chesapeake Bay, leaving Yorktown under naval blockade. General George Washington, commander of the American Continental Army, and General Jean-Baptiste Rochambeau, commander of a French expeditionary force, moved 16,000 troops to confront Cornwallis's army. Digging entrenchments opposite the British, the US and French launched an artillery bombardment and seized two crucial fortifications. With no escape, Cornwallis surrendered on 19 October. Britain soon accepted it would have to recognize US independence.

TIPPECANOE
TECUMSEH'S WAR

1811 ▪ MID-WESTERN USA ▪ USA
VS. SHAWNEE

Chief of the Shawnee tribe, Tecumseh, had tried to organize Native Americans to resist the transfer of their land to the US government. William Henry Harrison, governor of Indiana Territory, saw this as a threat and sought to increase the pace of settlement. In 1811, Harrison marched 1,000 soldiers and militia to Tecumseh's village at Prophetstown on the Tippecanoe river, and made camp. Tecumseh was away and had left his brother, Tenskwatawa, in charge. Early on 7 November, Tenskwatawa's 700 warriors attacked the camp. In confused, close-quarters fighting, 62 of Harrison's soldiers were killed or mortally wounded, but they fought off the attack. The Native Americans, who lost 50 warriors, abandoned Prophetstown, which Harrison burned to the ground.

▼ NAVARINO
GREEK WAR OF INDEPENDENCE

1827 ▪ SOUTHERN GREECE ▪ BRITISH,
FRENCH, AND RUSSIAN NAVIES VS.
TURKISH AND EGYPTIAN NAVIES

Navarino (now Pylos) was the last naval battle of the age of sail. In July 1827, Britain, France, and Russia joined in a war alongside Greece, fighting for independence from the Ottoman Empire. Admiral Sir Edward Codrington, the British naval commander in the Mediterranean, was trying to imposing a ceasefire. After an Egyptian fleet joined Ottoman warships off Navarino on the Peloponnese peninsula, the British blockaded the bay, where they were joined by French and Russian squadrons. As negotiations stalled, the Allied commanders decided to take action. On 20 October, their combined fleets sailed into Navarino bay,

This 19th-century Greek print depicts the aftermath of the battle at Navarino.

where more than 70 Egyptian and Ottoman ships were anchored. The Allies had only 22 ships, but their guns proved far superior. In four hours, 70 Ottoman and Egyptian ships were destroyed or disabled, with no Allied ship losses. Greece became independent in 1832.

SAN JACINTO
TEXAS REVOLUTION

1836 ■ SOUTHERN USA ■ TEXAS VS. MEXICO

In October 1835, American settlers in the Mexican province of Texas rebelled against the Mexican government. The Mexican president, Antonio López de Santa Anna, led an army to regain control of his territory. His forces initially defeated the Texans at the Alamo in March 1836. The Texan army, led by General Sam Houston, spent weeks in retreat, pursued by Santa Anna. Houston avoided direct clashes; his numbers grew with new recruits, and training improved. On 20 April, the two armies camped in swampland near the San Jacinto River, ready to engage. On 21 April, Houston's 900 men moved stealthily toward the Mexican camp, and fired at close range before charging on foot and horseback. Caught off-guard, almost all the Mexican force of 1,300 men were killed, wounded, or taken prisoner. Santa Anna was captured and signed a peace treaty on 14 May; Texas became an independent republic.

SOBRAON
FIRST ANGLO-SIKH WAR

1846 ■ NORTHERN INDIA ■ EAST INDIA COMPANY VS. SIKH EMPIRE

By the early 19th century, Britain – under the directorship of the East India Company – controlled most of India; the Sikh empire was based in the Punjab. In 1845, war broke out, and in December British forces narrowly avoided defeat by the Sikh army at Ferozeshah. The armies met again on 10 February 1846, at Sobraon by the Sutlej River. After cannon bombardments from each side, the British infantry attacked the Sikhs' fortified camp. Driven back with heavy losses, the British eventually breached the fortifications, and their cavalry penetrated the camp. Trapped between the British and the river, many Sikhs fought to the death, suffering 10,000 casualties – almost half their army. After this defeat, the Sikhs ceded part of the Punjab. After a war in 1849, the Sikh empire was absorbed into British India.

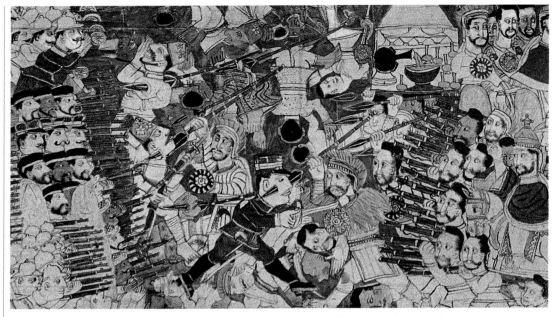

The **Ethiopian army** battles against Italian troops at the Battle of Adowa in this locally produced painting.

FIRST BULL RUN
AMERICAN CIVIL WAR

1861 ■ EASTERN USA ■ CONFEDERATES VS. UNION

Also known as First Manassas, this was the opening battle of the American Civil War, in which 11 southern states (the Confederates) broke away from the Union in a dispute over slavery. Each side had hastily assembled armies of raw volunteers. The Union forces, led by General Irvin McDowell, marched from Washington DC. They met Confederate troops under General Pierre Beauregard defending the Manassas railroad junction behind Bull Run river. McDowell sent his troops across a ford in a surprise attack on the Confederates, resulting in a savage and disorganized fight. Both sides were motivated but ill-trained, inexperienced, and badly equipped. The Confederates were reinforced by fresh troops arriving by train, and they mounted a general charge that dispelled the Union forces, who fled to Washington. For both sides, a long, hard war was ahead.

THIRD BATTLE OF NANJING
TAIPING REBELLION

1864 ■ EASTERN CHINA ■ TAIPING HEAVENLY KINGDOM VS. QING

The Taiping Rebellion was an uprising of a Christian faction led by Hong Xiuquan (self-proclaimed "Heavenly King") against the Qing Dynasty. In the 1850s, the Taiping ruled of much of southern China, but the Qing retaliated, backed by Western powers. From March 1864, the Qing besieged Nanjing, the rebel capital. Both armies were vast, with 500,000 Qing troops facing around 300,000 Taiping. On 1 June, Hong Xiuquan died, but his general Li Xiucheng continued the defence of the city. With supplies from Western allies, the Qing army launched a cannon bombardment of the city, while engineers dug tunnels under the walls. On 19 July, the Qing detonated explosives in the tunnels, allowing their troops to flood through the breach. After three days of fighting, around 100,000 Taipeng were dead, many by suicide in the face of surrender. Li Xiucheng was captured and executed. The rebellion did not last long.

▲ ADOWA
FIRST ITALO-ETHIOPIAN WAR

1896 ■ NORTHERN ETHIOPIA ■ ETHIOPIAN EMPIRE VS. KINGDOM OF ITALY

By the 1890s, Ethiopia was one of two African states entirely free of European control. The neighbouring state, Eritrea, was controlled by Italy, but Ethiopia's ruler, Menelik II, refused to accept Italian tutelage. In 1895, Menelik assembled an army to resist Italian incursions. The Italian army led by General Oreste Baratieri took up a defensive position at the town of Adowa. Baratieri had 18,000 men to Menelik's 100,000, but he had modern weaponry, and this prompted him to take the offensive. Baratieri's troops moved forward under cover of darkness for a dawn attack. However, by daybreak on 1 March his men were in disarray after an overnight move on difficult terrain, and dispersed groups of Italian soldiers were surrounded by Ethiopian warriors. More than 10,000 Italians were killed, wounded, or captured. Italy would not conquer Ethiopia until the 1930s.

OMDURMAN
MAHDIST WAR

1898 ■ CENTRAL SUDAN ■ ANGLO-EGYPTIAN ARMY VS. MAHDIST SUDANESE ARMY

The Islamic Mahdist movement in Sudan revolted against rule by Egypt, which itself had been dominated by Britain since 1882. In 1898, General Herbert Kitchener led a force of 26,000 British and Egyptian troops down the Nile into Sudan. At Omdurman, outside Khartoum, they met the 50,000-strong Mahdist Sudanese army. Kitchener's army positioned itself by the river, with gunboats providing covering fire. On 2 September, the Mahdists launched a frontal assault at dawn, but as they advanced over open ground they were cut down by the combined fire of artillery, gunboats, machine guns, and rifles. Kitchener then ordered his infantry and cavalry to take the offensive, which exposed them to counter-attacks and many suffered heavy casualties. The battle ended with Omdurman under British control, Kitchener's army having lost fewer than 500 men; the Mahdists lost around 10,000.

1900—PRESENT

- Mukden (1905)
- Tsushima (1905)
- Tannenberg (1914)
- First Marne (1914)
- Gallipoli (1915)
- Verdun (1916)
- Jutland (1916)
- The Somme (1916)
- Passchendaele (1917)
- Dunkirk (1940)
- Battle of Britain (1940)
- Pearl Harbor (1941)
- Midway (1942)
- Second Battle of El Alamein (1942)
- Stalingrad (1942-43)
- Kursk (1943)
- Operation Overlord (1944)
- Operation Market Garden (1944)
- Battle of the Bulge (1944)
- Iwo Jima (1945)
- Incheon (1950)
- Dien Bien Phu (1954)
- Six-Day War (1967)
- Tet Offensive (1968)
- Operation Desert Storm (1991)
- Directory:
  Spion Kop (1900) ■ Caporetto (1917)
  Warsaw (1920) ■ First and Second Battle of Inonu (1921)
  Madrid (1936) ■ Shanghai (1937)
  Imphal (1944) ■ Falaise Pocket (1944)
  Xuzhou (1948-49) ■ Falklands (1982)
  Invasion of Iraq (2003)

CHAPTER 5

Mukden

1905 ▪ NORTHEASTERN CHINA ▪ JAPAN VS. RUSSIA

RUSSO-JAPANESE WAR

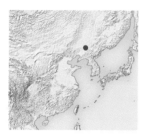

In February 1904, Russia and Japan went to war over their rival territorial claims in Manchuria and Korea. The Japanese besieged Russian troops stationed in Port Arthur (now Lüshunkou in eastern China). After attempting to break the siege and being defeated at the battle of Liaoyang in September that year, the Russian army retreated north to the Sha Ho River south of Mukden (now Shenyang). There, the two opposing armies dug into trenches 145 km (90 miles) long.

The Japanese took Port Arthur in January 1905, and the troops from the siege rejoined the main army at Mukden. This gave Japanese commander Field Marshal Oyama Iwao the chance to attack. Russia could reinforce its army with far greater resources than Japan, so Oyama sought to inflict a crushing defeat before Russia could mobilize any reserves. The Russian commander General Alexei Kuropatkin had

roughly 290,000 men in the field, against Oyama's 207,000. Although Kuropatkin was planning an offensive, the Japanese pre-empted him by attacking his left flank on 20 February. Fighting in snow, ice, and blizzards, Oyama lured Kuropatkin into shifting troops to his left, and on 27 February he unleashed his best troops against the Russian right. Kuropatkin frantically tried to reposition his forces to face this onslaught, but his army fell into disorder. Despite suffering heavy losses, the Japanese frontal assaults soon threatened to envelop the Russians; on 9 March, Kuropatkin withdrew. This battle, the largest ever fought at the time, turned the war in Japan's favour, preceding the naval clash at Tsushima (see pp.184–87).

▶ **A BLOODY VICTORY** As shown in this 20th-century lithograph, the Japanese at Mukden carried out repeated massed frontal assaults on entrenched troops, at a great cost: each side suffered around 70,000 casualties. Foreign military observers attributed the Japanese victory to a superior offensive spirit, mistakenly concluding that well-motivated infantry could overcome machine-guns and modern artillery.

In context

▼ **THE BIRTH OF TRENCH WARFARE** Japanese soldiers fire from trenches at Mukden. The battle prefigured the trench warfare of World War I: troops with rapid-fire rifles and machine-guns dug in behind barbed wire, while artillery fired high-explosive shells beyond line of sight, guided by forward observers via field telephones. Japan had the technological advantage, with twice as many machine-guns as Russia.

▲ **RETREAT FROM MUKDEN** Wounded Russian soldiers disembark at Vladivostok railway station. After the battle, the Russian army abandoned their equipment and their wounded in a stampede to the rear, but they avoided a total rout, reforming in defensive positions 160 km (100 miles) to the north. The Japanese victory at Tsushima (see pp.184–87) and upheavals in Russia helped to decide the war's outcome: in September 1905, Russia surrendered control of Korea to Japan, and evacuated southern Manchuria.

▲ **LETHAL BOMBARDMENT** A Russian battleship is struck by a high-explosive shell fired from the line of Japanese warships at Tsushima. Skilled Japanese naval gunners achieved numerous hits at ranges up to 6,000 m (20,000 ft). The Russians lost a total of six battleships in the two-day engagement.

Tsushima

1905 ▪ KOREA STRAIT ▪ JAPAN VS. RUSSIA

RUSSO-JAPANESE WAR

In October 1904, Russia dispatched a naval squadron, commanded by Admiral Zinovy Rozhestvensky, on an 18,000-nautical-mile (33,000-km) voyage from the Baltic to join the war it was fighting against the Japanese in the Pacific. The stakes could not have been higher. A Japanese victory would have forced Russia to abandon its expansionist policies in the Far East – leaving Japan to pursue its own – and Japan was already on the brink of winning the land war (see pp.180–81). After a gruelling seven-month journey, the squadron had to pass close to Japan to reach the port of Vladivostok. The Japanese Imperial Combined Fleet (a total of 89 ships), under Admiral Togo Heihachiro, was waiting to intercept them.

During the early hours of 27 May, the 38 Russian ships were spotted slipping through the Tsushima Strait under the cover of darkness. That afternoon, using wireless to organize a rapid response, Togo gave pursuit and engaged the Russian fleet. Through superior Japanese long-range gunnery, four Russian battleships were sunk by nightfall. Japanese destroyers and torpedo boats harassed the remnants of the Russian fleet through the night, and the following morning most surviving Russian vessels surrendered. A total of 20 Russian ships had been sunk at a cost of over 4,500 lives. It was the first time in the modern era that an Asian power had defeated a European military force, and it marked the beginning of the end of the Tsarist regime in Russia.

ADMIRAL **TOGO HEIHACHIRO** (1848–1934)

Togo Heihachiro was born into the Satsuma samurai clan, which provided most officers for the Imperial Navy. Sent to Britain for training in the 1870s, he took Nelson as his role model. He came to prominence in 1894 commanding a cruiser in the Sino-Japanese War. Leading the Imperial Combined Fleet, he opened the Russo-Japanese War with a surprise attack on Port Arthur and ended it with victory at Tsushima.

➤ **Admiral Togo's defeat** of the Russians made him a Japanese national hero.

In detail

Tsushima was the first fleet engagement fought between steel warships firing high-explosive shells. The Japanese had better-trained crews, more skilful gunnery, higher morale, and faster ships. They used their speed to manoeuvre around the Russian squadron, blocking its path to Vladivostok and bringing maximum firepower to bear. The first salvos were exchanged at 6,000 m (20,000 ft) as the two fleets steamed in line astern on a parallel course.

Togo then twice "crossed the T" – turning his fleet across the head of the Russian line, a manoeuvre that brought all his guns to bear on the hapless enemy. The Russian ships were battered by the Japanese shellfire and Admiral Rozhestvensky was put out of action by a shell fragment lodged in his skull. As the Russian fleet became disorganized they fell prey to smaller Japanese ships armed with torpedoes and equipped for night fighting.

▶ **TSUSHIMA, 1905** This sketch shows how Admiral Togo outmanoeuvred the Russian squadron during the first afternoon of the battle. Some of his manoeuvres were risky, especially the "turn in sequence" (3), which dangerously exposed his ships to enemy fire. The Russian gunners in fact achieved many hits on Japanese vessels, but the latter's armour proved highly effective.

1 **2:10pm:** The Japanese fleet steams northeast, blocking the Russians' path to Vladivostok.

3 **2:40pm:** Togo turns his fleet in sequence, keeping his flagship in the van, rather than having each ship turn individually and reversing the order of sailing.

5 **3pm:** Togo crosses the T for the second time, raining further destruction on the Russians.

6 **3pm:** The Russians suffer heavy losses, including Rozhestvensky's flagship *Knjaz Suvorov*.

2 **2:30pm:** Togo crosses the T, bringing all his main guns to bear on the Russian ships, while keeping them mostly out of the line of fire of all but the guns of the Russian lead ships.

4 **2:50pm:** Unable to find a way through to the north, the Russian fleet is forced to change course.

7 **6pm:** After a break in the fighting, Togo re-engages the disorganized Russians, inflicting yet more losses before nightfall.

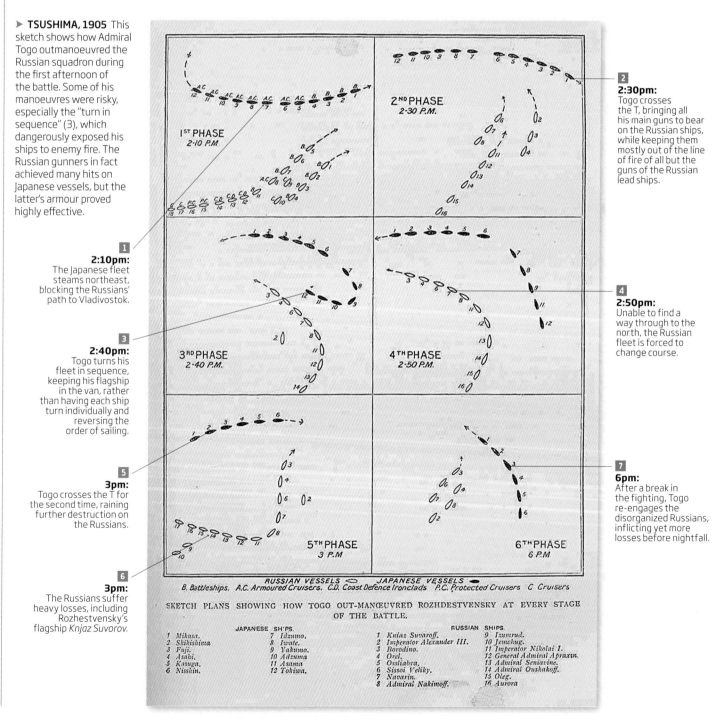

SKETCH PLANS SHOWING HOW TOGO OUT-MANŒUVRED ROZHDESTVENSKY AT EVERY STAGE OF THE BATTLE.

RUSSIAN VESSELS ⬎ JAPANESE VESSELS ⬑
B. Battleships. A.C. Armoured Cruisers. C.D. Coast Defence Ironclads P.C. Protected Cruisers C Cruisers

JAPANESE SH'PS.
1 Mikasa.
2 Shikishima.
3 Fuji.
4 Asahi.
5 Kasuga.
6 Nisshin.
7 Idzumo.
8 Iwate.
9 Yakumo.
10 Adzuma.
11 Asama.
12 Tokiwa.

RUSSIAN SHIPS.
1 Kniaz Suvaroff.
2 Imperator Alexander III.
3 Borodino.
4 Orel.
5 Ossliabya.
6 Sissoi Veliky.
7 Navarin.
8 Admiral Nakimoff.
9 Izumrud.
10 Jemchug.
11 Imperator Nikolai I.
12 General Admiral Apraxin.
13 Admiral Seniavine.
14 Admiral Oushakoff.
15 Oleg.
16 Aurora.

◄ **RUSSIA DEFEATED**
This depiction of Tsushima by Japanese artist Tojo Shotaro shows the two fleets unrealistically close together. The defeat of the Russian navy by an Asian fleet was a stinging blow to European assumptions of superiority in the imperialist era.

▼ **ROUTE TO TSUSHIMA**
This Russian map shows the route taken by Rozhestvensky's squadron from the Baltic. After mistakenly firing on British trawlers in the North Sea – known as the Dogger Bank Incident – the fleet was then denied passage through the British-controlled Suez Canal. Sailing around Africa, they had difficulty finding coaling stations at which to refuel. In southeast Asia, Rozhestvensky's squadron was joined by further ships that had taken the shorter Suez route.

▲ **HIJMS MIKASA** Admiral Togo's British-built flagship *Mikasa* was a state-of-the-art battleship when it was commissioned in 1902. It boasted four turret-mounted 12-in guns, as well as a range of lesser armaments, and Krupp steel plates for armour. *Mikasa* led the Japanese line at Tsushima.

◄ **WIRELESS COMMUNICATION** This Morse key from the battleship *Mikasa* was used to transmit messages by wireless telegraphy. Without this means of communication Admiral Togo would not have been able to organize such a rapid response to the Russian fleet's arrival.

Tannenberg

1914 ■ MODERN-DAY NORTHERN POLAND ■ GERMANY VS. RUSSIA

WORLD WAR I

At the start of World War I in August 1914, Germany committed most of its armies to attacking Belgium and France on the Western Front, leaving relatively limited forces to face Russia on the Eastern Front. They expected the Russians to be slow to mobilize, and were surprised when two Russian armies advanced on German soil in East Prussia in the third week of the war. The German Eighth Army commander, General Maximilian von Prittwitz, failed to halt the Russian advance at Gumbinnen (now Gusev, Russia), and ordered a general retreat. Shocked at the idea of sacrificing territory, German high command sacked Prittwitz, replacing him with General Paul von Hindenburg.

The commanders of the Russian First and Second Armies, generals Paul von Rennenkampf and Alexander Samsonov, were bitter enemies. Hindenburg and General Erich Ludendorff (see box, right) learned from intercepted radio messages that Samsonov planned to continue advancing, but that Rennenkampf had no intention of supporting him. They therefore concentrated almost all their forces on Samsonov's advancing Second Army, leaving only a light screen facing Rennenkampf. Moving troops swiftly by rail, the Germans executed a large-scale encirclement of Samsonov's army, a straggling mass after an overly rapid advance. Blocked at the front and attacked from both flanks, between 26 and 29 August the Second Army was reduced to disorder. Facing disaster, Samsonov shot himself. Over 90,000 Russians were trapped by the German pincer movement and taken prisoner. The battle made Hindenburg and Ludendorff German heroes; the Russian Empire continued to fight for another three years, but never truly recovered from this initial disaster.

PAUL VON HINDENBURG (1847-1934) AND ERICH LUDENDORFF (1865-1937)

A Prussian aristocrat, Hindenburg retired in 1911 after a solid military career. Recalled in August 1914, he commanded the Eastern Front with the intelligent, neurotic Ludendorff as his chief of staff. The stolid Hindenburg and volatile Ludendorff formed a strong partnership and from summer 1916, they ruled Germany, in effect, as a military dictatorship.

▲ **Hindenburg** (centre) and **Ludendorff** (front right) photographed at their command post at Tannenberg in 1914.

▼ **GERMAN INFANTRY ON THE MOVE** Wearing their traditional *pickelhaube* helmets, German soldiers march on the Eastern front. Many of Hindenburg's troops at Tannenberg were relatively elderly reserves or local *Landwehr* militia, the best formations having been deployed in the West.

German forces shown in blue encircling the Russian forces

Samsonov's Russian Second Army shown in red

German corps moved by train to south of Russian army

▲ **CONTEMPORARY MAP** The main map shows the encirclement of Samsonov's army (red) by German forces (blue) in the forests east of Tannenberg. The inset map shows the advance into East Prussia of Rennenkampf's First Army in the north and Samsonov's Second Army in the south.

First Marne

1914 ▪ NORTHERN FRANCE ▪ GERMANY VS. FRANCE AND BRITAIN

WORLD WAR I

In the first five weeks of World War I, from the start of August into September 1914, the German armies advanced unstoppably across Belgium and southward into France, driving French troops and the BEF (British Expeditionary Force) before them in headlong retreat. However, according to the Schlieffen Plan, the Germans to were turn to the west of Paris and then march south and east to encircle the French. In the event, weakened by the loss of 11 divisions that were needed elsewhere, the Germans turned to the east of Paris and headed south to the River Marne, which formed a barrier running east to west. This exposed their flank to a counterattack from the French Sixth Army, which was stationed north of Paris, and from the Paris garrison commanded by General Joseph Gallieni. Moreover, the Commander-in-Chief of the French forces, General Joseph Joffre, was an unflappable character who remained resolute in the face of huge losses.

The BEF, which had retreated south beyond the Marne, joined in the general counteroffensive with the French Fifth Army to their right. Unnerved by the Allied counterattacks, German Chief of Staff Helmuth von Moltke ordered a withdrawal. His First and Second Armies fell back to the River Aisne, where they entrenched in a strong defensive position on 12 September. With Paris safe, the prospect of a swift German victory – scheduled to take six weeks – had evaporated. By the year's end, the opposing armies were dug into trenches from the Channel to the Swiss border.

In context

◄ FRENCH CAVALRYMEN AFTER FIRST MARNE
Cavalry played a significant role in the early mobile stage of World War I, ranging over the countryside on reconnaissance missions and harassing enemy formations in retreat. However, horsemen were vulnerable to machine-gun and rapid rifle fire, and proved ineffectual once battlefields were strewn with trenches and barbed wire.

◄ 75MM FIELD GUN
The mobile "Soixante-Quinze" was the most effective rapid-fire artillery piece in any army at the start of the war. Capable of firing 30 rounds a minute, its chief function was to support the advance of massed French infantry over open ground. The 75s inflicted heavy losses on the Germans, but could not prevent enemy firepower from mowing down French troops.

▲ **FRENCH TROOPS DISEMBARK FROM TAXIS** For want of other transport, many French soldiers arrived at the battlefield in buses and taxis. The mobilization was enormous: two million men fought in the week-long battle, each side suffering 250,000 casualties.

Gallipoli

1915 ▪ NOTHWESTERN TURKEY ▪ OTTOMAN EMPIRE AND GERMANY VS. BRITAIN AND FRANCE

WORLD WAR I

In March 1915, British and French warships attempted to sail through the Dardanelles strait and bombard Constantinople, with the aim of knocking Turkey out of the war. Coming under fire from Turkish artillery, the naval attack failed, and the decision was made to land troops on the Gallipoli peninsula. These were to seize control of the shores of the strait and so enable the warships to get through. On 25 April, British troops landed at Cape Helles, supported by the French to the south while an Australian and New Zealand (ANZAC) force went ashore further north at Gaba Tepe. The landings faced stiff opposition, and troops made little progress inland. The ANZAC soldiers had also landed in the wrong place and were trapped by counter-attacking Turkish forces as they scrambled up from the beach through rocky ridges and ravines.

Led by German adviser Liman von Sanders and Turkish general Mustafa Kemal, the Turks held their ground. The Allies made fresh landings at Suvla Bay in August, accompanied by renewed attacks elsewhere on the peninsula. However, only limited gains were achieved at the cost of heavy losses in

Men, I am not ordering you to attack. I am ordering you to die.

GENERAL MUSTAFA KEMAL, ORDERS TO INFANTRY, 25 APRIL 1915

frontal assaults on prepared defences, while thousands also died of disease in the insanitary conditions. The British sacked their commander, General Sir Ian Hamilton, in October, and soon afterwards the decision was taken to withdraw. By January, 140,000 troops were evacuated without further loss. Some 44,000 Allied troops had died in the battle.

▼ **COMING ASHORE AT GALLIPOLI** Brought to Gallipoli aboard troop transports, British and French soldiers were ferried ashore in small boats, since specialist landing craft were not yet widely used. In many places they came under fire as they landed, suffering heavy losses. Elsewhere, the enemy counterattacked as troops attempted to advance inland.

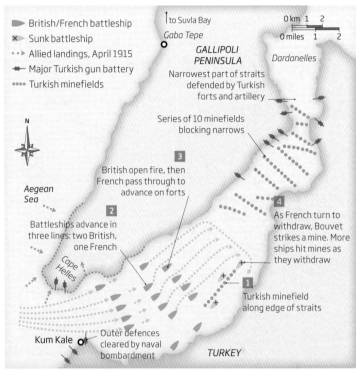

▲ **FAILED NAVAL ASSAULT** The Dardanelles strait connecting the Aegean Sea to the Sea of Marmara was blocked by sea mines and defended by Turkish guns in fortified positions. Allied troops were meant to take Gallipoli and seize the shores of the strait, but, blocked by Turkish troops holding high ground they never penetrated far beyond their landing sites.

THE **ANZACS**

At the outbreak of World War I, Australians and New Zealanders responded enthusiastically to their governments' call for volunteers to fight on the other side of the world. Together, they formed ANZAC, the Australian and New Zealand Army Corps. Trained initially in Egypt, ANZAC troops experienced a savage baptism of fire at Gallipoli. Moved to the Western front in 1916, they earned an enviable reputation as tough, skilful soldiers in the battles of the Somme and Passchendaele, and were used as spearhead troops in the victorious Allied offensives of 1918. Some 60,000 Australians and 17,000 New Zealanders died in the war.

▲ **Young Australians** are urged to join the ANZAC troops fighting at Gallipoli in this recruitment poster from 1915.

Verdun

1916 ▪ NORTHERN FRANCE ▪ GERMANY VS. FRANCE

WORLD WAR I

German Chief of Staff Erich von Falkenhayn chose the fortress city of Verdun in eastern France as the target for a major offensive in February 1916. His aim was to bleed France dry. The French forts defending Verdun had been stripped of most of their guns, taken for use on more active sectors of the front, and the French trenches were poorly constructed and undermanned. Falkenhayn assembled 1,200 guns for his offensive, including massive 420 mm howitzers. The French were slow to respond, and when the Germans attacked on 21 February they were outnumbered two to one. Pulverized by artillery fire, the French frontline positions were overrun. The largest Verdun fort, Fort Douaumont, fell on 25 February. Nevertheless, the French government decided that Verdun must be held at all costs – a task that was entrusted to General Philippe Pétain.

Supplied along a single road dubbed the *Voie Sacrée* ("Sacred Way"), the French army dug in to resist the German attacks. By June, German troops were close to taking Verdun, but from July many had to be transferred to meet Allied offensives on the Eastern front and the Somme. The French, now commanded by General Robert Nivelle, seized the initiative against the weakened German forces. By the time fighting subsided in December, French counteroffensives had regained much of the ground originally lost. The inconclusive battle is believed to have cost 700,000 French and German casualties.

PIGEONS AT WAR

Millions of animals served in World War I, including horses, mules, camels, dogs, and over 100,000 carrier pigeons. These birds were often the most efficient method of battlefield communication, carrying messages attached to their legs through shellfire and poison gas. At Verdun, pigeons won special celebrity when French troops under Major Sylvain Raynal were trapped inside Fort Vaux in June 1916. As they desperately resisted the Germans in the tunnels and passageways of the fortress, pigeons were their only mean of signalling to relief troops outside. One was even awarded the *Légion d'honneur* in gratitude.

▶ **This German pigeon** had a miniature camera attached to its breast so it could fly photo-reconnaissance missions.

▲ **FRENCH INFANTRY AT VERDUN** Shellfire inflicted the largest proportion of casualties on both sides in the 10-month battle at Verdun. Individual French units only served short spells on the battlefield. As a result of this rotation, three-quarters of the entire French army fought there at some time. French morale held up during the battle, but collapsed the following spring, causing many French soldiers to mutiny.

In detail

At the Battle of Verdun, both sides used innovative tactics. In their initial infantry attack, which followed a massive preparatory artillery bombardment, the Germans made use of "Stormtroopers" – specially trained assault troops equipped with hand grenades and flamethrowers – to clear French frontline trenches and penetrate beyond them in depth. When the French mounted successful counterattacks from August 1916, they implemented a form of close coordination between artillery and infantry known as the "creeping barrage". Instead of depending solely on a preparatory bombardment to suppress enemy defences before the infantry went "over the top", the French guns continued firing over the heads of the troops as they moved forwards, striking targets only a short distance in front of the advancing soldiers. Using this method, the French took enemy frontline positions with relative ease: deeper advances proved difficult to coordinate.

Aerial reconnaissance played a vital part in the fighting, since only aircraft could pinpoint targets for the heavy artillery firing far beyond visual range. The world's first struggle for air superiority took place over Verdun, as both sides organized fighter squadrons to protect their own reconnaissance aircraft and prevent the enemy from carrying out aerial observation. Despite such tactical innovations, however, the scale of firepower available to both sides ensured that any attack was costly and only gained very limited areas of territory.

◄ **GEORGES GUYNEMER** French pilot Georges Guynemer was one of the first fighter aces of World War I. He flew with one of the Cigogne fighter squadrons that combatted German aces such as Oswald Boelcke and Manfred von Richthofen over Verdun. Propagandists on both sides promoted their aces as invincible, but most had short lives. Guynemer had shot down 53 aircraft when he was killed in September 1917, aged just 22.

Front line at the start of battle, 20 February

▶ **THE VERDUN BATTLEFIELD** The battle of Verdun was fought on both banks of the River Meuse. The initial German offensive on the east bank in February made substantial initial progress, until French resistance stiffened. In March, the Germans renewed their offensive on the west bank, leading to desperate fighting for Hill 304 and Mort Homme. In a further advance in June, the Germans took Fort Vaux, but the following month they failed to seize Fort Souville. A series of French counteroffensives subsequently rolled back the line on the east bank.

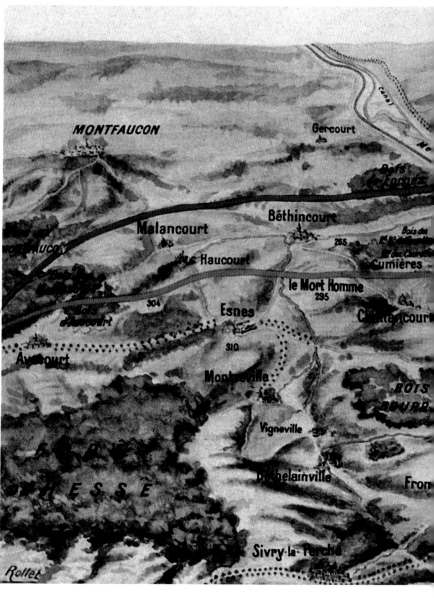

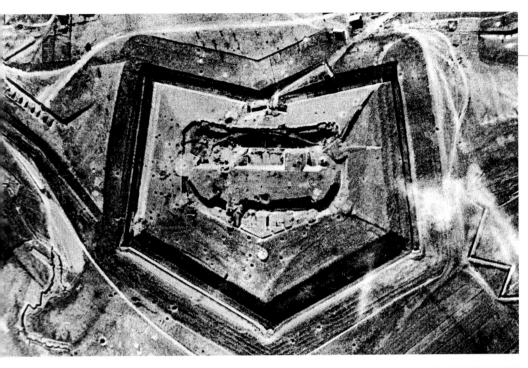

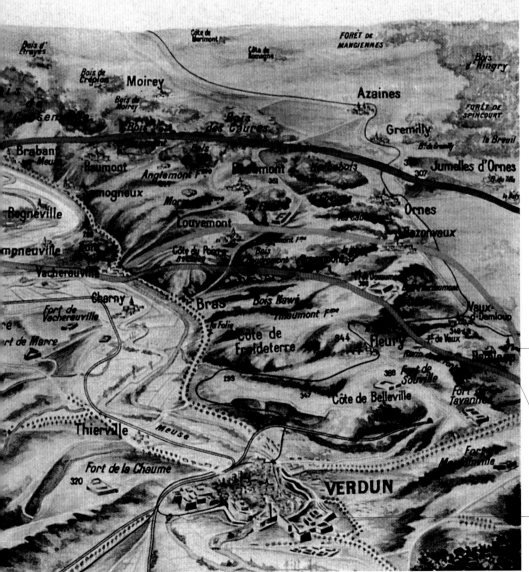

◄ FORT DOUAUMONT In the 1890s, the French ringed Verdun with concrete-and-steel forts, but by 1916 these were vulnerable to Krupp siege artillery. Still, the fall of Fort Douaumont, the largest fortress, to a German assault in the first week of the offensive came as a severe shock. It was recaptured after heavy fighting in October 1916.

▼ THEY SHALL NOT PASS In a message to his troops at Verdun 23 June 1916, General Nivelle urged his men not to let the enemy pass. Simplified to the phrase "On ne passe pas" ("They shall not pass"), this became a famous war slogan expressing the fortitude of the French infantrymen. In the last year of the war, it was used in this propaganda poster designed by Maurice Neumont.

Front line at the end of battle, 18 December (including red line to the left)

Line reached by the Germans by 1 July

Fortress city of Verdun

➤ **GERMAN IMPERIAL NAVY**
Despite a major shipbuilding programme before 1914, the German navy was outnumbered and outgunned by the Royal Navy. The German fleet spent most of World War I bottled up in port, apart from occasional sorties into the North Sea, such as the one that led to the Battle of Jutland. Here, part of the German High Seas Fleet steams in line astern before the battle.

Jutland

1916 ∎ NORTH SEA ∎ BRITAIN VS. GERMANY

WORLD WAR I

In World War I, the Royal Navy's Grand Fleet, commanded by Admiral John Jellicoe, dominated the North Sea. In late May 1916, Vice-Admiral Reinhard Scheer led the German High Seas Fleet on a rare sortie, hoping to achieve surprise. But British naval intelligence, monitoring German radio traffic, spotted the move. Sensing a chance to destroy the German fleet, Jellicoe set sail with 151 warships, including 28 battleships. Scheer had only 99 warships, including 22 battleships.

The British and Germans met on the misty afternoon of 31 May. In initial exchanges between the two sides' battlecruiser squadrons the British fared badly. Superior German gunnery and inferior British armour saw two British battlecruisers destroyed. However, when the Grand Fleet appeared out of the mist, Scheer realised he was in danger. The German fleet fled for home. Jellicoe twice subjected it to heavy fire, but his pursuit was inhibited by his fear of losing battleships to German destroyers' torpedoes. During the following night, the High Seas Fleet carved a passage through the British line, and in the morning Jellicoe found that they had

escaped him. Britain had lost 14 ships and suffered almost 7,000 casualties to Germany's 11 ships and 3,000 casualties. This allowed Germany to claim a victory. However, Britain had reaffirmed control of the North Sea, and the German surface fleet remained in port for much of the war afterwards.

DREADNOUGHT **BATTLESHIPS**

In response to German naval expansion, Britain launched the first of the Dreadnought class of battleships in 1906. Mounting ten 12-in guns and capable of a speed of 21 knots, the Dreadnought rendered all existing battleships obsolete. Over the following years, all of the world's major powers built their own Dreadnought-style ships, but the Royal Navy stayed ahead by developing even more powerful battleships, dubbed the "super-Dreadnoughts". Too valuable to risk losing, the German and British battleships only exchanged fire once in World War I, at the battle of Jutland.

▲ **A Dreadnought-style** battleship that entered service in 1914, the USS *New York* remained in service during World War II.

▶ **JUTLAND, 1916** The German fleet sailed north from Wilhelmshaven while the British fleet sailed south from Scapa Flow. Both fleets were preceded by squadrons of battlecruisers, and when these met off Jutland each tried to draw the other into the fire of their battleships, which were hidden by mist. Once the Germans realised that the entire British fleet was bearing down on them, they fled back for Wilhelmshaven. Pursuing them southward through the night, the British eventually gave up and let the German fleet slip away.

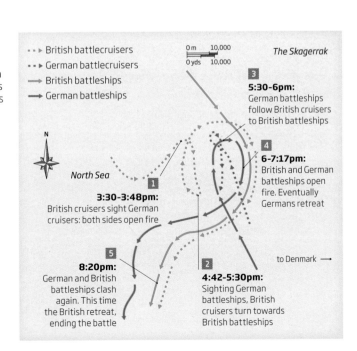

··▶ British battlecruisers
··▶ German battlecruisers
⟶ British battleships
⟶ German battleships

0 m   10,000
0 yds   10,000

The Skagerrak

N

North Sea

3
5:30–6pm:
German battleships follow British cruisers to British battleships

4
6–7:17pm:
British and German battleships open fire. Eventually Germans retreat

1
3:30–3:48pm:
British cruisers sight German cruisers: both sides open fire

5
8:20pm:
German and British battleships clash again. This time the British retreat, ending the battle

2
4:42–5:30pm:
Sighting German battleships, British cruisers turn towards British battleships

to Denmark ⟶

> The spell of Trafalgar has been broken. You have started a new chapter in world history. 🙶

KAISER WILHELM, PROCLAIMING GERMAN SUCCESS AFTER THE BATTLE, 1916

▲ **BRITISH TROOPS AT THE SOMME** Field artillery moves forwards through the shattered remnants of Delville Wood, a position on the Somme front that was fought over by British Commonwealth and German troops for seven weeks from July to September 1916. The ground conditions on the heavily shelled battlefield deteriorated as the fighting dragged on from the summer into the autumn, making the prospect of a decisive breakthrough ever more remote.

The Somme

1916 ▪ NORTHERN FRANCE ▪ BRITAIN AND FRANCE VS. GERMANY

WORLD WAR I

The British and French planned a joint offensive in summer 1916 in the Somme sector of the Western front. Due to French commitments at Verdun, the offensive became a British-led operation. British commander Sir Douglas Haig assembled around 1,500 guns and an army of half a million men, many entering combat for the first time. Doubtful of the fighting quality of his unblooded troops, Haig depended on an eight-day preliminary artillery bombardment to destroy the German defences. However, the Germans sheltered safely in concrete bunkers, and when the British went "over the top" on 1 July they faced intact barbed wire and dense rifle and machine-gun fire. French infantry made a substantial advance, but in parts of the British sector, troops did not even reach the German front line. The first day of the Somme was the worst military disaster in British history, with 57,470 casualties including 19,240 killed.

Despite these losses, Haig was determined to continue the offensive. Further major attacks were mounted in mid-July and mid-September. Intense, local fighting for objectives such as the fortified village of Pozières and nearby Mouquet Farm, which was taken and held by the Australians at a cost of 23,000 casualties, wore down the armies of both sides. Thiepval, marked as an objective for the first day of the battle, was not taken until 26 September. In mid-November, in worsening weather, Haig finally called the battle off. It was believed to have cost around 400,000 British, 200,000 French, and 500,000 German casualties.

A **CALL TO ARMS**

The bulk of the British Army that fought on the Somme consisted of volunteers who had joined up in response to an appeal for troops launched by the Secretary for War, Lord Kitchener, at the start of the conflict. Some 2.5 million volunteers from all walks of life signed up for service, many forming Pals Battalions made up of men from the same town, occupation, school, or even sports club. Due to the difficulty of training and equipping Britain's first mass citizen army, few of these volunteers entered combat before autumn 1915. For most, the Somme was their first battle, and for many it was their last.

▶ **On recruitment posters** all over Britain, the stern, moustached face of Lord Kitchener appeared calling for volunteers to join the British Army.

In detail

On the first day of the Somme, British troops were ordered to advance in lines at walking pace. This disastrous decision was motivated by the belief that British artillery would by then have annihilated the German defences, and led to thousands being slaughtered; but it was not typical of the battle as a whole. British commanders constantly sought innovation in tactics and technology. Although the first use of tanks attracted much attention, the vital issue was the coordination of artillery and infantry. As well as the "creeping barrage" advancing ahead of attacking infantry, the British experimented with the "lightning bombardment", in which infantry attacked after a brief but intense burst of shelling.

Aircraft flew photo-reconnaissance missions, pinpointing targets for the guns. On the ground, infantry learned to make intelligent use of weapons such as portable Lewis light machine-guns, rifle grenades, and the Mills bomb.

However, many problems on the Western Front were intractable. Without portable radios, advancing troops soon lost contact with supporting artillery. The inability of cavalry to operate on a battlefield dominated by artillery and machine-guns made it difficult to exploit local breakthroughs. Both sides made tactical errors, the German counterattacks aimed at retaking lost ground costing as many casualties as the repeated British offensives.

▼ **THE FIRST TANKS** A British invention, the Mk1 tank was first delivered to the Western front during the battle of the Somme. Haig threw them into an offensive at Flers-Courcelette on 15 September, but, being slow and vulnerable to artillery fire, they had limited impact. Later in the war, tanks performed vital service in an infantry support role, helping advancing troops to neutralize enemy strongpoints.

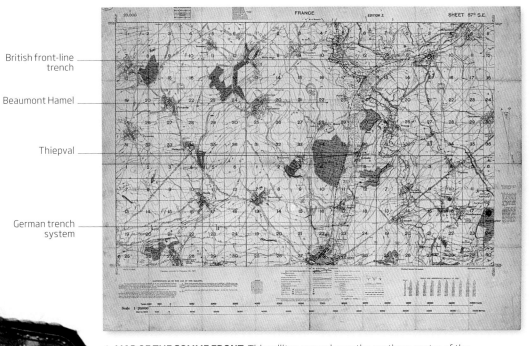

British front-line trench

Beaumont Hamel

Thiepval

German trench system

▲ **MAP OF THE SOMME FRONT** This military map shows the northern sector of the battlefield – the scene of Britain's worst military disaster. The fortified German positions at Thiepval and Beaumont Hamel, both first-day objectives, remained in German hands until the end of September and mid-November respectively. The furthest advance of Allied troops after four and a half months' fighting was 12km (7½ miles).

▼ **TRENCHES AT BEAUMONT HAMEL** An aerial reconnaissance photograph shows the British trench line, bottom left, facing the German front line. Massive shell craters are clearly visible in the no-man's land between the two sides. Trenches were always dug in a zigzag pattern to stop enemy fire or the force of an explosion travelling the whole length of the trench.

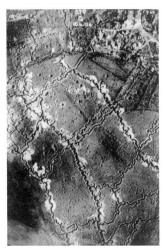

▼ **UNDERGROUND WARFARE** In preparation for the battle, thousands of British engineers dug tunnels under the no-man's land between the opposing front-line trenches and packed them with explosives. These mines were detonated just before the infantry went into action. German engineers dug their own tunnels, seeking to locate and disable the British mines. Here, a British soldier listens for German countermining.

▲ **THE LOST REGIMENT** The Royal Newfoundland Regiment were volunteers from Britain's smallest dominion. On the first day of the Somme, they were ordered forwards in a second-wave attack at Beaumont Hamel, unaware that the first wave had failed to reach the enemy front line. Advancing unsupported across open ground into German machine-gun fire, they were mown down, suffering 684 casualties out of a total of 780 men.

Passchendaele

1917 ▪ BELGIUM ▪ BRITAIN, FRANCE, AND BELGIUM VS. GERMANY

WORLD WAR I

In the summer of 1917, British commander-in-chief General Douglas Haig planned a major offensive on the Western Front in Flanders, intending to break through the German lines and capture the Belgian ports that were serving as bases for enemy U-boats. A preparatory assault on the Messines Ridge in June was a success, but long delays followed. After a prolonged artillery bombardment, the main battle, officially known as Third Ypres, was launched on 31 July.

Advancing behind a creeping artillery barrage, British infantry took German front lines with relative ease, but then ran into a dense network of concrete blockhouses and machine-gun nests. German counter-attacks drove the British back from much of the ground gained. In August, heavy rain and shelling turned the battlefield into a sea of mud across which men and supplies could only move on duckboards.

In September, the weather improved and the British seized some positions with infantry and artillery attacks. The loss of Broodseinde Ridge in early October was a serious blow to German morale. However, Haig continued the offensive under worsening conditions to no clear purpose. By the time the fighting ended with the capture of Passchendaele Ridge on 10 November, each side had suffered around a quarter of a million casualties, with no strategic objective achieved.

DOUGLAS HAIG (1861–1928)

Field Marshal Douglas Haig was a cavalry officer blooded in Britain's colonial wars before World War I. A corps commander in 1914, he led British First Army at the Battle of Loos in 1915. Raised to commander-in-chief, he was responsible for the costly offensives at the Somme in 1916 and Third Ypres in 1917.

An intelligent modernizer, Haig promoted improved artillery and infantry tactics, and the use of aircraft and tanks. However, stubborn over-optimism led him to persist with offensives under hopeless conditions. Sustained by the belief he was "a tool in the hands of the Divine Power", Haig eventually won a string of victories in 1918.

▲ **Haig was a controversial** commander who had an unshakeable faith in taking the offensive.

In detail

▶ **BATTLEFIELD MAP** This map shows the Zonnebeke Redoubt part of the battlefield, which saw heavy fighting. Thanks to air reconaissance, British officers had detailed maps of the Germans' defensive positions. The German "defence in depth" created a complex battlefield dotted with barbed wire obstacles, machine-gun posts, and fortified strongpoints.

Dugout enclosed by trenches

Machine-gun nest protected by barbed wire

▲ **THE MENIN ROAD** Artist Paul Nash's painting conveys the appalling conditions of the war: waterlogged ground churned up by shellfire hampered any advance. Nevertheless, the offensive along the Menin Road was one of the most successful operations of Third Ypres.

◄ **TAKING THE RIDGE** Passchendaele Ridge became the final objective of Third Ypres and gave the offensive its popular name. It was taken by Canadian troops in an operation lasting from 26 October to 10 November 1917, at a cost of almost 16,000 casualties. The position was later abandoned without a fight.

▲ **THE WITHDRAWAL FROM DUNKIRK** Troops and rescue vessels were at the mercy of Luftwaffe bombs at Dunkirk, despite the best efforts of the RAF, as depicted in this painting by Charles Cundall. Sunken ships blocked the approach to the beaches, so smaller boats became essential to ferry the evacuees to the ships waiting offshore in deeper waters.

Dunkirk

1940 ■ NORTHERN FRANCE ■ ALLIED FORCES VS. GERMANY

WORLD WAR II

After Adolf Hitler invaded Poland on 1 September 1939 and Britain responded by declaring war on Germany, soldiers of the British Expeditionary Force were sent over to Europe. They joined the French Army defending the Maginot Line, a series of fortifications along the border with Germany. In May 1940, Hitler ordered the invasion of France, his tanks bypassing the Maginot Line to punch through the Allied lines at Ardennes. The defenders were forced into a scrambled retreat to the beaches at Dunkirk in northern France, around 10 km (6 miles) from the Belgian border.

Rather than advance on Dunkirk, the German forces halted to consolidate and prevent an Allied breakout. Seizing the opportunity, British Prime Minister Winston Churchill launched Operation Dynamo, in which ships from the Royal Navy were sent across the Channel to evacuate as many troops as possible.

The evacuations began on 27 May, under heavy fire from German aircraft. As well as naval vessels, nearly 700 privately-owned small boats from all over the south coast of England were also pressed into service. Some were requisitioned and sailed by naval crews, but others were independently piloted by their owners. In nine days, 338,226 Allied soldiers escaped in what came to be known as the "Miracle of Dunkirk". It provided a huge morale boost for the Allies – despite France's surrender soon after – and saved an army that could be re-equipped to fight another day.

◄ GERMAN PROPAGANDA
During the evacuation, the German Luftwaffe dropped thousands of propaganda leaflets on the Allied troops, urging them to surrender. As the leaflet showed, the German Army had them surrounded with nowhere left to go. The success of the improvised sea evacuation was a great surprise, and one that turned defeat for the Allies into a great propaganda coup of their own.

Battle of Britain

1940 ▪ BRITISH AIRSPACE ▪ BRITAIN VS. GERMANY

WORLD WAR II

On 21 June 1940, in a railway carriage in the Forest of Compiègne in France, Adolf Hitler accepted the surrender of France, only six weeks after his armies had invaded the country. It was expected that the British would now seek peace. They chose not to, and so Hitler began to prepare for an invasion of Britain, codenamed Operation Sea Lion. For this to succeed, the Germans' first priority was for its air force, the Luftwaffe, to destroy the Royal Air Force and establish control of the skies over southern England.

The Germans began by attacking coastal targets and British shipping in the English Channel, and then Royal Air Force (RAF) bases in late August and early September. RAF Fighter Command, led by Sir Hugh Dowding, faced the threat with its squadrons organized into four Groups, each covering a different area. The critical phase came from 7 September, when the Luftwaffe shifted its attacks to civilian targets in London. The effects on the city were devastating, but it also gave the RAF time to recover. By mid-September, it became clear that the Luftwaffe had failed to establish air superiority, which made Operation Sea Lion all but impossible, meaning that Britain was able to stay in the war. Four years later, the Allies would launch a counter-invasion of Nazi-occupied Europe from British shores that would ultimately see the defeat of Hitler's Germany.

▼ **RAF FIGHTERS SCRAMBLING** The German Luftwaffe had superior numbers of fighters and bombers, but the RAF met the challenge with arguably better aircraft, notably the Supermarine Spitfire. Here pilots run to their Spitfires before a mission.

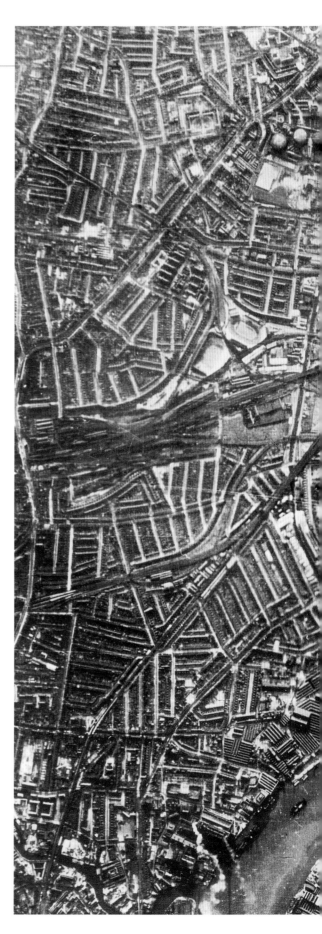

▼ **LUFTWAFFE OVER LONDON** A Heinkel III bomber flies over London's Docklands – the commercial hub of the capital – in September 1940. Over 25,000 bombs were dropped on the area, making it the most heavily damaged civilian target in Britain.

In detail

What became known as the Battle of Britain began in late June with German aircraft making "nuisance" attacks on coastal targets and English shipping in the Channel. In mid-July, this intensified to larger attacks on English ports, RAF airfields, and aircraft factories. In mid-August, the Germans began large-scale daylight attacks against RAF airfields in an attempt to cripple Britain's aerial defence capabilities. Soon after, the Luftwaffe also began day and night attacks on London. The turning point came on 15 September 1940, when the Luftwaffe threw everything it had into an attack that lasted all day and night. In the wake of this onslaught, the RAF was still able to put fighter aircraft

▶ **THE LUFTWAFFE** The German air force had 2,600 aircraft, of which 1,200 were twin-engine bombers and 760 were single-engine fighters. It also had several hundred Messerschmidt 110 twin-engine fighter-bombers, one of which is shown here flying near Dover in southern England.

◀ **AIR DEFENCES** As part of Britain's defences, giant barrage balloons were floated above the potential targets of the German bombers. These forced the German aircraft to fly at higher altitudes, which reduced the accuracy of their bombing. Radar was also used to track incoming enemy aircraft.

THE **BLITZ**

The Blitz (German for "lightning") was the name given to the heavy bombing of British towns and cities that began during the Battle of Britain. Designed to crush public morale, the raids began on London in early September 1940. In just that one month, the Luftwaffe dropped 5,300 tonnes of high explosives on the city. The raids then expanded to include targets across the country, including Birmingham, Coventry, Liverpool, and Plymouth. During that time, London continued to be bombed: for 57 consecutive nights many in the city chose to sleep down in the deep-level Underground stations for safety. The bombing eased off after May 1941, when Germany turned its attentions to Russia.

▲ **A bus lies** in a crater in Balham, south London, after a German bombing raid in October 1940.

◄ **V-1 FLYING BOMB** Well after the Battle of Britain had ended, the Germans continued to bomb London. In June 1944, they began sending pilotless V-1 Flying Bombs, otherwise known as Doodlebugs. Later that year, London was also targeted by V-2 rockets, which were the forerunners of the modern ballistic missile.

into the air. German bombing had failed to halt the British production of aircraft, so when a British plane was shot down, the pilot, if he was able to parachute to safety, could fly again in a new machine. By contrast, the Germans suffered from a lack of aircraft reserves and from downed pilots being captured as prisoners of war. Britain's radar technology also played a role, enabling air attacks to be detected in advance. After 15 September, Hitler considered the air battle lost, and, although the bombing raids continued, he abandoned his plans for a ground invasion.

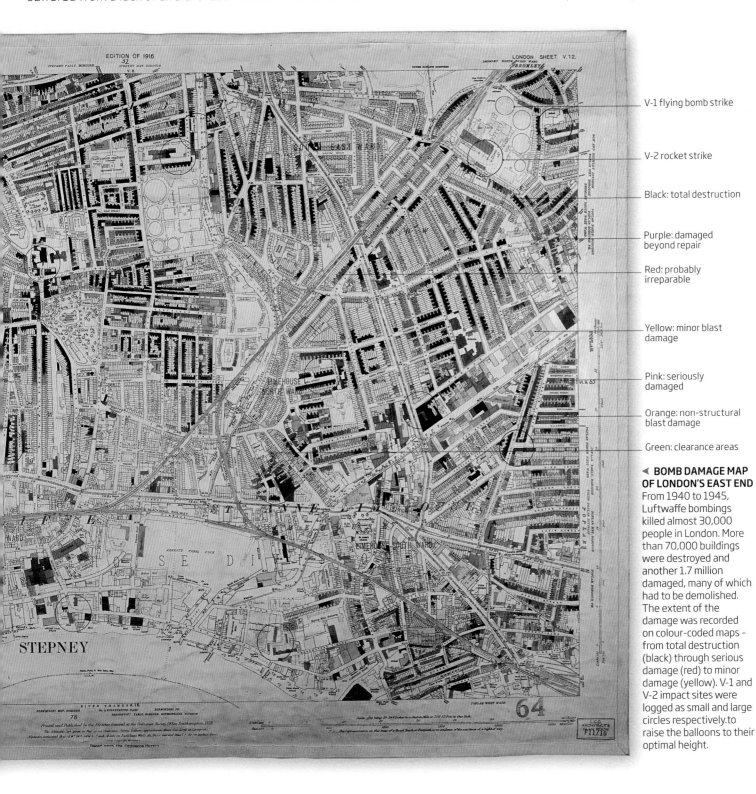

V-1 flying bomb strike

V-2 rocket strike

Black: total destruction

Purple: damaged beyond repair

Red: probably irreparable

Yellow: minor blast damage

Pink: seriously damaged

Orange: non-structural blast damage

Green: clearance areas

◄ **BOMB DAMAGE MAP OF LONDON'S EAST END** From 1940 to 1945, Luftwaffe bombings killed almost 30,000 people in London. More than 70,000 buildings were destroyed and another 1.7 million damaged, many of which had to be demolished. The extent of the damage was recorded on colour-coded maps – from total destruction (black) through serious damage (red) to minor damage (yellow). V-1 and V-2 impact sites were logged as small and large circles respectively.to raise the balloons to their optimal height.

Pearl Harbor

1941 ■ HAWAII ■ USA VS. JAPAN

WORLD WAR II

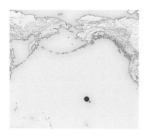

At dawn on Sunday 7 December 1941, the first of two waves of Japanese aircraft banked and began the approach for their bombing run on the US Pacific Fleet moored at Pearl Harbor on the Pacific island of Oahu, Hawaii. Over 350 Japanese aircraft took part in the surprise attack, supported by midget submarines: they succeeded in sinking, exploding, or capsizing six warships and damaging 10 others, with three non-combat ships also knocked out. A total of 188 US aircraft were destroyed, and over 2,400 Americans killed, with a further 1,178 wounded. The Japanese, by contrast, lost just 29 aircraft and 64 servicemen.

The attack was the latest in a series of acts of aggression by Imperial Japan in the western Pacific region. In 1937, Japan had invaded China, which led to war between the two countries, and in 1940 it had attacked French Indochina. The following year, hoping to check Japanese ambitions, the US had moved its naval fleet from San Diego to Hawaii and imposed an oil embargo on Japan, which was reliant on American oil. Japan viewed this as a provocation, and so launched its raid on Pearl Harbor. Its immediate aim was to neutralize the American navy and then invade the oil-rich islands of the Dutch East Indies.

The US had known that conflict in the Pacific was almost inevitable, but it had not imagined that Japan would mount such an audacious attack without first declaring war. For Japan, Pearl Harbor was an overwhelming success: it crippled the Pacific Fleet and prevented the US from interfering with Japan's planned further conquests. However, it also united the US in favour of entering a war it had so far tried to stay out of.

▶ **THE PACIFIC FLEET** This photograph shows the Pacific Fleet anchored at Pearl Harbor the day before the attack. The base was attacked from all sides by a mixture of fighter planes, bombers, and torpedo bombers.

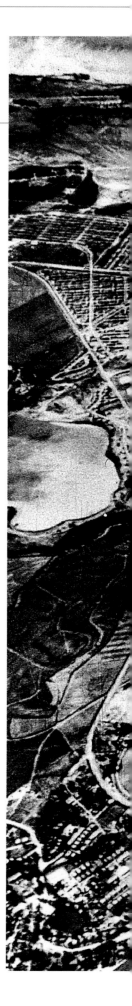

In detail

▼ **US BATTLESHIPS MOMENTS AFTER THE ATTACK**
Of the ships damaged or sunk in Pearl Harbor, only three were damaged beyond repair. By chance, the Pacific Fleet's three aircraft carriers were out at sea on 7 December, and survived. The attack gave the US the chance to rebuild its fleet and enter the war with superior resources.

AVENGE PEARL HARBOR

OUR BULLETS WILL DO IT

◀ **ENTERING THE WAR**
Prior to Pearl Harbor, the US had been divided on whether to join the Allies in the war in Europe. The day after the attack, President Roosevelt called for a formal declaration of war not just on Japan, but also Japan's allies: Germany and Italy. Without American intervention, the defeat of Nazi Germany would not have been possible.

And then I saw **a glint in the sun** that looked like **a beautiful silver waterfall.** It was the **dive-bombers** coming in **"**

JIMMY THACH, US FIGHTER PILOT

Midway

1942 ▪ PACIFIC OCEAN ▪ USA VS. JAPAN

WORLD WAR II

▼ **YORKTOWN ABLAZE** The *Yorktown* survived bombing by Japanese aircraft, only to be sunk by a torpedo fired from a Japanese submarine. It was the only major loss suffered by the US Pacific Fleet at Midway.

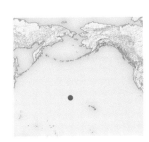

After its success at Pearl Harbor (see pp.212–13), the Japanese Imperial Navy commanded the Pacific. From there it conquered Malaysia and Singapore, sank British warships in the Indian Ocean, and even used its carriers to launch a devastating bombing raid on Darwin in northern Australia. In April 1942, the Americans made a daring attack on Tokyo, with 16 bombers launched from an aircraft carrier. The raid caused little damage, but it was a boost to American morale. Shocked that their homeland and the life of their emperor had been threatened, the Japanese decided to destroy the American carrier fleet.

Japanese admiral Yamamoto Isoroku planned to launch a diversionary attack on the Alaskan coast, intended to draw the US fleet north, and then to attack Midway, an island halfway across the Pacific that was used as an American airbase. He hoped that the US fleet would come to the rescue and fall into a carefully arranged ambush. Instead, the Americans deciphered the Japanese radio code, which enabled Pacific Fleet commander Admiral Chester W. Nimitz to surprise his opponents. The Americans sank all four large Japanese aircraft carriers, destroying 292 Japanese aircraft in the process. The victory was a decisive turning point in the Pacific and sent the Japanese forces into retreat.

THE IMPORTANCE **OF INTELLIGENCE**

A crucial element of the battle of Midway was the Americans' interception of Japanese radio signals. The Japanese fleet was widely dispersed and had to communicate by radio. The Americans picked up the orders that Yamamoto had sent out to prepare his forces for the operation. Once the Americans had cracked the code, they were forewarned of the forthcoming Japanese operation, and knew where and on what day the attack was going to take place. US admiral Nimitz was able to direct his limited forces to inflict maximum damage on the Japanese fleet based upon the operational intelligence.

▶ **US naval radio operators** were crucial to success at the battle of Midway.

In detail

On the morning of 4 June 1942, the date on which US intelligence had predicted a Japanese attack on Midway, US scout aircraft located the Imperial invasion fleet. The US force consisted of three carriers, eight cruisers, and 15 destroyers, while the Japanese had four large and two medium carriers, 11 battleships, 16 cruisers, and 46 destroyers. However, the Japanese force was divided into two battle groups: one was to the north of Midway, while another was at the Aleutian islands near Alaska, landing a small invasion party. As a result, just four Japanese carriers, three cruisers, three battleships, and a number of destroyers took part in the battle itself.

The US carriers were waiting in ambush near Midway Island. When the Japanese launched an aerial attack on the airfields at Midway, the US carriers launched their own dive-bombers at the Imperial fleet. The US bombers caught the Japanese as their aircraft were rearming and refuelling. The decks were full of ordnance and fuel hoses and it took only a few hits to set the ships ablaze.

A sole surviving Japanese carrier, the *Hiryu*, made a counterattack, following the retreating American aircraft to the *Yorktown*, which they bombed. Later that afternoon, the Americans countered and sunk the *Hiryu*. Deprived of aerial support by the loss of all of their carriers, the Japanese forces withdrew.

▶ **PLAN OF THE JAPANESE ATTACK**
Traditionally, sea battles were fought between ships armed with guns. Midway was a battle fought between ships armed with aircraft. It involved strike and counterstrike by carrier-based fighter-bombers, and ended when Japan's loss of its carriers left its other ships too vulnerable to air attack.

1 Japanese aircraft fly to Midway

2 US aircraft target the Japanese fleet

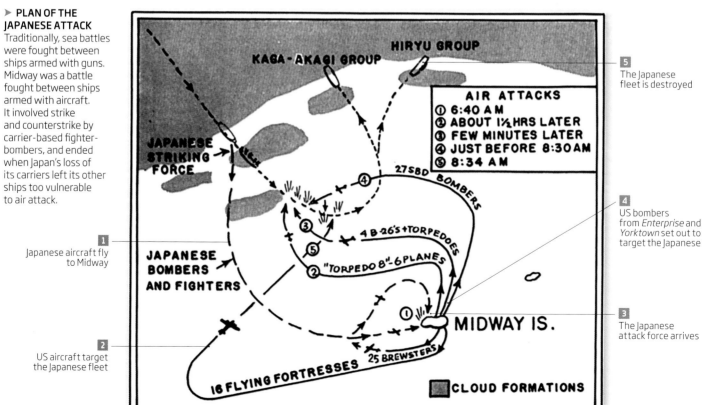

5 The Japanese fleet is destroyed

4 US bombers from *Enterprise* and *Yorktown* set out to target the Japanese

3 The Japanese attack force arrives

◄ **YORKTOWN ATTACKED** This diorama, made by Norman Bel Geddes for the US Navy, shows a wave of Japanese bombers targeting the *Yorktown*. The attack crippled the ship, which was later sunk by a Japanese submarine. It was the last attack mounted by the Japanese carrier *Hiryu* before it was destroyed.

▲ **JAPANESE AERIAL FORCES** Here a Nakajima B5N torpedo bomber attacks, flying incredibly low under heavy enemy fire. Other notable Japaneseaircraft used at midway include the Mitsubishi Zero, a formidable long-range fighter used by the Imperial Japanese Navy.

▲ **USS ENTERPRISE** One of three similar carriers deployed in the Battle of Midway, the *Enterprise* was commanded by Rear Admiral Raymond Spruance. Pilots from the carrier were given credit for the sinking of the Japanese carriers *Kaga* and *Akagi*. She returned to Pearl Harbor undamaged.

◄ **MIDWAY ISLAND** A small atoll roughly halfway between North America and Asia, Midway was an important refuelling point for US Navy ships. When war broke out with Japan in 1941, the island was second in importance only to Pearl Harbor for the protection of the west coast of America.

Second Battle of El Alamein

1942 ▪ NORTHERN EGYPT ▪ ALLIED FORCES VS. AXIS FORCES

WORLD WAR II

The German-Italian army had been advancing east through Libya since March 1941, heading for Egypt and the Suez Canal – a vital link with British India – and the oilfields of Iraq and Iran. El Alamein, a remote town on the north coast of Egypt, 106 km (66 miles) west of Alexandria, had the Mediterranean Sea to the north and a large area of quicksand known as the Qattara Depression to the south, forming a natural tactical bottleneck. In the First Battle of El Alamein, fought on 1–27 July 1942, the Allies had repelled the Axis forces and retained control of the town; in August, the Allies once more faced the advancing Axis armies.

Lieutenant-General Bernard Montgomery took command of over 190,000 men, along with 1,000 tanks, 900 artillery pieces, and 1,400 anti-tank guns. The opposing army was under the command of Field Marshall Erwin Rommel, who had 116,000 soldiers, 540 tanks, 500 artillery pieces, and 490 anti-tank guns, as well as a dangerously low level of supplies – for the second battle at El Alamein, the advantage was with the Allies.

Montgomery unleashed his offensive on the night of 23 October with an artillery barrage; after this, engineers cleared a path through the German minefields. Despite punishing losses from anti-tank guns, the Allies achieved a decisive breakthrough on 4 November, and the Germans were driven back into Libya and Tunisia. El Alamein was the Germans' first major defeat in the west.

ERWIN **ROMMEL** (1891-1944)

The commander of the Axis forces at El Alamein, Erwin Rommel was a highly decorated officer in World War I. In World War II, he led the 7th Panzer Division during the 1940 invasion of France. Under his command, German and Italian forces achieved a string of victories in North Africa, which earned him the nickname "Desert Fox". Despite the loss at El Alamein, he later commanded the German forces in France against the Allied invasion of Normandy in 1944. After being implicated in a plot to kill Hitler, he was allowed to commit suicide using a cyanide pill rather than face a trial.

▶ **A talented tactical leader**, Field Marshall Erwin Rommel is pictured here during the North African campaign wearing the medals he received in World War I.

▲ **ALLIED TANKS IN THE LIBYAN DESERT**
The UK fielded over 200 of these British Crusader MkII tanks, and around 300 US-made Sherman M4s – their first use in combat by British forces – as well as numerous US Grant and M3 tanks. German armour mainly consisted of Panzer II, III, and IV variants. A lack of fuel prevented Rommel from conducting his usual highly mobile tank warfare, instead relying on dug-in defences.

Now this is **not the end**… But it is, perhaps, the **end of the beginning**.

WINSTON CHURCHILL ON SECOND EL ALAMEIN, IN A SPEECH MADE IN 1942

This **struggle** is one of ideologies and **racial differences,** and will have to be conducted with **unprecedented, unmerciful,** and **unrelenting harshness.**

ADOLF HITLER, RECORDED IN THE DIARY OF THE HEAD OF GERMAN GENERAL STAFF FRANZ HALDER, 1941

▲ **SOVIET VICTORY** A victorious Red Army soldier raises the Soviet flag over the ruins of Stalingrad in February 1943. Lasting five and a half months, this was the single bloodiest battle in the history of warfare, leaving almost two million combatants and civilians dead or wounded. In halting the German advance into the Soviet Union, this battle marked the turning of the tide of war in the Allies' favour.

Stalingrad

1942-43 ■ SOUTHWESTERN RUSSIA ■ SOVIET UNION VS. GERMANY

WORLD WAR II

Following the launch of Operation Barbarossa (see below), the German forces invading Russia divided into two, with one group moving south to capture the oil fields of the Caucasus, and the other attacking Stalingrad in August 1942. Having learned of the plan, on 28 July the Soviet leader Joseph Stalin had decreed that the city's defenders would take "Not one step back". He forbade the evacuation of residents, saying that their presence would make the army fight harder. The assault began with an intensive Luftwaffe bombing, which reduced much of the city to rubble. The German ground forces then advanced into the city. By mid-September, they had pushed the defending Soviet forces in Stalingrad back to just a narrow strip of the city along the west bank of the Volga River. At this point, the city became the scene of some of the fiercest fighting of the war, as streets and individual buildings were battled over, often changing hands several times.

The turning point came on 19 November, when the Soviets launched a two-pronged attack on the Romanian and Hungarian armies protecting the Germans' rear flank. The two prongs met to encircle the Germans in Stalingrad, but Hitler ordered his forces to continue the fight to the death. The Germans attempted to break through the Soviet ring and to resupply the trapped army by air, but to no avail. On 31 January 1943, the German field marshal in command at Stalingrad, Friedrich Paulus, surrendered to the Soviets. Had the German forces not divided, reducing the Stalingrad attack force, the outcome might have been very different. The Axis forces are thought to have suffered nearly 800,000 dead, wounded, or missing; Soviet casualties were estimated to be approximately 1.1 million.

OPERATION **BARBAROSSA** (JUNE-DECEMBER 1941)

In June 1941, Adolf Hitler launched a massive invasion of the Soviet Union. Its codename was Operation Barbarossa, and its aim was to seize *lebensraum* ("living space") for the German people, to take slaves to aid the German war effort, and to capture key oil fields. In the early stages, German forces penetrated deep into Soviet territory. The offensive stalled as it approached Moscow. By then, Russian winter had set in, and melting snow turned roads and open areas into muddy quagmires. This slowed German armour, allowing the Soviet forces to counterattack. Suffering heavy losses, the Germans began a slow retreat, and revised plans for the quick defeat of the Soviet Union. Instead, Hitler focused on the oilfields of the Caucasus and the capture of Stalingrad.

▶ **German tanks** and other vehicles arrive in a small rural village on the Eastern Front – a small part of the largest invasion force in history,

In detail

As the Germans advanced on Stalingrad, any residents who could fight were called to arms, and many others, including children, were put to work building barricades. Factory workers and college students were formed into militias, while the 1077th Anti-aircraft Regiment, a unit made up mainly of young women volunteers, was given the task of stopping the German 16th Tank Division. The city's defences were strengthened by the arrival of regular Soviet forces, however, to get to the front lines they had to make perilous crossings of the Volga River, under constant bombardment from German artillery and aircraft.

The Soviet defenders' strategy was to fight for every building. They converted housing blocks, factories, and offices into fortifications held by small units, and if the Germans captured a position, the Soviets tried to retake it. Fighting on and around Mamayev Kurgan, a hill above the city, was particularly merciless, and the position changed hands frequently. After three months of brutal engagement, the Germans finally reached the river Volga and took control of around 90 per cent of the city. Nevertheless, the defenders kept fighting, notably on the slopes of Mamayev Kurgan and in the industrial area in the north of the city, and did not stop until the Germans surrendered.

▲ **STRATEGIC CAPTURE** Here, German soldiers capture the Stalingrad tractor factory in late 1942. Despite the ongoing devastation of the city, some factories remained open, including the tractor factory, which had been repurposed to build tanks from leftover spare parts. These tanks, unpainted and lacking many basic features, were driven directly from the factory floor to the front lines, and production only stopped when German forces stormed the plant.

➤ **STREET FIGHTING**
Bitter fighting raged for every ruin on every street. Soldiers cleared buildings room by room and floor by floor. In some cases, the Red Army found itself occupying one floor of a building while the Germans held another in the same building. Fighting even took place in the sewers. The Germans called this highly urban warfare *rattenkrieg* ("rat war").

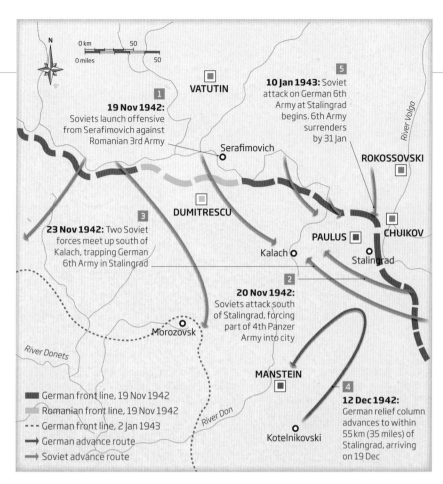

1 **19 Nov 1942:** Soviets launch offensive from Serafimovich against Romanian 3rd Army

5 **10 Jan 1943:** Soviet attack on German 6th Army at Stalingrad begins. 6th Army surrenders by 31 Jan

VATUTIN

Serafimovich

ROKOSSOVSKI

DUMITRESCU

3 **23 Nov 1942:** Two Soviet forces meet up south of Kalach, trapping German 6th Army in Stalingrad

PAULUS   CHUIKOV

Kalach

Stalingrad

River Volga

2 **20 Nov 1942:** Soviets attack south of Stalingrad, forcing part of 4th Panzer Army into city

Morozovsk

River Donets

MANSTEIN

4 **12 Dec 1942:** German relief column advances to within 55 km (35 miles) of Stalingrad, arriving on 19 Dec

River Don

Kotelnikovski

■ German front line, 19 Nov 1942
■ Romanian front line, 19 Nov 1942
--- German front line, 2 Jan 1943
→ German advance route
→ Soviet advance route

◀ **SOVIET COUNTER-OFFENSIVES** The decisive action in the battle for Stalingrad took place away from the city, when the Soviets launched offensives, from the north and south, converging on the German rearguard. The pincer movement succeeded in encircling the German forces at Stalingrad and cutting off all their supplies.

◀ **CASUALTIES** A volunteer army nurse helps a wounded Russian soldier at Stalingrad. The casualties on the Russian side were immense: of the 10,000 soldiers of the Soviet 13th Guards Rifle Division who fought in the battle, only 320 (3 per cent) survived.

▲ **DEFEAT OF THE GERMAN ARMY** On 22 January 1943, General Paulus, the German commander in charge at Stalingrad, requested permission from his superiors to surrender. His men were running out of food and ammunition. Hitler refused, and nine days later the German headquarters in Stalingrad was overrun by the Red Army. The Russians captured around 91,000 exhausted, sick, wounded, and starving German soldiers.

Kursk

1943 ▪ WESTERN RUSSIA ▪ SOVIET UNION VS. GERMANY

WORLD WAR II

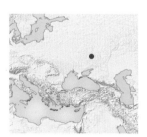

After their successful defence of Stalingrad (see pp.220–23), the Red Army pushed the Germans back across southern USSR, until a German counter-offensive in March 1943 halted the Soviet advance. The two armies reached a stalemate, so the Germans had a choice: either wait for the Red Army to attack, or to launch another counter-offensive of their own. The German command chose the latter, opting to target an area around the city of Kursk where Soviet forces had pushed on ahead of their own front line, creating an inroad into the German lines. However, they also chose to delay the attack during the first half of 1943 to build up their forces, and hurried rail shipments of their new tanks to the Eastern Front. This in turn gave the Soviets time to prepare their defences by laying minefields and digging trenches, bunkers, and tank traps.

The German plan was to advance from the north and south in a pincer movement. On 4 July 1943, with nearly 800,000 men and around 2,700 tanks, the Germans attacked. However, they were heavily outnumbered: the Red Army had 1.9 million soldiers, supported by close to 5,000 tanks. The German attack from the north became mired from the start. The southern forces advanced around 35 km (22 miles) to the town of Prokhorovka, where the Soviets pinned them down on 12 July, and the two armies fought one of the largest ever tank battles.

The German offensive failed to achieve its objectives. Meanwhile, Hitler received the news that the Allied forces had invaded the Mediterranean island of Sicily, so he withdrew his forces and redirected them to Italy. This allowed the Eastern Front initiative to pass to the USSR.

➤ **PANZER IV TANKS DEPLOYED AT KURSK** Taken in July 1943, this photograph shows a German Panzer Group on the move in fields at Kursk. The Panzer IV was a heavier variant of the German Panzer tank family. The Soviet forces sustained the heaviest losses in the battle, but neither side could claim a decisive victory.

In detail

◀ **TANKS AT KURSK** The Soviets mostly used their stalwart T-34 tanks at the battle for Kursk. Shown here in training crossing a trench of Red Army soldiers, the T-34 was fast, reliable, heavily armed, and easy to manufacture. The Germans had fewer tanks in the field, but one of Hitler's reasons for delaying the counter-offensive had been to ensure that their newer, superior vehicles, most notably the heavily armoured and highly effective Tiger and Panther tanks, could be used.

➤ **BATTLE FORMATION AT KURSK** This battlefield map shows the Red Army advance through the German lines around the city of Kursk. The front line stretched 240 km (150 miles) from north to south and protruded 160 km (100 miles) into the German lines. The Germans' plan had been to attack north and south of this bulge, and then squeeze inwards, to trap a sizeable part of the Red Army.

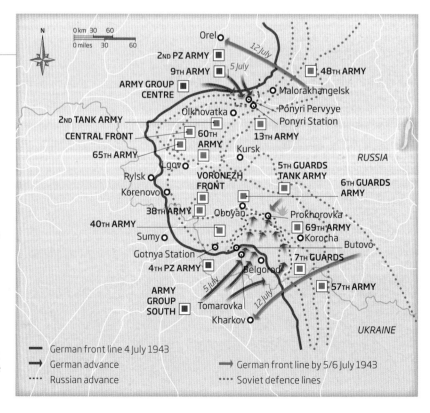

You're quite right. Whenever I think of this attack, my stomach turns over.

ADOLF HITLER TO TANK WARFARE SPECIALIST HEINZ GUDERIAN PRIOR TO THE ASSAULT ON KURSK, 1943

With our brave Allies and brothers-in-arms… you will bring about the destruction of the German war machine…

GENERAL DWIGHT EISENHOWER IN A LETTER TO THE ALLIED FORCES BEFORE OPERATION OVERLORD, 1944

Operation Overlord

1944 ▪ NORTHERN FRANCE ▪ WESTERN ALLIES VS. GERMANY

WORLD WAR II

On 6 June 1944, Allied forces in England launched a combined naval, air, and land assault on German-occupied France. Known as D-Day, this marked the start of Operation Overlord – the campaign to liberate northwest Europe from the Germans. The ultimate aim was to push the Germans out of France – in what became known as the Battle of Normandy – and all the way back to Berlin, forcing Adolf Hitler's surrender. An Allied attack on France would also relieve pressure on the Soviet Union in the east.

Preparation for the invasion began in late 1943. British armaments factories increased production, and the US and Canada sent millions of tons of supplies and equipment across the Atlantic. Over 1.4 million American servicemen also arrived in Britain during 1943 and 1944 to take part in the landings. After an assessment of the alternatives, Allied command decided that the invading force should land on the beaches of Normandy. Under the direction of the supreme commander of the Allied Expeditionary Force, US general Dwight D. Eisenhower, Allied commanders worked on the details of this plan during the winter of 1943. On 1 April 1944, heavy bombers began to soften up the German defences all along the French coast. Sixty-six days later, at a little after midnight, planes full of paratroopers took off heading for drop zones over northern France, while an invasion fleet of assault troops set off for the Normandy beaches.

▲ **AMPHIBIOUS ASSAULT** Nearly 7,000 naval vessels took part in the Normandy landings, including 1,213 naval combat ships, 4,126 landing craft, and hundreds of ancillary craft and merchant ships. Minesweepers secured the route first, then the vast armada of battleships, cruisers, and destroyers crossed the English Channel. On D-Day alone, some 150,000 troops landed on the Normandy beaches.

THE **ATLANTIC WALL**

In expectation of an Allied invasion, Hitler ordered the construction of fortifications all along the Atlantic coast, from Norway to the French border with Spain. However, due to shortages of materials and labour, little of this "Atlantic Wall" was ever built. Instead, the Germans lay minefields and placed guns at the likeliest landing spots – such as Calais, the French town closest to England. An Allied deception campaign encouraged the idea of a Calais attack, intended to maintain the secrecy of the real destination of the landings.

▲ **German soldiers patrol** the beach in front of a gun emplacement on the northern French coast in early 1944. An allied attack was expected at any time.

In detail

The D-Day invasion consisted of two phases: an airborne assault and a series of amphibious landings. Shortly after midnight on 6 June, around 24,000 paratroopers dropped into the invasion area to neutralize the German coastal defences. Naval forces then landed troops along an 80-km (50-mile) stretch of beaches divided into five sectors, codenamed Utah, Omaha, Gold, Juno, and Sword. Despite the efforts of the paratroopers, the Allied troops came ashore under heavy fire from gun emplacements overlooking the beaches, which were also mined and strewn with barbed wire. Some soldiers had to wade ashore through deep water directly into gunfire, and many drowned; those that reached the beach were thrown into fierce fighting. Amphibious tanks and other vehicles also landed, some of which sank or were destroyed. Only two of the beachheads were captured on the first day, and it took until 12 June for all five to be fully secured. The Allied army then had a coastal foothold from which it could advance.

Over the next three months the Allies fought the Battle of Normandy, advancing through sunken lanes with high hedgerows favoured the German defenders. Nevertheless, by the end of August 1944 the German Army was in full retreat from France, and the Allies could advance on Germany.

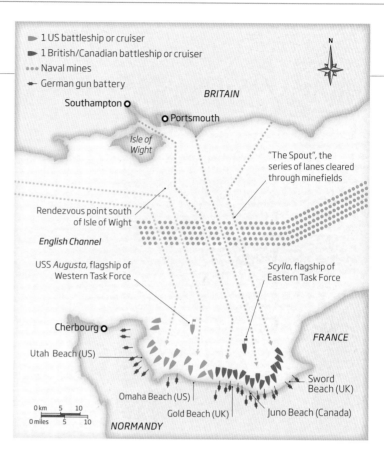

▲ **BEACH LANDINGS** The English Channel was wider at Normandy than elsewhere, but the Allies chose Normandy as its beaches were closest to the major UK ports Southampton and Portsmouth. Also, the strategically important French harbour Cherbourg was nearby. British and Canadian forces put ashore at Gold, Juno, and Sword, while the Americans landed at Omaha and Utah. Defences varied from beach to beach depending on the effectiveness of Allied shelling.

▲ **LIMBERING UP FOR THE INVASION** As soldiers exercised on the dockside before boarding the ships destined for Normandy, the man who masterminded the operation, General Dwight D. Eisenhower, was by no means certain of its success. He had already written a letter accepting full responsibility if D-Day turned out to be a disaster.

▲ FOR A SINGLE VICTORY As this French poster reads: "All Together, for a Single Victory". The Allied forces that took part in D-Day and the greater Operation Overland were drawn from over 15 nations. In addition to the large contingents of American, British, and Canadian troops, servicemen from Australia, Belgium, Czechoslovakia, Holland, France, Greece, New Zealand, Norway, Rhodesia, and Poland took part in the operation.

▼ AMERICANS LAND AT OMAHA BEACH In this famous image, titled "Into the Jaws of Death", soldiers of US Army 1st Infantry Division disembark from a landing craft and wade towards Omaha beach. Of the five zones, this was the bloodiest. The Allied soldiers were met with an unexpectedly strong defence from German forces occupying high cliffs overlooking the beach. US casualties at Omaha were around 2,400; overall, there were 10,000 Allied casualites on D-Day.

FIRST **PARIS, THEN BERLIN**

Operation Overlord did not end to the war in Europe, but it did begin the final act of the war. Following the strategically important capture of Caen, another significant result was the liberation of Paris, which had been under German occupation since June 1940. Little actual fighting took place in the city, because the Germans largely withdrew in the face of the Allied advance. A remaining German garrison officially surrendered the city on 25 August 1944, providing a huge morale boost for the Allies. Nine months later, the German garrison in Berlin surrendered to the Russian army.

▲ Jubilant Parisians line the Champs Élysées on 26 August 1944 as French soldiers drive down the avenue in the newly liberated city.

Operation Market Garden

1944 ■ SOUTHEASTERN NETHERLANDS ■ ALLIED FORCES VS. GERMANY

WORLD WAR II

In the summer of 1944, the Allied armies advanced across Europe after the retreating German army. To avoid the German defences along the Siegfried Line, which stretched south from the Netherlands to Switzerland, Field Marshal Montgomery devised a plan in which Allied airborne divisions would drop into the Netherlands and secure strategic bridges in and around the towns of Eindhoven, Nijmegen, and Arnhem. If successful, this would secure the way through northern Germany into the Ruhr, Germany's industrial heartland, and hopefully hasten the end of the war. Montgomery also intended that the British would spearhead the action, not his rivals the US.

Operation Market Garden, as it was called, began on 17 September. It was one of the largest airborne operations in history, and it delivered over 14,000 men by glider and 20,000 by parachute. Once on the ground, the soldiers were to seize the Rhine bridges for the armoured ground divisions that would follow. On the day, bridges around Eindhoven and Nijmegen were taken and held. However, at Arnhem, the most distant objective from the Allied front line, the paratroopers were unable to hold out for four days until the supporting tanks and infantry arrived. On 21 September, the Germans overwhelmed the paratroopers and retook the bridge. The disaster at Arnhem meant that the Allies failed to secure a foothold over the Rhine, which crushed all hope of ending the war by Christmas 1944.

In detail

◄ CROSSING AT NIJMEGEN BRIDGE
The Allied ground assault intended to link up quickly with the airborne forces. However, the forward units encountered fierce opposition from German infantry equipped with hand-held anti-tank weapons. As a result, they were not able to reach Arnhem in time to stop the British and Polish paratroopers being overrun by a German counterattack.

◄ GERMAN DEFENCES
Parts of the 9th and 10th Panzer Divisions defended the all-important bridge over the Lower Rhine at Arnhem. Attacked by the British 1st Airborne Division and the 1st Polish Independent Parachute Brigade, the German defenders (left) repelled the assault, which led to the withdrawal of the Allies across the Rhine. In the famous phrase, Arnhem was "a bridge too far".

▲ AIRBORNE INVASION
Waves of 1st Allied Airborne Army paratroopers land in the Netherlands on 17 September 1944. Some 20,000 troops landed by parachute, and another 14,000 or more by glider. The operation required the use of over 1,750 aircraft, the drops taking place in daylight over two days. Thanks to the Allies' control of the air, this part of the operation was a complete success.

THE **FIRST PARATROOPERS**

During World War I the US Army Air Service had plans to equip infantry with parachutes and to drop them off the wings of converted bombers over France as part of an offensive against German lines. The war ended before the plan could be put into action. Instead, Germany became the first nation to drop troops into combat, which it did during the 1940 invasions of Denmark and Norway. However, a disastrous attempted airborne invasion of Crete, in which troop-carrying German aircraft were cut to pieces by Allied anti-aircraft fire, led German commanders to abandon similar actions for the rest of the war.

▶ **British paratroopers** on their way to Arnhem in a USAAF C-47 aircraft on 17 September 1944. The survivors were forced to surrender or withdraw.

▲ **ALLIED ADVANCE** American soldiers of the 289th Infantry Regiment march through the snowy forests of the Ardennes. Their task was to cut off the road between St. Vith and Houffalize, in Belgium; they did so successfully, which stalled the advance of the 6th Panzer Army.

Battle of the Bulge

1944-45 ▪ SOUTHERN BELGIUM ▪ ALLIED FORCES VS. GERMANY

WORLD WAR II

By autumn 1944, the Allied advance across Europe (see pp.226-31) had lost its momentum. In mid-December, Germany launched an unexpected counteroffensive. The territory through which they chose to attack was equally unexpected - the densely forested Ardennes region of eastern Belgium. This was difficult terrain, and the Allies, who were stretched out along a front of nearly 1,000 km (600 miles), had left it sparsely defended. The German plan was to break through Allied lines and isolate the British and American forces. The British forces to the north could then be encircled and destroyed, and Hitler could negotiate a peace from a position of strength.

The US units in the Ardennes were caught completely by surprise, and the Germans drove a wedge, or "bulge", into the Allied lines, starting on 16 December 1944. However, the US forces held several strategic locations, which slowed the offensive. The British were then able to reinforce the US units defending the northern line of the battle, while US General George Patton's Third Army drove up from the south. Patton's successful relief of the beleaguered troops at Bastogne played a key role in halting the German offensive.

Between 8 and 16 January, the Allied armies attempted to retake the bulge driven into their lines, and the Germans had to carry out a rapid withdrawal to escape. Losses were heavy on both sides, but the Germans lost a great deal of equipment and stores, and the battle effectively ended their resistance on the Western Front.

In detail

▼ **THE ARDENNES FRONT LINE** This map shows the American front line at the Ardennes forest before and during the battle. The Germans advanced almost 160 km (100 miles) west, forcing the Allies from the Ardennes. By 26 December, Patton's Third Army had reached Bastogne, and by 16 January 1945 all of the German gains had been retaken.

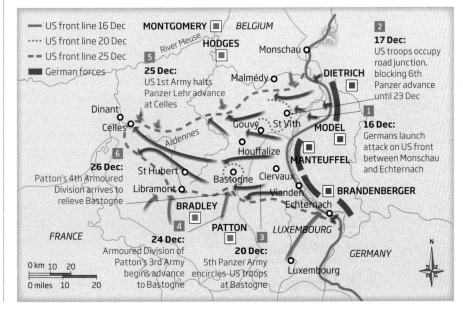

▲ **THE GERMAN ADVANCE** Waffen SS troops pass a wrecked US M3 half-track during the offensive. The thick woods of the Ardennes provided concealment for the massing of forces, while the high ground offered a drier terrain for German tanks. To minimize the danger from Allied air power, German forces struck when the forecast promised mist, rain, and snowy skies.

Iwo Jima

1945 ▪ PHILIPPINE SEA ▪ USA VS. JAPAN

WORLD WAR II

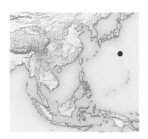

During World War II, the Imperial Japanese Army used the tiny volcanic island of Iwo Jima as an early warning station that sent radio reports of incoming bombers back to the mainland, around 1,300 km (800 miles) away. The US wanted to capture the island, knowing that it would deprive the Japanese of this facility; its three runways could also provide their forces with an air base within fighter range of Japan. Aware of the US plan to attack, the Japanese began to fortify the island. They knew they could not win the battle, but they hoped to inflict enough damage on the Americans to stall an invasion of Japan.

US forces bombed the island for 70 days, followed by three days of naval shelling. Then, on 19 February 1945, US Marines landed and established a beachhead, thinking the Japanese must have been wiped out by the bombardment. But roughly 23,000 troops lay in wait in a network of bunkers, artillery positions, and 18 km (11 miles) of tunnels dug into the rock. Although the invaders initially gained ground, within an hour they came under heavy fire from the concealed positions. The battle for the island lasted over a month and, while the Americans were ultimately victorious at Iwo Jima, it came at a terrible price on both sides. The entire Japanese garrison was wiped out, except for some 216 prisoners, while more than 6,800 US servicemen died, with 19,000 wounded.

RAISING THE FLAG **AT IWO JIMA**

Iwo Jima's Mount Suribachi dominates the southwest tip of the island. On 23 February, US Marines seized its summit and raised a US flag to boost the morale of the soldiers down on the beaches. Later that day they replaced it with a larger, more visible flag.

US photographer Joe Rosenthal's image of the raising of the second flag provided the US with one of the most iconic images of the Pacific Campaign, and was the inspiration behind the US Marine Corps War Memorial that stands at the Arlington National Cemetary for service members and veterans, in Virginia.

▶ **Three of the six marines** in Joe Rosenthal's famous photograph were killed in fighting over the next few days.

▲ **LANDING AT IWO JIMA** Unlike in traditional engagements, the defenders did not meet the invaders on the beaches, but allowed them to land first. Once the beaches were crowded with US forces, the Japanese attacked. By sundown on the first day, the Americans had already incurred 2,420 casualties. US troops are seen here unloading heavy crates from landing craft as they set up depots.

▲ **AMPHIBIOUS ASSAULT** After aerial and naval bombardment on 14 September, the
following day US Marines attacked Wolmi Island off the South Korean coast, which was
connected to Incheon by a causeway. A second wave of infantry landed at Incheon itself.
Led by tanks, the invading force pushed inland under covering fire from aircraft. The
allied landing forces were the largest assembled anywhere since World War II.

Incheon

1950 ▪ SOUTH KOREA ▪ SOUTH KOREA AND UNITED NATIONS ALLIED FORCES VS. NORTH KOREA

KOREAN WAR

On 25 June 1950, Soviet-backed North Korean forces invaded South Korea, pushing back the South Korean army and its UN allies to a perimeter around the city of Pusan on the southwest coast. As the South Koreans and the UN held on, American general Douglas MacArthur, who had commanded US forces in the Pacific during World War II, proposed a plan to land behind North Korean lines at Incheon, the port for Seoul, and cut off the north's supply lines. The approach was difficult, passing through a narrow channel dotted with mines and prone to extreme tides, but the North Koreans would not expect an attack there.

US warplanes dropped napalm on North Korean coastal defences on 10 September 1950, and then battleships shelled them. The landings, codenamed Operation Chromite, went ahead on 15 September: some 50,000 US-led UN troops, including a tank brigade, secured the landing sites, and began the slow and bloody battle towards Seoul, overcoming resistance from infantry, tanks, and artillery.

THE **DIVISION OF KOREA**

Japan ruled Korea as a colony from 1910 until its defeat in World War II. Korea then became a divided territory: the Soviet Union administered the north and the US oversaw the south. A Soviet–US commission tried and failed to establish a national government, and two separate nations formed in 1948; Soviet troops left, and the south had a US-supervised election. Border clashes soon began, with both north and south claiming sovereignty over the peninsula, and war broke out in 1950.

▲ **During Korean War hostilities**, South Korean troops move an anti-tank gun at Suwon Airfield in 1950.

Meanwhile, the South Korean and UN forces fighting at Pusan broke out of the Pusan Perimeter and drove the North Koreans back north. Incheon changed the course of the war and is widely regarded as one of the most decisive military operations in modern warfare.

In context

▲ **FOR PUSAN!** A North Korean propaganda poster from 1950 urges solidarity with the communist side of the Korean peninsula. The tanks shown are Russian T-34s: the Soviet Union supplied armaments and other material support to the North Koreans in their fight against US-backed South Korea.

▲ **AFTER INCHEON** The 19th Infantry Regiment of the US Army on the Kumsong front send a New Year's greeting home. Although the course of the war changed at Incheon, MacArthur advanced too far north and provoked China's involvement, leading to stalemate. An armistice ended the war in July 1953.

Dien Bien Phu

1954 ▪ NORTHWESTERN VIETNAM ▪ VIET MINH REVOLUTIONARIES VS. FRANCE

FIRST INDOCHINA WAR

The Vietnamese fight for independence from French rule (the First Indochina War, 1946–54) was led by the Viet Minh, a nationalist group under revolutionary leader Ho Chi Minh. Eight years of guerilla warfare against the French culminated at Dien Bien Phu, a small hilltop town in northwest Vietnam, near the Laos border. Viet Minh forces had infiltrated Laos, and the French hoped to cut off their supply lines by establishing a camp at Dien Bien Phu. In 1953, the French deployed 10,000 troops, mostly paratroopers, to fortify a base and clear an airstrip that would provide their sole means of resupply.

This site was later described as a "rice bowl", with the French occupying the bottom. The "sides" were a ring of jungle-covered mountains, which the French considered a natural defence. However, they had significantly underestimated the determination of their enemy. Under the command of General Võ Nguyên Giáp, the Viet Minh hauled heavy artillery up the rear slopes of the mountains, dug tunnels through the rock, and positioned guns overlooking the French camp. Five additional Viet Minh divisions, totalling 50,000 men, surrounded the French. On 13 March 1954, the Viet Minh unleashed an artillery attack and within 24 hours the airstrip was damaged beyond use. On 30 March, they began infantry assaults against French defensive positions. The French surrendered on 7 May, signalling the end of both the war and French power in Indochina. On 21 July, Vietnam officially split into a communist north and a non-communist south – a divide that would result in the Vietnam War (see p.243).

▶ **MOVING ARTILLERY THROUGH THE FOREST** The tenacity and skill of Viet Minh artillery troops enabled them to transport their equipment over difficult terrain. From mountain caves above the French camp, they could fire with devastating accuracy, while French artillery could not spot them to return fire.

In detail

▶ **AERIAL SUPPLY LINES** The French initially landed troops into Dien Bien Phu via a paratroop drop in November 1953. They mistakenly believed that the Viet Minh had no anti-aircraft capability, and so planned to resupply their position by air. However, the Viet Minh attacked the French with vast amounts of artillery and anti-aircraft guns. These shut down the French airstrip and prevented any vital supply drops.

▲ **FRENCH SOLDIERS IN THE VALLEY** The French camp was located in an isolated airbase at the bottom of Dien Bien Phu valley. The Viet Minh were able to surround this exposed area in cover, leaving the French outnumbered, outmanoeuvered, and vulnerable. Around 1,500 French soldiers died at Dien Bien Phu, with around 4,000 wounded and around 1,600 missing.

Six-Day War

1967 ▪ MIDDLE EAST ▪ ISRAEL VS. EGYPT, JORDAN, AND SYRIA

ARAB-ISRAELI WARS

In 1948, under the auspices of the UN, the state of Israel was created in what had been a majority Arab territory known as Palestine. The 1948 Arab-Israeli war that followed, between Israel and their Arab neighbours, the Egyptians, Jordanians, and Syrians, ensured the survival of this newly founded state, but there was no peace. By 1967, tensions were rising dangerously. Syria was facilitating Palestinian guerrilla raids on Israel, so Israel made threats against the Syrian capital Damascus. In response, the self-styled leader of the Arab world, President Nasser of Egypt, entered into a dangerous game of brinkmanship by blockading one of Israel's main ports and expelling UN peacekeepers from their shared border.

On the morning of 5 June 1967, Israel launched a preemptive strike. Its fighter-bombers hit Egyptian air bases, destroying virtually the entire Egyptian air force, then later that day they attacked other Arab air forces. Within three days, Israeli ground forces had advanced into Egypt and conquered the Sinai Peninsula. At the same time the Israeli infantry assaulted the Syrian-held Golan Heights, and pushed the Jordanian army back across the River Jordan. By the time a ceasefire was agreed on 10 June, Israel had massively extended its territories, including land occupied by around a million Arabs. It was a spectacular military victory, but one that created unrest in the region for years to come.

▶ **EMBATTLED REGION**
In just six days of fighting in 1967, Israel managed to more than double the size of the territory the country occupied before the war. This proved to be something of a burden. The Sinai Peninsula was returned to Egypt after 1979 as part of the Israel–Egypt peace treaty, but Israel's continued occupation of parts of the West Bank has ensured that the conflict remains live.

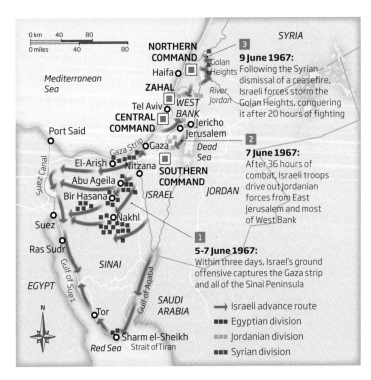

3 9 June 1967: Following the Syrian dismissal of a ceasefire, Israeli forces storm the Golan Heights, conquering it after 20 hours of fighting

2 7 June 1967: After 36 hours of combat, Israeli troops drive out Jordanian forces from East Jerusalem and most of West Bank

1 5-7 June 1967: Within three days, Israel's ground offensive captures the Gaza strip and all of the Sinai Peninsula

→ Israeli advance route
▪▪▪ Egyptian division
▪▪▪ Jordanian division
▪▪▪ Syrian division

▲ **ISRAEL FORCES IN THE SINAI PENINSULA** The Israeli army, shown here in action crossing the Sinai Desert, were equipped with US-built tanks, while the Soviet Union was advising and supplying weapons to the armies of Syria and Egypt. Although the Six-Day War was primarily a conflict between Arab countries and Israel, it was also very much part of the Cold War struggle for global influence being fought between the world's superpowers.

In context

◄ ARAB REFUGEES
This war, like the first Arab-Israeli war of 1948, resulted in displacement of populations in the captured territories. Around 300,000 Palestinian refugees fled to neighbouring Arab countries. Those shown here are trying to cross the remains of the Allenby Bridge, which links the West Bank and Jordan. It had been blown up by the Arab forces to prevent Israeli pursuit.

◄ A DIVIDED JERUSALEM Before the 1967 conflict, the city was split into East and West Jerusalem, each separated by concrete walls and barriers such as this. East Jerusalem was administered by the Jordanians; the West by the Israelis. On 7 June, Israeli forces captured the Old City of East Jerusalem; the walls were torn down, and the city was reunited under Israeli rule.

Tet Offensive

1968 ▪ VIETNAM ▪ NORTH VIETNAM AND VIET CONG VS. SOUTH VIETNAM AND USA

VIETNAM WAR

Tet, the Vietnamese celebration of the lunar New Year, is the most important holiday in the Vietnamese calendar, usually falling in late January or early February. During the war in Vietnam, ongoing since 1959, this holiday was often marked by an unofficial truce in the fighting. In 1968, Tet fell on the 30 January, and the North Vietnamese and their southern-based communist faction, the Viet Cong, used it to launch a series of attacks on South Vietnamese government troops and US forces in more than 100 towns, cities, and outposts.

Their aims were threefold: to break the stalemate in the war, to instigate rebellion among the South Vietnamese population, and to encourage the US to scale back their involvement. Among the Viet Cong's many targets was the US Embassy (left) in the South Vietnamese capital, Saigon; one Viet Cong platoon managed to breach the compound, but was killed in a gun battle. The most intense fighting took place in the city of Hue, 80 km (50 miles) south of the border between North and South Vietnam. The Viet Cong took the city and a battle raged for more than three weeks. US and South Vietnamese forces recaptured Hue and managed to hold off other attacks; despite this victory, news coverage of the offensive so shocked the American public that their support for the war began to wane. Despite heavy casualties, North Vietnam achieved a strategic victory, as this marked the beginning of the US withdrawal.

◀ **EMBASSY ATTACK** US soldiers patrol the embassy in Saigon, seen through a hole blasted in the perimeter wall in a Viet Cong attack during the Tet Offensive. The Viet Cong held the embassy for six hours until they were fought off by US paratroopers, who landed on the roof by helicopter.

THE **VIETNAM WAR** (1959-75)

Vietnam had been under French rule since the 19th century. In 1954, the French lost power after the first Indochina War. Split between a communist north and pro-western south, the North Vietnamese government looked to unify the country under a single communist regime. It promised country-wide elections, but this never happened. Instead, the communists of the north, supported by communist elements in the south (the Viet Cong), launched a guerrilla war on the government in the south. The US sent hundreds of thousands of troops to help the South's fight against communism in a costly – and ultimately unsuccessful – war.

▶ **A group of South Vietnamese** and US troops shelter from the rotor wash of an American UH-1 Huey helicopter in Vietnamese countryside.

Operation Desert Storm

1991 ■ PERSIAN GULF ■ US-LED COALITION VS. IRAQ

GULF WAR

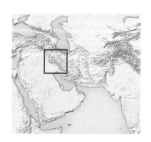

In August 1990, the Iraqi leader Saddam Hussein ordered his army to invade and occupy neighbouring Kuwait. The invasion was met with international condemnation, and the UN Security Council imposed economic sanctions on Iraq. One of the West's greatest concerns was the threat Iraq now posed to Kuwait's neighbour, Saudi Arabia, and its oilfields. Out of fear that Saddam Hussein might invade Saudi Arabia, the US began building up its military presence in the region – Operation Desert Shield. On 29 November, the UN Security Council gave Iraq a deadline of 15 January 1991 to withdraw from Kuwait, threatening the use of force if it failed to comply. An international coalition assembled, headed by the US and including Saudia Arabia, the UK, Egypt, and more than 30 other countries.

Iraq failed to comply with the ultimatum, and so on the morning of 17 January the coalition launched an aerial bombardment of Iraq that ran for 42 consecutive days and nights. They used sophisticated weapons such as cruise missiles, smart bombs, and drones for the first time in a conflict. This was followed by a major ground assault on 24 February. Just three days later, US president George Bush claimed victory and a ceasefire took effect on 28 February. The coalition stopped short of capturing Iraq's capital, Baghdad, and overthrowing Hussein. This became the objective of the second Gulf War in 2003 (see p.247).

▲ **AIR OFFENSIVE** The coalition forces subjected Iraq to one of the most intensive air bombardments in military history. Together they flew more than 100,000 sorties during the 42-day bombardment. Here, US Air Force F-16 and F-15s fly over a desert ablaze with burning oil wells, the latter sabotaged by the retreating Iraqi army.

In context

▶ **GROUND ASSAULT**
The coalition launched a massive allied ground offensive into southern Iraq and Kuwait from Saudi Arabia. Their well-equipped forces quickly overwhelmed the Iraqis, who were mainly using older Soviet technology, and they had liberated Kuwait by 27 February. In total the coalition lost 292 combatants out of 956,600. Iraqi wounded and dead is estimated at 100,000, and 80,000 were captured.

▼ **LIVE FROM THE BATTLEFIELD** Desert Storm was the first war to be televised around the globe. The American TV channel CNN streamed the war 24 hours a day, providing reports and live broadcasts from the front line. Coverage also included satellite footage of guided missile attacks, which earned the conflict its nickname: "the video game war".

Directory: 1900–present

CAPORETTO
WORLD WAR I

1917 ▪ MODERN-DAY SLOVENIA ▪
ITALY VS AUSTRO-HUNGARY
AND GERMANY

Italy joined World War I as an ally
of Britain and France in 1915, and by
late 1917 was locked in a stalemate
with Austro-Hungarian forces on
the northern Italian border. Germany,
now allied with Austria, sent in
reinforcements, and on 24 October
the Austro-German forces launched
poison gas at the Italian lines, followed
by an artillery bombardment. Platoons
equipped with flamethrowers and
grenades advanced rapidly towards
Venice, while Italian forces retreated. A
new line of defence was prepared at the
Tagliamento River but this only held for
two days. The Italians withdrew to the
Piave River, near Venice. Here the
Austro-German advance was finally
halted, but by now the Italians had lost
10,000 men, with 30,000 wounded and
265,000 taken prisoner. The battle was
a national catastrophe.

WARSAW
POLISH-SOVIET WAR

1920 ▪ CENTRAL POLAND ▪
POLAND VS. RUSSIA

After triumphing in the 1917 Russian
Revolution, the newly installed leader,
Vladimir Lenin, decided to extend
Bolshevik rule westward. The first
target was Poland, where the Bolsheviks
hoped to incite Polish communists to rise
up and help establish a new Polish
Revolutionary Government. Within six
weeks of launching the campaign, the
Russians were on the outskirts of Warsaw.
However, the invasion of Poland united its
people against the Russians. The Polish
army began a fierce defence of the city,
while additional units launched an attack
from the south, severing the Russian supply
lines and encircling Lenin's Red Army
outside Warsaw. The Russians surrendered,
and Lenin was forced to agree to peace
terms that ceded large amounts of
territory to Poland. However, the Soviet
Army returned to reclaim it in 1939.

FIRST AND SECOND BATTLE OF INONU
GRECO-TURKISH WAR

1921 ▪ NORTHWESTERN TURKEY ▪
GREECE VS. TURKEY

The Ottoman Empire collapsed in the early
20th century; following World War I, its
lands were divided between the European
powers. Britain had promised certain
Ottoman territories to Greece in exchange
for their support during the war, and
once the war ended in the Allies' favour,
Britain offered logistical support to Greece
as it landed troops at Smyrna (now
Izmir) in 1919. The Greeks advanced into
Anatolia but were halted by Turkish
forces during the First Battle of Inönü
on 11 January 1921.The Greeks chose to
withdraw rather than engage in a major
confrontation, then suffered a second
defeat by the Turkish troops on 27–30
March. In recognition of the victories,
the Turkish commander Mustafa İsmet
took the name Inönü; two years later
he became the first prime minister of
Turkey, and was later president.

▲ MADRID
SPANISH CIVIL WAR

1936 ▪ CENTRAL SPAIN ▪
NATIONALISTS VS. REPUBLICANS

In 1936, Nationalist forces led by
insurgent commander Emilio Mola
marched on Republican-controlled
Madrid. Mola had launched his attack
through the open ground of the Casa
de Campo park on 8 November. However,
the previous day, Republicans had learned
of the attack and so concentrated their
own troops in the Casa de Campo
to meet the Nationalist forces. The
Republicans had superior numbers
but they were a citizen army, not
trained soldiers, and were poorly
armed. They fought the Nationalist
invasion for 10 days until on
19 November the Nationalists made a
final assault under the cover of artillery
and managed to fight their way into
the university quarter, but no further.
Mola decided not to risk losing more
troops and called a halt to the attempt
to take Madrid.

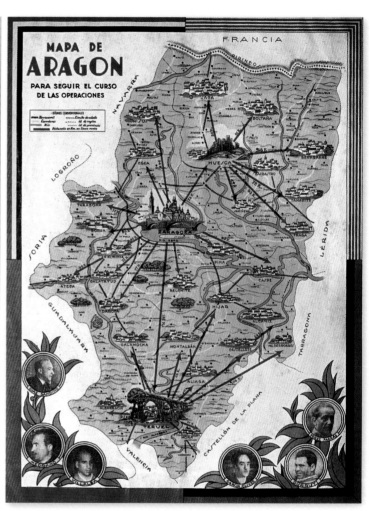

This map shows military operations in Aragón during the Spanish Civil War,
including the Battle for Madrid.

▶ SHANGHAI
SECOND SINO-JAPANESE WAR

1937 ▪ EASTERN CHINA ▪
CHINA VS. JAPAN

China and Japan had been in conflict
since Japan invaded Manchuria in 1931.
In 1937, Japan seized Beijing, and later
that year the shooting of a Japanese
officer in Shanghai escalated tensions
in the city. The Chinese attacked Japanese
garrisons along the Huangpu River,
hoping to seize control of the waterway
and prevent Japanese landings. Although
vastly outnumbered, the Japanese
soldiers resisted and successfully
landed reinforcements. From mid-August
Shanghai became a battleground with
civilians caught in the middle – during
three months of street-fighting and aerial
bombardment, 300,000 people died. By
November, the Japanese had landed more
troops and Chinese casualties were so
high that they were forced to abandon the
city. The Chinese moved west where they
joined the final defence lines to stop
the Japanese reaching Nanjing.

IMPHAL
BURMA CAMPAIGN

1944 ▪ NORTHEAST INDIA ▪
BRITAIN AND INDIA VS. JAPAN

In March 1944, the Japanese attempted to
invade India through the northeast state
of Manipur, via the towns of Imphal and
Kohima. Imphal was defended by four
divisions of British and Indian troops while
Kohima was defended by just 1,500
men. However, they held off 15,000

invading Japanese for two weeks until reinforcements arrived, and for four months British and Indian forces defended against Japanese attacks. The Japanese exhausted themselves, and the long distance to their bases meant they were unable to bring in reinforcements or supplies. In June they ended the battle at Kohima, and by July they began to retreat from Imphal, having suffered around 55,000 killed or wounded.

FALAISE GAP
WORLD WAR II

1944 ■ NORTHERN FRANCE ■
ALLIED FORCES VS. GERMANY

The D-Day beach landings of June 1944 launched Operation Overlord (the Normandy Invasion – see pp.226–29). This secured the Allies a coastal foothold and led to the battle for Normandy. Despite continued fierce fighting in cities such as Caen, the German army was in retreat, and Allied commanders were determined to cut off its escape route. In early August, the Allied forces converged on Falaise to encircle the Germans, the Americans advancing from the south, the Canadians from the north, and the British from the west. By 21 August, the Germans were surrounded. The cordon was eventually breached by German tanks, but it is estimated that of the 80,000– 100,000 troops caught within the cordon, 10,000–15,000 were killed, 40,000–50,000 taken prisoner, and 20,000–50,000 escaped. Falaise was the decisive Allied victory in Normandy and opened the way to the German border.

XUZHOU
CHINESE CIVIL WAR

1948-49 ■ EASTERN CHINA ■ REPUBLIC
OF CHINA VS. COMMUNIST PARTY

The Chinese Civil War between the Nationalists led by Chiang Kai-Shek and the Communists under Mao Zedong began in 1927. It was suspended in the late 1930s, when both sides united to fight Japanese invaders, then resumed in 1946. Initially the Nationalists had been the stronger side, but following the Russian liberation of Manchuria from the Japanese, the Russians turned over huge stockpiles of captured weapons to the Communists, and

the balance of power shifted. By September 1948, the Communists had control of Manchuria. To prevent them from moving south, the Nationalist army advanced to Xuzhou; however defections, leaked intelligence, and poor leadership weakened the Nationalists and within two months the Communists secured a series of military victories. By 10 January 1949, the Nationalist forces in Xuhou were defeated.

INVASION OF IRAQ
IRAQ WAR

2003 ■ IRAQ ■ COALITION FORCES
VS. IRAQ

On 20 March 2003 over 200,000 troops from the US, Britain, Australia, and Poland invaded Iraq, ostensibly over Saddam Hussein's possession of weapons of mass destruction, although none were ever found. The assault, via Kuwait, was preceded by extensive airstrikes on Baghdad and other cities, and Iraqi troop concentrations. The coalition forces met with little resistance and on 1 May President George W. Bush declared an end to combat operations. Saddam Hussein was captured in December 2003 and executed in 2006. The US army remained in occupation of Iraq until 2011, although the country was wracked by conflict between armed factions.

SYRIAN CIVIL WAR
ARAB SPRING

2011-PRESENT ■ SYRIA ■ GOVERNMENT
OF SYRIA VS. OPPOSITION FACTIONS

Opposition protests during the wider Arab Spring movement were met with a harsh clamp-down by the Syrian regime of Bashar al-Assad. In response, the opposition formed militias and a full-scale civil war broke out. The opposition Free Syrian Army obtained support from Turkey, Qatar, and Saudi Arabia, while the Syrian government received arms from Iran and fighters from the pro-Iranian Hezbollah militia in Lebanon. The opposition took much of the key city of Aleppo in mid-2012, but thereafter the conflict devolved into a stalemate. Increasing numbers of Islamist fighters from the al-Nusrah Front and ISIS joined the anti-government side, sapping Western support for the rebels against whom the US launched air-strikes in 2013. In 2015, Russia began active support for the Syrian regime, facilitating air and land offensives that gradually pushed the opposition back. Aleppo fell in 2016, and by 2019 the Assad regime had recovered most of its territory except Kurdish-controlled areas in the east and Idlib region. The fighting devastated much of Syria, causing nearly 7 million refugees to flee the country.

INVASION OF UKRAINE
RUSSIA-UKRAINE CONFLICT

2014-PRESENT ■ UKRAINE ■ RUSSIA
VS. UKRAINE

After popular protests unseated a pro-Russian president in February 2014, clandestine Russian forces took control of Crimea, long claimed by Russia. In April, pro-Russian separatists seized government buildings in southeastern Ukraine. Clashes erupted, but in the summer a full-scale Ukrainian counter-offensive was driven back by a Russian intervention that secured the establishment of pro-Russian regimes in Luhansk and Donetsk. Sporadic fighting continued, and in February 2022, after months of rising tension, Russia launched a full-scale invasion of Ukraine. Unexpectedly strong resistance and Russian logistical problems stalled the attack just short of the capital Kyiv, from where the Russians withdrew in April. Assisted by growing supplies of military equipment provided by western allies, the Ukrainian military overcame the overwhelming numerical superiority of the Russians and stabilized the line. In October and November 2022 they made gains around Kharkiv and recaptured the regional capital of Kherson. Russia's hopes of an easy victory turned into a protracted conflict costing tens of thousands of lives.

Japanese naval landing forces take cover behind a building wearing gas masks during a chemical attack at Battle of Shanghai.

INDEX

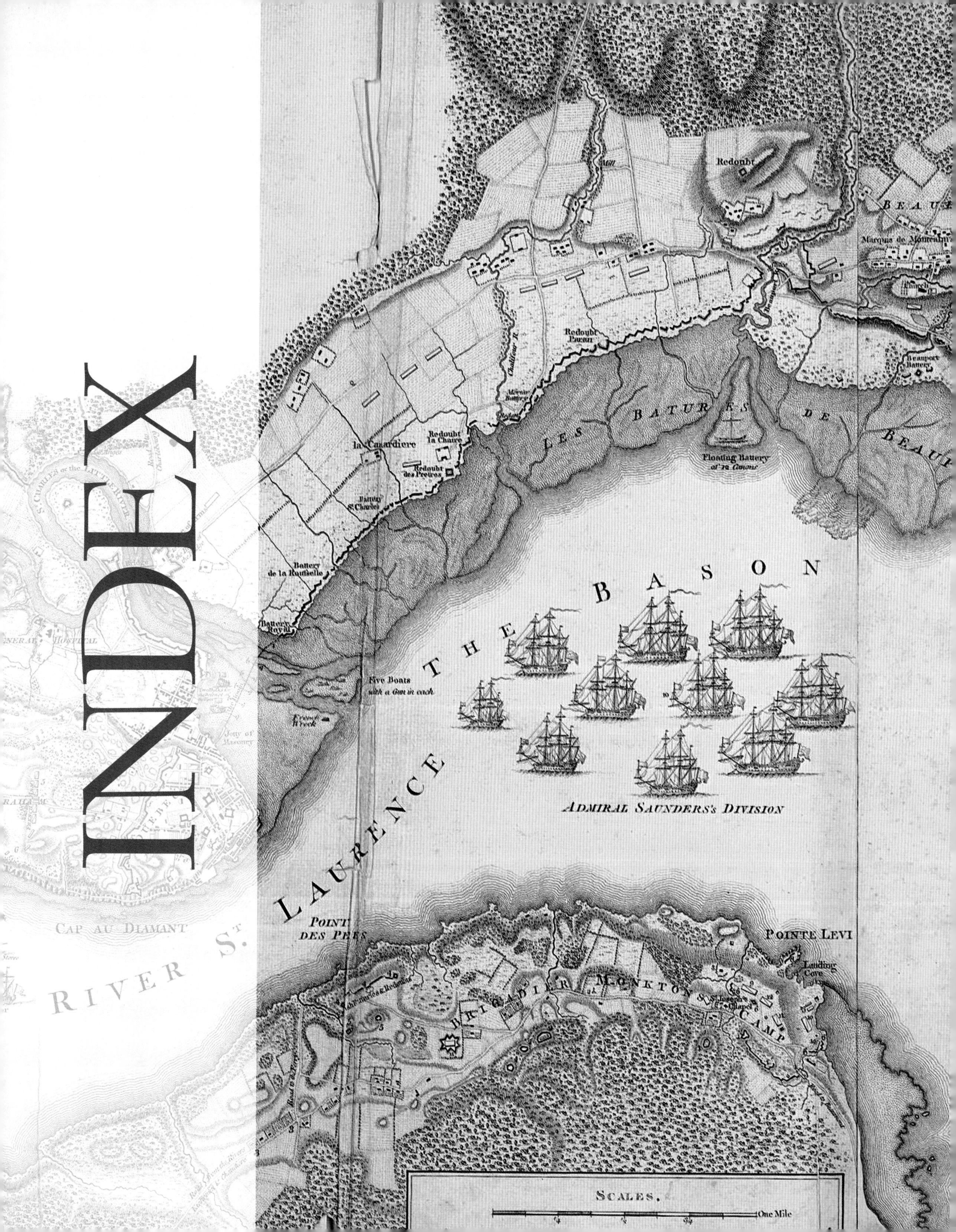

BEAU...

Redoubt

Marquis de Montcalm

Beauport Battery

Redoubt Perin

LES BATURES DE BEAU...

la Canardiere

Redoubt la Chaire

Redoubt des Prestres

Battery St Charles

Floating Battery of 12 Canons

Battery de la Rouffelle

THE BASON

Battery Royal

Five Boats with a Gun in each

Wreck

ADMIRAL SAUNDERS's DIVISION

CAP AU DIAMANT

RIVER ST. LAURENCE

POINT DES PEES

POINTE LEVI

Landing Cove

BRIGADIER MONKTON's CAMP

SCALES.

One Mile

Index

Acknowledgments

Dorling Kindersley would like to thank the following people for their assistance with this book:

Gadi Farfour, Steve Crozier, Meenal Goel, and Simran Saini for design assistance; Kate Taylor, Frankie Piscitelli, Rishi Bryan, Michael Clark, Jane Perlmutter, and Megan Douglass for editorial assistance; Margaret McCormack for indexing. DTP designers: Sachin Gupta, Anita Yadav.

The publisher would like to thank the following for their kind permission to reproduce their photographs:

(Key: a-above; b-below/bottom; c-centre; f-far; l-left; r-right; t-top)

Endpaper: front and back: Getty Images: nik wheeler. **1 Alamy Stock Photo:** Everett Collection Inc (cr); Granger Historical Picture Archive (c). **Getty Images:** Werner Forman (cl). **2-3 Alamy Stock Photo:** Peter Horree. **4-5 Alamy Stock Photo:** Granger Historical Picture Archive. **6 akg-images:** ullstein bild / Haeckel (b). **Getty Images:** DEA / A. DAGLI ORTI (c). **Rex by Shutterstock:** The Art Archive (t). **8 Bridgeman Images:** Museum of Fine Arts, Boston, Massachusetts, USA / William Sturgis Bigelow Collection (b). **9 Dorling Kindersley:** Powell-Cotton Museum, Kent. **10-11 Bridgeman Images:** Pushkin Museum, Moscow, Russia. **12-13 National Museums of Scotland. 13 Getty Images:** DEA / G. Nimatallah / De Agostini (bc). **14 Alamy Stock Photo:** Classic Image (bl); www.BibleLandPictures.com / Zev Radovan (tr). **14-15 Photo Scala, Florence. 15 Getty Images:** Universal History Archive (tl). **16 Alamy Stock Photo:** Antiqua Print Gallery. **17 Alamy Stock Photo:** Panagiotis Karapanagiotis (tr). **Bridgeman Images:** Silverfish Press / National Geographic Creative. **18-19 AF Fotografie. 19 Getty Images:** Universal Images Group / Leemage (br). **20-21 Alamy Stock Photo:** Adam Eastland. **20 Alamy Stock Photo:** Adam Eastland (br). **22 Bridgeman Images:** (tc). **22-23 Bridgeman Images:** Mondadori Electa. **23 Alamy Stock Photo:** ART Collection (bc). **Getty Images:** (cr); De Agostini / G. Dagli Orti (tr). **24 Alamy Stock Photo:** Classic Image (bl); Peter Horree (cr). **25 The Metropolitan Museum of Art, New York. 26-27 Getty Images:** Hulton Archive / Henry Guttmann. **26 Alamy Stock Photo:** North Wind Picture Archives (bc). **27 Alamy Stock Photo:** Eye Ubiquitous / Paul Seheult (bc). **28 Photo Scala, Florence:** bpk, Bildagentur. **29 akg-images:** Album / Kurwenal / Prisma (bc). **Alamy Stock Photo:** Science History Images (cr). **Getty Images:** Corbis / Leemage (br). **30-31 Bridgeman Images:** De Agostini Picture Library. **31 Getty Images:** Print Collector / Ann Ronan Pictures. **32-33 Bridgeman Images:** North Carolina Museum of Art, Raleigh, USA / Gift of the Sameul H. Kress Foundation. **33 The Trustees of the British Museum:** (tl). **Getty Images:** Print Collector / Art Media (tr). **SuperStock:** age fotostock / José Lucas (tc). **34 The Trustees of the British Museum:** (br). **34-35 Imagine China:** Niu Shupei. **35 Getty Images:** Corbis / Asian Art & Archaeology, Inc. (br). **36-37 akg-images:** Pictures From History. **37 Alamy Stock Photo:** Lanmas (br). **38 Getty Images:** Universal Images Group / Leemage. **39 The Metropolitan Museum of Art, New York:** John Stewart Kennedy Fund, 1913 (br). **40-41 Alamy Stock Photo:** INTERFOTO. **41 akg-images. Alamy Stock Photo:** Science History Images / Photo Reseaarchers (br). **42 Getty Images:** DEA / G. DAGLI ORTI (bl). **43 Bridgeman Images:** Pushkin Museum, Moscow, Russia (tl). **44-45 Rex by Shutterstock:** Alfredo Dagli Orti. **46-47 Getty Images:** Photo 12. **47 Getty Images:** Danita Delimont (br). **48 Alamy Stock Photo:** Granger Historical Picture Archive (bl). **48-49 Bridgeman Images:** Musée de la Tapisserie, Bayeux, France (t). **Getty Images:** nik wheeler (b). **49 Alamy Stock Photo:** Antiqua Print Gallery (tr). **Getty Images:** UniversalImagesGroup (br). **50-51 Getty Images:** Werner Forman. **51 Alamy Stock Photo:** Paul Fearn (br). **52 Alamy Stock Photo:** www.BibleLandPictures.com (bc). **Getty Images:** Ann Ronan Pictures / Print Collector (clb). **53 Alamy Stock Photo:** Science History Images. **54-55 Bridgeman Images:** Museum of Fine Arts, Boston, Massachusetts, USA / William Sturgis Bigelow Collection (t). **55 Bridgeman Images:** Pictures from History (cra, crb). **56-57 Bridgeman Images:** Pictures from History. **57 Alamy Stock Photo:** Chronicle (br); Heritage Image Partnership Ltd (tr). **58-59 akg-images:** Album / sfgp. **59 Alamy Stock Photo:** Granger Historical Picture Archive (br). **60 Alamy Stock Photo:** GL Archive (cra); World History Archive (bc). **Getty Images:** Dea / G. Dagli Orti (bl). **61 Getty Images:** Heritage Images. **62 Getty Images:** Heritage Images. **63 © FSUE Russian Post:** (crb). **Getty Images:** Wojtek Radwanski / Stringer (c). **64 © KHM-Museumsverband:** (br). **Rex by Shutterstock:** The Art Archive (cb). **65 Alamy Stock Photo:** Paul Fearn. **66 Bridgeman Images:** Edward III, c.1600 (oil on panel), English School, (16th century) / Royal Collection Trust © Her Majesty Queen Elizabeth II, 2018 (bc). **66-67 Bridgeman Images:** Bibliotheque Nationale, Paris, France. **68-69 akg-images:** Jérôme da Cunha (c). **69 Alamy Stock Photo:** North Wind Picture Archives (br). **Bridgeman Images:** Musee Dobree, Nantes, France (tr). **Dorling Kindersley:** © The Board of Trustees of the Armouries (cr). **70-71 Getty Images:** Universal History Archive. **71 Getty Images:** Heritage Images (br). **72 Getty Images:** Universal History Archive (bc). **72-73 Alamy Stock Photo:** Granger Historical Picture Archive (t). **74-75 akg-images:** Erich Lessing. **75 akg-images. 76 Mary Evans Picture Library. 77 Alamy Stock Photo:** Granger Historical Picture Archive (bl). **78 Alamy Stock Photo:** Heritage Image Partnership Ltd (cra). **79 Getty Images:** DEA PICTURE LIBRARY. **80-81 Rex by Shutterstock:** Alfredo Dagli Orti (t). **81 Alamy Stock Photo:** Danita Delimont (bl). **Dreamstime.com:** Ciaobucarest (br). **82 akg-images:** Jérôme da Cunha (bl). **83 Getty Images:** DEA / A. DAGLI ORTI (tr). **84-85 akg-images:** Nemeth. **86 Alamy Stock Photo:** ART Collection (bc). **86-87 Alamy Stock Photo:** Lebrecht Music and Arts Photo Library (b). **88-89 Bridgeman Images:** Museo di Capodimonte, Naples, Campania, Italy. **89 Alamy Stock Photo:** Walker Art Library (br). **90 Alamy Stock Photo:** ART Collection (clb). **Bridgeman Images:** British Library, London, UK / © British Library Board (br). **91 Dorling Kindersley:** National Museum, New Delhi. **92 Alamy Stock Photo:** Science History Images. **93 Alamy Stock Photo:** MARKA (clb). **Bridgeman Images:** Bibliotheque Nationale, Paris, France (br). **94-95 Alamy Stock Photo:** Adam Eastland Art + Architecture (All Images Used On The Spread). **96 Alamy Stock Photo:** Paul Fearn. **97 Bridgeman Images:** Pictures from History (cra). **Rex by Shutterstock:** Granger (bc). **98-99 Alamy Stock Photo:** Science History Images. **99 Bridgeman Images:** Private Collection / Peter Newark Pictures (br). **100-101 akg-images:** Album / sfgp (t). **101 Getty Images:** De Agostini (br). **102 Alamy Stock Photo:** The Granger Collection (bc). **Getty Images:** Mansell (bl); whitemay (cl). **102-103 Getty Images:** Granger Historical Picture Archive (c). **103 Getty Images:** Universal History Archive (bl, br). **104 Alamy Stock Photo:** HD SIGNATURE CO.,LTD (bc). **104-105 Alamy Stock Photo:** Science History Images (b). **106 Augsburg University Library:** 02.IV.13.2.26-1 = Theatrum Europaeum vol. 1, plate after (bc). **SuperStock:** Oronoz (clb). **106-107 Getty Images:** DEA / G. NIMATALLAH. **108 Getty Images:** DEA PICTURE LIBRARY (bl). **108-109 Bridgeman Images:** Deutsches Historisches Museum, Berlin, Germany / © DHM (b). **109 Bridgeman Images:** Deutsches Historisches Museum, Berlin, Germany / © DHM (cl, cr, ca). **110-111 Alamy Stock Photo:** FALKENSTEINFOTO (t). **111 Alamy Stock Photo:** FLHC 1 (bl). **Livrustkammaren Museum:** http://emuseumplus.lsh.se/eMuseumPlus?service=ExternalInterface&module= literature&objectId=30083&viewType=detailView (br). **112-113 Bridgeman Images:** The Cheltenham Trust and Cheltenham Borough Council (b). **113 Alamy Stock Photo:** The Granger Collection (tr). **114-115 Alamy Stock Photo:** World History Archive. **115 Getty Images:** Hulton Archive / Stringer (br). **116 Rijksmuseum, Amsterdam:** (bc). **116-117 Rijksmuseum, Amsterdam:** (b). **118-119 Getty Images:** Leemage (t). **118 Getty Images:** Leemage (bl, br). **119 Getty Images:** Leemage (bl, br). **120 Getty Images:** Heritage Images (bc). **120-121 akg-images:** Nemeth (b). **121 akg-images:** Erich Lessing (cra). **Alamy Stock Photo:** Geoffrey Taunton (br). **122 Getty Images:** Godong (cla). **123 Alamy Stock Photo:** Science History Images (br). **124-125 Alamy Stock Photo:** Niday Picture Library. **126 Getty Images:** Print Collector (bl). **126-127 Bridgeman Images:** National Army Museum, London. **128-129 Bridgeman Images:** Peterhof Palace, Petrodvorets, St. Petersburg, Russia. **129 akg-images. 130 Alamy Stock Photo:** The Granger Collection (bl). **Getty Images:** Print Collector (cb). **130-131 Rex by Shutterstock:** British Library / Robana. **132 SuperStock:** Interfoto. **133 Getty Images:** UniversalImagesGroup (br). **134-135 Alamy Stock Photo:** The National Trust Photolibrary (t). **134 Library of Congress, Washington, D.C.:** Jefferys, Thomas, -1771, Cartographer G3454.Q4S1 1760 .J4 (bc). **135 Alamy Stock Photo:** World History Archive (bc). **Bridgeman Images:** Jackson, Peter (1922-2003) / Private Collection / © Look and Learn (bl). **136-137 Getty Images:** Mpi / Stringer. **137 Alamy Stock Photo:** Danita Delimont (br). **138-139 Alamy Stock Photo:** World History Archive (t). **138 Alamy Stock Photo:** ClassicStock (crb); North Wind Picture Archives (bc). **139 Bridgeman Images:** Private Collection / Photo © Don Troiani (cb). **Getty Images:** Bettmann (br). **140-141 Alamy Stock Photo:** Granger Historical Picture Archive. **140 Alamy Stock Photo:** Granger Historical Picture Archive (bc). **142-143 Alamy Stock Photo:** Heritage Image Partnership Ltd (t). **143 Alamy Stock Photo:** Josse Christophel (br). **144-145 Alamy Stock Photo:** Granger Historical Picture Archive. **146-147 Alamy Stock Photo:** GL Archive (t). **147 Alamy Stock Photo:** Chronicle (br). **148-149 Bridgeman Images:** Hue, Jean-Francois (1751-1823) / Château de Versailles, France (tc). **Getty Images:** Heritage Images (b). **149 Alamy Stock Photo:** Art Collection 2 (cra); Artepics (tc). **150-151 Alamy Stock Photo:** Antiqua Print Gallery. **151 Alamy Stock Photo:** Niday Picture Library (br). **152-153 Getty Images:** Heritage Images. **153 Alamy Stock Photo:** Antiqua Print Gallery (cr); Heritage Image

Partnership Ltd (tc). **Bridgeman Images:** Chelminski, Jan van (1851-1925) / Private Collection / Photo © Christie's Images (br). **154-155 Alamy Stock Photo:** Granger Historical Picture Archive (t). **155 Alamy Stock Photo:** Niday Picture Library (clb). **Library of Congress, Washington, D.C.:** LC-DIG-pga-11931 (br). **156-157 Alamy Stock Photo:** GL Archive (b). **158-159 Getty Images:** DEA / M. SEEMULLER. **159 Bridgeman Images:** Private Collection / Archives Charmet (br). **160-161 Alamy Stock Photo:** Heritage Image Partnership Ltd (b). **161 Dorling Kindersley:** National Museums of Scotland (crb). **162-163 Getty Images:** DEA / A. DAGLI ORTI (t). **163 Getty Images:** DEA / G. DAGLI ORTI (br). **164-165 Library of Congress, Washington, D.C.:** G3844.S43S5 1862 .W55. **165 Library of Congress, Washington, D.C.:** LC-DIG-pga-04031 (clb); LC-DIG-ppmsca-23719 (crb). **166 Getty Images:** The LIFE Picture Collection / Alexander Gardner (bc). **166-167 Alamy Stock Photo:** Niday Picture Library. **168-169 Library of Congress, Washington, D.C.:** LC-DIG-cwpb-03652 (b). **169 Dorling Kindersley:** Gettysburg National Military Park, PA (cra); Jacob Termansen and Pia Marie Molbech / Peter Keim (ca). **Getty Images:** Science & Society Picture Library (crb). **Rex by Shutterstock:** Granger (cla). **170-171 akg-images. 171 Alamy Stock Photo:** Chronicle (cra); The Granger Collection (crb). **172 akg-images. Alamy Stock Photo:** Stefano Bianchetti (bc). **172-173 Getty Images:** ullstein bild Dtl. **174-175 Alamy Stock Photo:** Granger Historical Picture Archive (b). **175 Dorling Kindersley:** American Museum of Natural History (crb). **Library of Congress, Washington, D.C.:** LC-USZ62-12277 (cra). **176-177 Bridgeman Images:** National Army Museum, London. **177 Alamy Stock Photo:** GL Archive (bc). **Dorling Kindersley:** Board of Trustees of the Royal Armouries (crb/Spear); Powell-Cotton Museum, Kent (crb). **178 Getty Images:** Historical Picture Archive (br). **179 akg-images:** Fototeca Gilardi (t). **180-181 Getty Images:** Larry Burrows / Time Magazine / The LIFE Picture Collection. **182 Alamy Stock Photo:** Granger Historical Picture Archive (bl). **TopFoto. co.uk:** Sputnik (br). **183 Bridgeman Images:** Private Collection / © Look and Learn. **184-185 Alamy Stock Photo:** Granger Historical Picture Archive. **185 Getty Images:** Culture Club (br). **187 Alamy Stock Photo:** Granger Historical Picture Archive (t). **Dorling Kindersley:** Chester Ong / Mikasa Preservation Society (bl). **Getty Images:** Hulton Archive (cl). **188 akg-images:** ullstein bild / Haeckel (b). **Getty Images:** Imagno (c). **189 Imperial War Museum:** © IWM (Art.IWM PST 7652). **190-191 TopFoto.co.uk:** © Roger-Viollet. **190 Bridgeman Images:** Granger (c). **Dorling Kindersley:** The Tank Museum, Bovington. (b). **192-193 Bridgeman Images:** Australian War Memorial, Canberra, Australia. **193 Imperial War Museum:** © IWM (Art.IWM PST 0398) (br). **194 Bridgeman Images:** SZ Photo / Scherl (bl). **194-195 Getty Images:** General Photographic Agency. **196 Getty Images:** Print Collector (t). **196-197 Getty Images:** Galerie Bilderwelt (b). **197 Getty Images:** Galerie Bilderwelt (cr); ullstein bild Dtl. (t). **198 Bridgeman Images:** SZ Photo. **199 Alamy Stock Photo:** Classic Image (tr). **Getty Images:** Universal History Archive (b). **200-201 Getty Images:** Windmill Books. **201 Bridgeman Images:** Granger (br). **202-203 Bridgeman Images. 203 Alamy Stock Photo:** PF-(wararchive) (br). **Imperial War Museum:** © IWM (Q 70254) (tl); © IWM (Q 61479) (tr). **Mary Evans Picture Library:** Illustrated London News Ltd (bl). **204-205 Bridgeman Images:** Imperial War Museum, London (t). **204 Getty Images:** Universal History Archive (bl). **205 Alamy Stock Photo:** Chronicle (br). **National Army Museum:** (bc). **206-207 Bridgeman Images:** Imperial War Museum, London. **208 Getty Images:** Topical Press Agency (bl). **208-209 Getty Images:** Fotosearch. **210-211 Dorling Kindersley:** Gary Ombler, RAF Cosford. (t). **London Metropolitan Archives:** (b). **210 Alamy Stock Photo:** Chronicle (cl). **Getty Images:** ullstein bild Dtl. (cla); William Vandivert / The LIFE Picture Collection (bl). **212 Alamy Stock Photo:** Granger Historical Picture Archive (bl). **Getty Images:** Smith Collection / Gado (br). **212-213 Alamy Stock Photo:** Granger Historical Picture Archive. **214-215 The US National Archives and Records Administration. 215 Alamy Stock Photo:** Stocktrek Images, Inc. (br). **216 Mary Evans Picture Library:** Sueddeutsche Zeitung Photo (cr). **216-217 Alamy Stock Photo:** PJF Military Collection. **217 Alamy Stock Photo:** Niday Picture Library (bl); Photo 12 (br). **218 Getty Images:** Michael Nicholson (bl). **218-219 Getty Images. 220-221 Colourised by Olga Shirnina:** Media Drum World. **221 Getty Images:** Hulton Archive (br). **222 akg-images. 222-223 Getty Images:** Universal History Archive (b). **223 Getty Images:** Ullstein Bild (br); Pictorial Parade (tr). **224 Rex by Shutterstock:** Sovfoto / Universal Images Group (bl). **225 Getty Images:** Ullstein Bild. **226-227 Alamy Stock Photo:** Prisma by Dukas Presseagentur GmbH. **227 Alamy Stock Photo:** dpa picture alliance (br). **228 Alamy Stock Photo:** Chronicle (bl). **228-229 Getty Images:** Smith Collection / Gado (b). **229 Alamy Stock Photo:** World History Archive (tr). **Imperial War Museum:** (tl). **230 Alamy Stock Photo:** War Archive (bl). **Getty Images:** Ullstein Bild (br). **230-231 Alamy Stock Photo:** Everett Collection Inc (t). **231 Imperial War Museum:** (b). **232 akg-images. 233 Alamy Stock Photo:** INTERFOTO (br). **234 Getty Images:** Photo 12 (bl). **234-235 Getty Images:** U.S. Coast Guard. **236 Getty Images:** Hank Walker / The LIFE Picture Collection. **237 Getty Images:** Sovfoto (bl). **The US National Archives and Records Administration:** (tr, br). **238 Getty Images:** Ullstein Bild (br); SeM (bl). **238-239 Getty Images:** Collection Jean-Claude LABBE. **240-241 Getty Images:** AFP (t). **241 Getty Images:** Terry Fincher (bl); Jacoby / Ullstein Bild (br). **242-243 Getty Images:** Dick Swanson / The LIFE Images Collection. **243 Getty Images:** Larry Burrows / Time Magazine / The LIFE Picture Collection (br). **244-245 Bridgeman Images:** Pictures from History. **245 Getty Images:** Chip HIRES (br); Mike Nelson (bl).

246 SuperStock: Oronoz (cra). **247 Alamy Stock Photo:** World History Archive (br). **248 Library of Congress, Washington, D.C.:** Jefferys, Thomas, -1771, Cartographer G3454.Q4S1 1760 .J4

All other images © Dorling Kindersley

For further information see:

www.dkimages.com